CORRECT YOUR FRENCH BLUNDERS

second edition

How to Avoid 99% of the Common Mistakes Made by Learners of French

VÉRONIQUE MAZET

New York Chicago San Francisco Lisbon London Madrid Mexico City
Milan New Delhi San Juan Seoul Singapore Sydney Toronto

The McGraw-Hill Companies

1 2 3 4 5 6 7 8 9 10 11 12 13 14 15 16 17 QFR/QFR 1 9 8 7 6 5 4 3 2

ISBN 978-0-07-178824-3
MHID 0-07-178824-7

e-ISBN 978-0-07-178825-0
e-MHID 0-07-178825-5

This book is printed on acid-free paper.

CORRECT YOUR FRENCH BLUNDERS

second edition

Thanks to all the dedicated students of French
who are willing to go the extra mile to learn
this beautiful but difficult language.
Especially my students here in Texas!

CONTENTS

INTRODUCTION

This book identifies the most common trouble spots for English speakers learning French. It provides a basis for understanding why these trouble spots cause difficulty, and offers guidance and practice for avoiding potential *blunders*.

In the process of learning a foreign language, most errors occur when the learner transfers the patterns of his or her native language directly to the target language. The most effective way to identify these trouble spots is to take the point of view of the learner—your point of view—and start like you would, from English. For instance, what potential blunders could we find in trying to express "This is the woman I wanted to work with" in French? We see three potential sources of error: how to express "this is," where to place the preposition "with" in the French sentence, and which past tense to use for "wanted." This book shows you the reasons behind many common blunders by emphasizing how patterns in French differ from those in English. You will learn potential trouble spots and how to break bad habits, as well as correct your own mistakes.

The book is divided into three parts: Spelling, Grammar, and Vocabulary. The units in each part explain and illustrate particular grammar points and provide many examples of the potential blunders to avoid in Avoid the Blunder boxes, printed in blue type and marked by ✗. The words and sentences marked by ✗ are unacceptable in French.

Because the individual words and phrases of a language are related to other words and phrases, you will find that most grammar topics are mentioned in more than one place. The book tries to avoid technical grammar terms, but some concepts cannot be explained without traditional terminology. If you are unfamiliar with these terms, it may help to go directly to the Avoid the Blunder box. Read the examples, then read the related explanation. In this way, you will understand the idea even if you are not familiar with the grammar term.

At the end of each unit are exercises to test your comprehension and help you avoid the mistakes encountered when translating word for word, or pattern for pattern, from English. A final Catch the Blunders unit includes exercises that round out your understanding of what you have learned from the book as a whole.

This book should make you aware of the traps you may fall into when translating from English to French, and I hope that it puts you on the right track to being blunder-free in French. Happy French studies!

CORRECT YOUR FRENCH BLUNDERS

second edition

PRONUNCIATION AND SPELLING

PRONUNCIATION

French uses the same alphabet as English. Many letters, however, are pronounced differently in the two languages. The pronunciation material included in this unit is intended to give you a very basic guide to pronouncing French words. For more exact French pronunciation, consult a book on French phonetics that includes the International Phonetic Alphabet (IPA).

Consonants

Single Consonants

The French letters *b, d, f, k, m, n, p, r, v, x, y,* and *z* are generally pronounced like their English counterparts. Other French consonants are pronounced as follows.

c pronounced like the *c* in "cup" when it occurs before *a, o,* or *u*

le cadeau	*the gift*
le cou	*the neck*
curieux	*curious*

pronounced like the *s* in "see" when it occurs before *e* or *i*

la céramique	*ceramics*
le divorce	*divorce*
un citron	*a lemon*

pronounced like the *s* in "see" when it is written with a cedilla (see the section on the cedilla in this unit)

soupçonner	*to suspect*

g pronounced like the *g* in "goal" when it occurs before *a, o,* or *u* or when it occurs before a consonant

le garçon	*the boy*
le frigo	*the refrigerator*
la guitare	*the guitar*
gros	*fat*

g pronounced like the *s* in "pleasure" when it occurs before *e, i,* or *y*

la génération	*the generation*
un régime	*a diet*
la gymnastique	*gymnastics*

h silent, as in "honor" (for elision with words beginning with *h,* see the unit on spelling)

j pronounced like the *s* in "pleasure"

le jardin	*the garden*
jeune	*young*

AVOID THE 

Don't use the English /d/ sound before the *j* in French words. Only foreign words like *jeans* use this sound.

l pronounced like the *y* in "yes" when it occurs in *-ill-* or in final *-eil* or *-euil* after a vowel

la fille	*the girl*
la bouteille	*the bottle*
le soleil	*the sun*
l'écureuil	*the squirrel*

otherwise pronounced like the *l* in "tell"

le lait	*milk*

s pronounced like the *s* in "sip" when it begins a word, when it occurs before a consonant, or when it is doubled

le soleil	*the sun*
l'espace	*space*
le poisson	*the fish*

pronounced like the *z* in "zip" when it occurs between two vowels

une chanteuse	*a singer*
le poison	*the poison*
la rose	*the rose*

t pronounced like the *s* in "sip" in endings that begin with *-ti* (e.g., *-tion* and *-tiel*).

l'action	*action*
la nation	*the nation*
partiel	*partial*

AVOID THE Blunder

Don't pronounce French *-tion* with a /sh/ sound as in English.

t otherwise pronounced like the *t* in "top"

tenir	*to hold*
la table	*the table*
actuel	*current*

w pronounced like the *v* in "vine" or the *w* in "weekend" (*w* occurs only in loanwords and typically follows the pronunciation of the original language)

le wagon (/v/)	*the car*
le week-end (/w/)	*the weekend*

In general, consonants at the end of French words are silent, but *c, f, l,* and *r* in this position are usually pronounced.

Nasal Sounds

When *m* or *n* follows certain vowels, the *m* or *n* is not pronounced; instead, the combination of vowel + *m/n* is a nasal sound. However, if the combination is followed by a vowel or by *m/n* + a vowel, the *m* or *n* is pronounced as a separate consonant. The French word *infini* "infinite" has both types of sounds: The first *in* is nasal (*in* + consonant), but the second is not (*in* + vowel).

THE COMBINATIONS *i/u/y + m/n*

im	important (*important*), simple (*easy*)
in	intelligent (*smart*), le cousin (*the (male) cousin*), la meringue (*meringue*)
aim	la faim (*hunger*)
ain	le pain (*bread*), craindre (*to fear*)
eim	Reims (*city of Reims*)
ein	la peinture (*painting*)
um	le parfum (*perfume*), humble (*humble*)
un	lundi (*Monday*), un (*one*), commun (*common*)
ym	la symphonie (*the symphony*)
yn	la synthèse (*synthesis*)

Certain combinations with *en* have the same pronunciation.

éen	européen (*European*)
ien	canadien (*Canadian*), bien (*well*), il vient (*he is coming*)
yen	moyen (*average*)

In certain loanwords, the combination *en* also has this pronunciation: *l'examen* "the exam" and *l'agenda* "the planner."

AVOID THE Blunder

Don't pronounce the *n* in *les Martin* "the Martins" as a separate consonant.

When these combinations are followed by a vowel or by *m/n* + a vowel, the *m* or *n* is pronounced as a separate consonant.

l'image	*the picture*
immédiat	*immediate*
la cousine	*the (female) cousin*
la graine	*the seed*
la synagogue	*the synagogue*
parfumer	*to perfume*
la lune	*the moon*

The change from a nasal sound with *n* to the *n* being pronounced separately often occurs when an adjective ending in *-ain, -an, -éen, -ein, -en, -ien, -in, -on,* or *-un* is put in the feminine form, that is, when *-e* is added.

NASAL SOUND	*n* PRONOUNCED
américain	américaine
brun	brune

AVOID THE Blunder

Don't forget to pronounce the *n* in *Martine* as a separate consonant.

THE COMBINATIONS *a/e* + *m/n*

am	la chambre (*the bedroom*)
an	maman (*Mom*), chanter (*to sing*)
em	sembler (*to seem*), remplir (*to fill*)
en	l'enfant (*the child*), le client (*the client*)

When these combinations are followed by a vowel or by *m/n* + a vowel, the *m* or *n* is pronounced as a separate consonant.

un ami	*a friend*
un âne	*a donkey*
un année	*a year*

THE COMBINATIONS *o* + *m/n*

om	tomber (*to fall*), le nom (*the name*)
on	monter (*to go up*), le pardon (*pardon*)

AVOID THE Blunder

Don't pronounce the final *n* in *bourguignon* "from Bourgogne" as a separate consonant.

When these combinations are followed by a vowel or by *m/n* + a vowel, the *m* or *n* is pronounced as a separate consonant.

la pomme	*the apple*
monotone	*monotonous*
pardonner	*to forgive*

Consonant Combinations

Certain consonant combinations require special attention.

cc pronounced like the *k* in "kit" before *a, o,* or *u*

accompagner	*to accompany*

pronounced like the *cc* in "accent" before *e* or *i*

accepter	*to accept*

ch usually pronounced like the *sh* in "ship" (not like the *ch* in "church")

la chambre	*the room*
la recherche	*the research*
la bronchite	*bronchitis*

sometimes pronounced like the *c* in "cup"

une chiromancienne	*a palm reader*
le chlore	*chlorine*

gn usually pronounced like the *ny* in "canyon" but as one sound

la montagne	*the mountain*

sometimes pronounced as separate sounds

un gnome	*a gnome*
agnostique	*agnostic*

qu usually pronounced like the *k* in "kit"

quand	*when*

qu sometimes pronounced like the *qu* in "quit"

l'aquarium	*the aquarium*
l'équateur	*the equator*

th pronounced like the *t* in "tall" (not like the *th* in "think" or "this")

le théâtre	*the theater*
la méthode	*the method*

AVOID THE *Blunder*

Don't pronounce *th* in French words like the /th/ sound in English "theology."

Vowels

Vowels without accent marks are pronounced as follows.

a pronounced like the *a* in "father"

malade	*sick*
le pas	*the step*

e pronounced like the *e* in "the" in a monosyllabic word ending in *-e* or at the end of a syllable that is not word-final

je	*I*
me	*me*
te	*you* (sing.)
le	*the* (m. sing.)
se	*oneself*
ce	*this, that*
que	*that; than*
de	*of*
ne	*no, not*
petit	*little*

pronounced like the *e* in "get" before a double consonant or in a syllable that ends in a pronounced consonant (this is also the pronunciation of *è* and *ê*; see below)

belle	*beautiful*
la fillette	*the little girl*
avec	*with*

pronounced like the *ée* in *(crème) brulée* in word-final *-ed, -er,* or *-ez* or in a monosyllabic word ending in *-es* (this is also the pronunciation of *é*; see below)

le pied	*the foot*
lancer	*to throw*
le nez	*the nose*
Marchez!	*Walk!*

AVOID THE *Blunder*

Don't pronounce the *r* or *z* of a verb ending.

e usually silent when it occurs at the end of a word, when it occurs in the plural noun or adjective ending *-es* or the verb ending *-es* or *-ent*

la table	*the table*	les tables	*the tables*
un rêve	*a dream*	les rêves	*dreams*
belle	*beautiful* (f. sing.)	belles	*beautiful* (f. pl.)

AVOID THE *Blunder*

Don't pronounce the *s* at the end of plural nouns and adjectives.

(tu) parles	*(you) talk*
(ils) mangent	*(they) eat*

Note that the *je, tu, il/elle,* and *ils/elles* forms of an *-er* verb have the same pronunciation in the present tense.

je mange
tu manges
il mange
ils mangent

AVOID THE *Blunder*

Don't pronounce the *-e* or *-ent* endings of verb forms.

i pronounced like the *y* in "yes" when it precedes another pronounced vowel

la société	*society*

otherwise pronounced like the *i* in "sushi"

il	*he*
difficile	*difficult*

o pronounced like the *o* in "go" when it precedes a /z/ sound or when it is the last sound in a word

la chose	*the thing*
vos	*your* (pl.)

otherwise pronounced like the *ou* in "ought"

la sortie	*the exit*
la compote	*the compote*

u pronounced by forming the lips to say the *oo* in "pool," then saying the *ee* in "peel" instead

une	*a* (sing.)

Don't pronounce the *u* in *gue* or *gui* combinations in words such as *guerre* and *guitare.*

Written Accent Marks and the Cedilla

In French, accents are used to change the pronunciation of the vowel *e,* as well as to distinguish two otherwise identical words, like *ou* "or" and *où* "where." They do not indicate syllable stress. Accents are used on both capital and lowercase vowels (see page 21 in the unit on spelling).

The Acute Accent

The acute accent (*l'accent aigu*: ´), which can be placed only over the letter *e,* indicates that the *e* is pronounced with the lips stretched out.

It is particularly important to write the acute accent on the *é* of the past participle of *-er* verbs.

je FORM OF PRESENT TENSE	**PAST PARTICIPLE**
mange	mangé
parle	parlé
écoute	écouté

AVOID THE Blunder

✗ J'ai mange.
✗ Il est arrive.

AVOID THE Blunder

Make sure you pronounce *é* differently from *e, è,* and *ê.*

The Grave Accent

The grave accent (*l'accent grave*: `) can be placed over the letters *e, a,* and *o.*

The grave accent over an *e* indicates that the *e* is pronounced like the *e* in English "let."

très	*very*
la pièce	*the play*
cinquième	*fifth*
le père	*the father*

The grave accent over the letters *a* and *u* does not change their pronunciation. Instead, it distinguishes between homonyms (words that are spelled and pronounced alike but have different meanings). See page 20 in the unit on spelling.

The Circumflex

The circumflex (*l'accent circonflexe*: ˆ) over the letter *e* indicates that the pronunciation of *e* is similar to the sound of *è.*

la forêt	*the forest*
le même	*the same*

The circumflex also occurs over the letters *a, i, o,* and *u,* without a change in pronunciation. (For more information on the use of the circumflex over *i* and *u* (with a few exceptions), see the unit on spelling.)

le château	*the castle*
il croît	*he is growing*
la côte	*the coast*
sûr	*certain*

Note that in French, the letter *a* with a grave accent (*à*) occurs *only* in the last syllable of a word, but the letter *a* with a circumflex (*â*) *never* appears as the last letter of a word.

déjà	*already*
voilà	*there (is)*
la grâce	*grace*
le mâle	*the male*

AVOID THE *Blunder*

✗ déjâ

The Dieresis

The dieresis (*le tréma*: ¨) over one of two adjacent vowels indicates that the vowels otherwise pronounced as one sound are to be pronounced separately.

mais	/ai/ (*one vowel sound*)	*but*
le maïs	/a + i/ (*two vowel sounds*)	*corn*
la sœur	/oe/ (*one vowel sound*)	*the sister*
Noël	/o + e/ (*two vowel sounds*)	*Christmas*

The Cedilla

The cedilla under a *c* softens its pronunciation from /k/ to /s/ before *a, o,* and *u*.

- *c* without a cedilla

c before *a* → /k/	le placard	*the closet*
c before *o* → /k/	le chocolat	*chocolate*
c before *u* → /k/	le curé	*the priest*
c before *e* → /s/	la glace	*ice cream*
c before *i* → /s/	la cigale	*the cicada*
c before *y* → /s/	cynique	*cynical*

- *c* with a cedilla

ç before *a* → /s/	je commençais	*I was beginning*
ç before *o* → /s/	le soupçon	*suspicion*
ç before *u* → /s/	reçu	*received*

AVOID THE Blunder

✗ çe pain-çi
✗ çes arbres

The cedilla is particularly important in the conjugation of verbs like *commencer* "to begin," *prononcer* "to pronounce," and *remplacer* "to replace," where the verb ending begins with *-o* (the *nous* form of the present tense) or *-a* (most *imparfait* forms, for example). Use of the cedilla is required to maintain the /s/ sound throughout.

tu commences *you* (sing.) *begin*	nous commençons *we begin*
il prononcera *he will pronounce*	ils prononçaient *they were pronouncing*
nous remplacions *we were replacing*	elle remplaçait *she was replacing*

LIAISON

Liaison is pronunciation of an ordinarily silent word-final consonant before a word that begins with a vowel or mute *h*.

Liaison does not occur before an aspirated *h* or before the words *oui, onze, onzième,* and *un* (when it means "one"); see the unit on spelling.

The sound created by liaison is one of the following:

/z/ for a word ending in *-s* or *-x*
/t/ for a word ending in *-t* or *-d*
/n/ for a word ending in *-n*
/p/ for a word ending in *-p*
/v/ for a word ending in *-f*
/r/ for a word ending in *-r*
/g/ for a word ending in *-g*

■ Liaison is required in the following situations.

- After a determiner

un‿enfant *a child*
ton‿école *your school*
mes‿amis *my friends*

- Between an adjective and a noun (but not between a noun and an adjective)

le petit‿enfant	*the small child*
un grand‿ami	*a great friend*
les beaux‿oiseaux	*the beautiful birds*
le premier‿échelon	*the first step*

- After a monosyllabic preposition and after certain short adverbs

en‿Amérique	*in America*
dans‿un bateau	*in a boat*
en‿or	*in gold*
très‿ému	*very touched*
plus‿ouvert	*more open*
bien‿assaisonné	*spiced*

AVOID THE Blunder

Don't use liaison between a monosyllabic preposition and a word beginning with an aspirated *h*.

✗ en‿haut

- Between a subject or object pronoun and the verb

on‿est	*one is*
nous‿aimons	*we like*
ils‿ont	*they have*
j'en‿ai	*I have some*
il les‿aime	*he likes them*
tu nous‿écoutes	*you listen to us*

- Between the verb and a subject pronoun (in inversion) and between the verb and an object pronoun (in the imperative)

Prend‿elle le thé?	*Is she having tea?*
Parles‿en!	*Talk about it!*

- After third-person singular and plural forms of the verb *être*

C'est‿important.	*It is important.*
Ils sont‿intelligents.	*They are clever.*
il était‿une fois	*once upon a time*

- After *quand* (as a conjunction, not as a question word) and *dont* (as a relative pronoun)

quand‿il est parti — *when he left*
le livre dont‿elle parle — *the book she talks about*

- Liaison is not used in the following situations.

- After a proper name

Robert | est petit. — *Robert is short.*

- Between a singular noun and an adjective

l'enfant | amusant — *the funny child*
l'accident | idiot — *the stupid accident*

AVOID THE *Blunder*

Don't use liaison between a noun and an adjective.

✗ étudiant‿américain
✗ enfant‿intelligent

Liaison between a plural noun and adjective is often considered "optional." In fact, it is rarely used in everyday language.

des gens | agréables — *pleasant people*

- After a plural noun when it is the subject of the following verb

Mes parents | aiment le golf. — *My parents like golf.*
Les enfants | ont peur. — *The children are afraid.*

- Between the subject pronoun *on, ils,* or *elles* and a past participle or infinitive that follows (in inversion)

Vont-ils | arriver? — *Will they arrive?*
Ont-elles | écouté? — *Did they listen?*

- After *et* "and"

lui et | elle — *he and she*
Paul et | Anne — *Paul and Anne*

- After a question word

Combien | y en a-t-il? — *How many are there?*
Comment | on fait? — *How is it done?*

There are, however, two fixed phrases that are exceptions:

Comment‿allez-vous? — *How are you?*
Quand‿est-ce que…? — *When is it that . . . ?*

Exercise

A *Rewrite the following sentences and phrases, using a cedilla under the letter* c *where necessary.*

1. Ils ont commencé.

 ____

2. Des glacons.

 ____

3. Nous remplacons la vitre.

 ____

4. Je l'ai apercu.

 ____

5. Elle aime la glace.

 ____

6. Avancons lentement.

 ____

7. Ca m'intéresse.

 ____

8. Ils prononcaient mal.

 ____

9. Ils s'est fiancé l'an dernier.

 ____

SPELLING

Cognate Nouns

Many French nouns look very similar to English nouns. Most of these are cognates (words that have a similar spelling and a similar meaning in two languages), and sometimes the only difference between the French noun and the English noun is its ending.

la déité	*the deity*
l'égalité	*equality*
la fraternité	*fraternity*

When writing in French, make sure that all the words "look" French. Here are a few guidelines to help you.

- The French ending *-té* corresponds to the *-ty* ending in English.

la difficulté	*the difficulty*
la liberté	*liberty*
la société	*the society*
la stabilité	*stability*

AVOID THE Blunder

✗ la liberty
✗ la mentality

- The French endings *-ie* and *-ogie* correspond to the *-y* and *-ogy* endings in English.

l'astronomie	*astronomy*
la géologie	*geology*

AVOID THE Blunder

✗ la géography
✗ la philosophy

- The French ending *-ique* corresponds to the *-ic* ending in English.

la clinique	*the clinic*
démocratique (*adj.*)	*democratic*
la république	*the republic*

AVOID THE Blunder

✗ la républic

- The French ending *-isme* corresponds to the *-ism* ending in English.

le journalisme	*journalism*
le tourisme	*tourism*

- The French ending *-eur* corresponds to the *-or* ending in English.

le directeur	*the director*
le professeur	*the professor*

AVOID THE Blunder

✗ le professor

Nouns and Verbs That Sound Alike

Some verbs whose stems end in *-l,* like *appeler* "to call," *réveiller* "to wake up," and *travailler* "to work," have a noun and more than one verb form that sound alike.

un appel	*a call*
j'appelle	*I call*
il appelle	*he calls*
le réveil	*the alarm clock*
je me réveille	*I wake up*
il se réveille	*he wakes up*
le travail	*work*
je travaille	*I work*
il travaille	*he works*

To distinguish the verb form from the noun, try to put the word into the *imparfait.* If the sentence still makes sense, then the original word is a verb form (and takes the ending *-lle*).

AVOID THE *Blunder*

Don't write a noun as a verb form.

✗ J'ai beaucoup de travaille.
✗ Il a reçu un appelle.

Adding *s-* or *-t-* Between a Verb and Pronoun

■ In the *tu* form of the imperative of *-er* verbs, *s-* is added before the object pronouns *en* and *y*.

REGULAR PRESENT TENSE FORM	IMPERATIVE FORM
tu vas	va
tu manges	mange

Va au lit!	*Go to bed!*
Vas-y!	*Go!*
Mange des fruits!	*Eat some fruit!*
Manges-en!	*Eat some!*

Note that *s-* is not added to verbs that keep the *-s* ending in the imperative (*-re* and *-ir* verbs).

REGULAR PRESENT TENSE FORM	IMPERATIVE FORM
tu prends	prends

Prends des bonbons!	*Take some candy!*
Prends-en!	*Take some!*

■ In questions formed by inversion, *-t-* is added between a verb form that ends in a vowel and *il*, *elle,* or *on*.

Parle-t-il chinois?	*Does he speak Chinese?*
Finira-t-elle son travail à temps?	*Will she finish her work on time?*
Mange-t-on bien ici?	*Is this a good place to eat?*

AVOID THE *Blunder*

Don't confuse the *s-* and *-t-* additions.

✗ Va-t-y.
✗ Parle-t-en.
✗ Mange-s-on bien ici?

The Spelling Reform of 1990

According to the French spelling reform of 1990, the circumflex accent is no longer used on the letters *i* or *u,* except over the words *mûr* "ripe," *sûr* "certain," *dû* "owed," *le jeûne* "the fast," and certain forms of the verb *croitre* "to grow," where the circumflex is needed to distinguish these words from their homonyms. The *passé simple* conjugations also maintain the accent.

FORMER SPELLING	CURRENT RECOMMENDED SPELLING
le coût	le cout
le goût	le gout
paraître	paraitre

Written Accents to Distinguish Homonyms

In French, accents can be used to distinguish between homonyms (words that are spelled and pronounced alike but that differ in meaning), such as *ou* "or" and *où* "where."

A grave accent over *a* or *u* does not affect the pronunciation of these vowels; it serves instead to distinguish between homonyms.

Cache ces bonbons, ou je les mangerai.	*Hide this candy, or I will eat it.*
Cache ces bonbons où je les mangerai.	*Hide this candy where I will eat it.*
Je me repose ou je travaille.	*I rest or I work.*
Je me repose où je travaille.	*I rest where I work.*
Il est à la maison.	*He is at home.*
Il a une maison.	*He has a house.*

If you are not sure whether the letter *a* needs a grave accent or not, try restating the sentence in the *imparfait.*

Il a une maison.
Il avait une maison.

If the sentence still makes sense, the word *a* is a form of the verb *avoir* and does not take the accent. If the sentence does not make sense in the *imparfait,* the word is likely to be the preposition *à* with a grave accent.

AVOID THE Blunder

✗ Il à une maison.

Following is a list of pairs of common homonyms that are distinguished only by the use of an accent mark.

a	(*present tense form of* avoir)	à	*at*
âge	*age*	âgé	*old*
aie	(*subjunctive form of* avoir)	aïe!	*ouch!*
bronze	*bronze*	bronzé	*tanned*
cure	*treatment*	curé	*priest*
des	(*pl. indefinite article*)	dès	*as soon as*
du	*some*	dû	(*past participle of* devoir)
entre	*between*	entré	(*past participle of* entrer)
jeune	*young*	jeûne	*a fast*
la	(*f. definite article*)	là	*there*
mais	*but*	maïs	*corn*
marche	*walk*	marché	*market*
mur	*wall*	mûr	*ripe*
ou	*or*	où	*where*
pécheur	*sinner*	pêcheur	*fisherman*
sale	*dirty*	salé	*salty*
sur	*on*	sûr	*sure, certain*

Accents on Capital Letters

An accent on a capital letter is mandatory only with proper names, such as the names of people, organizations, and countries.

Émile André	ÉMILE ANDRÉ
l'Équipe	L'ÉQUIPE
Les États-Unis	LES ÉTATS-UNIS

Either of the following, however, is correct.

LES ETUDIANTS
LES ÉTUDIANTS

Sometimes common sense demands the use of an accent on a capital letter, even though it is not mandatory. Compare the following announcements.

MARCHE DU PRADO DIMANCHE DE 8 HEURES A 13 HEURES
MARCHÉ DU PRADO DIMANCHE DE 8 HEURES A 13 HEURES

Without the accent on *marche,* "a walk" is announced; with the accent, "a market day" is announced.

As a general rule, use a written accent over an initial capital letter if that letter takes an accent when not capitalized.

Écoutez vos parents.

Elision

Elision consists of dropping the vowel of a monosyllabic word before a word beginning with a vowel or mute *h*. An apostrophe substitutes for the dropped vowel and joins the consonant of the monosyllabic word with the following word. Many of these monosyllabic words are articles or pronouns.

le arbre	→	l'arbre	*the tree*
la hirondelle	→	l'hirondelle	*the swallow* (bird)
se aimer	→	s'aimer	*to love one another*
je arrête	→	j'arrête	*I stop*

■ The articles *le* and *la* become *l'* before a word beginning with a vowel or mute *h*.

l'eau (*f.*)	*the water*
l'homme (*m.*)	*the man*
l'Italie (*f.*)	*Italy*
l'ours (*m.*)	*the bear*

AVOID THE Blunder

✗ la histoire
✗ la organisation

■ The object pronouns *me, te, se, le,* and *la* become *m', t', s',* and *l'* before a word beginning with a vowel or mute *h*.

Nous t'admirons.	*We admire you.*
Ils s'aiment.	*They love one another.*
Elle l'accepte.	*She accepts it.*

AVOID THE Blunder

✗ Il la écoute.
✗ Je aurais peur.

The object pronoun *lui* is never elided to *l'*.

✗ Elle l'a dit merci.

■ In commands, when the object pronouns *me* and *te* become *moi* and *toi,* these are further changed to *m'* and *t'* before the pronoun *en*.

Donne-m'en!	*Give me some!*
Sers-t'en!	*Use it!*

■ The subject pronoun *je* becomes *j'* before a verb form that begins with a vowel or mute *h*.

j'aime	*I love*
j'habite	*I live*
j'organise	*I organize*

AVOID THE Blunder

The subject pronoun *tu* is never elided.

✗ T'as pas fini.
✗ T'attends.
✗ T'écoutes la radio.

■ The negative particle *ne* becomes *n'* before a verb or pronoun that begins with a vowel or mute *h*.

Tu n'as pas entendu.	*You did not hear.*
Je n'aime pas ça.	*I don't like that.*
N'oublie pas!	*Don't forget!*
Il n'y arrive pas.	*He's not getting there.*
Il n'en a pas.	*He doesn't have any.*
Il n'habite pas ici.	*He doesn't live here.*

■ The word *que* always changes to *qu'* before a word that begins with a vowel or mute *h*.

- *que* as a relative pronoun

le prof qu'il admire	*the professor that he admires*
la femme qu'il aime	*the woman that he loves*

AVOID THE *Blunder*

The relative pronoun *qui* never changes to *qu'*.

✗ un enfant qu'aime le chocolat

- *que* used in a comparison

Il est plus petit qu'elle.	*He is shorter than she.*
Marie est aussi jolie qu'Alice.	*Marie is as pretty as Alice.*

- *que* used as the conjunction "that"

Je pense qu'il est content.	*I think that he is happy.*
Il faut qu'on parte.	*We must leave.*

- *que* used in the expressions *jusqu', lorsqu', avant qu', pour qu',* etc.

jusqu'à demain	*until tomorrow*
avant qu'il parte	*before he leaves*
pour qu'elle comprenne	*so that she understands*

- The subject pronoun *ce* changes to *c'* before any form of the verb *être* that begins with a vowel.

C'est une conque.	*It's a conch.*
C'était intéressant.	*It was interesting.*

The demonstrative adjective *ce* "this" never changes to *c'*. Instead, *cet* is used before a masculine noun that begins with a vowel.

cet éléphant	*this elephant*
cet été	*this summer*

AVOID THE *Blunder*

✗ c'arbre
✗ c'enfant

- *De* always changes to *d'* before a vowel.

D'où viens-tu?	*Where are you coming from?*
Il a besoin d'eau.	*He needs water.*
Il a beaucoup d'argent.	*He has a lot of money.*

- *Si* changes to *s'* only before *il* and *ils*.

S'il fait beau...	*If the weather is nice . . .*
S'ils étaient plus sympa...	*If they were nicer . . .*

AVOID THE Blunder

Don't change *si* to *s'* before *a, e, o,* or *u.*

✗ S'Alain arrive en retard...
✗ S'elle réussit...
✗ S'on changeait de voiture...

Cases Where Elision Never Occurs

- Before a plural noun

les arbres	*the trees*
les oiseaux	*the birds*

✗ l'innocents
✗ l'omelettes

- Before the words *oui, onze, onzième,* or *un* (when it means "one"—the expression *l'un l'autre* is an exception)

le onzième étage	*the eleventh floor*
le oui et le non	*yes and no*

AVOID THE Blunder

✗ l'onzième jour de la grève

- Before an aspirated *h*

la haine	*hatred*
le homard	*the lobster*
la honte	*shame*
le hors-d'œuvre	*appetizer*
le huit mai	*May 8*

AVOID THE Blunder

✗ l'honte
✗ l'huit mai

- The feminine possessive adjectives *ma, ta,* and *sa* borrow the masculine forms *mon, ton,* and *son* before a vowel or mute *h* (rather than changing to *m', t',* and *s'*).

mon amie	*my (female) friend*
ton école (*f.*)	*your school*
son heure (*f.*)	*his time*

AVOID THE Blunder

✗ m'amie Julie

Exercises

A *Fill in the blanks with either* à *or* a.

1. Le chien _____ marché _____ côté de son maitre jusqu'_____ la porte, puis il _____ pris la fuite.
2. Il _____ réussi _____ faire des économies et il _____ enfin acheté une nouvelle machine _____ café.
3. Pierre _____ dix ans aujourd'hui. Sa mère _____ préparé un bon gâteau.
4. _____ dix ans, un petit garçon commence _____ être un petit homme.
5. Quand elle _____ voyagé _____ Paris, elle _____ visité tous les monuments et elle _____ parlé _____ beaucoup de gens.
6. _____ quelle heure _____-t-il commencé _____ travailler?

B *Write the French equivalent of the following English words.*

1. certain _______________
2. salty _______________
3. at _______________
4. market _______________
5. as soon as _______________
6. on _______________

C *Rewrite the following sentences, correcting the spelling of the words in bold type where necessary. You may modify them by using elision or by changing their form.*

1. **Que** est-ce **que** elle veut?
____
2. **Qui** a dit ça?
____
3. **Le** homme a prononcé **le** oui **que** on attendait.
____
4. **Ma** amie **se** appelle Emma.
____
5. **Tu** as vu **ce** arbre? **Ce** est un centenaire.
____
6. **Ce** enfant **ne** est pas sage.
____
7. **Jusque** où est-ce **que tu** iras?
____
8. **Que** est-ce qui **te** est arrivé? **Tu** es pâle.
____
9. **Je** ai autant **de** amis **que** eux.
____
10. Est-ce **que** ils **se** sont amusés?
____
11. Tu **la** as lue?
____
12. Il **le** a mis là.
____

CAPITALIZATION

Capitalization is not used as much in French as it is in English. The two languages vary in their capitalization conventions.

Words That Must Be Capitalized

- As in English, the first letter of a sentence in French is capitalized, as is the first letter of a quotation or an independent statement or expression.

Il pleut aujourd'hui. Ça sera bon pour le jardin.	*It is raining today. It will be good for the yard.*
—Savez-vous si le train a du retard?	*"Do you know if the train is late?"*
—Toujours en retard. Jamais à l'heure.	*"Always late. Never on time."*

- Nouns referring to nationalities are capitalized. This even includes inhabitants of a region or town.

les Suisses	*the Swiss*
un Français	*a Frenchman*
les Bretons	*the Bretons*
un Marseillais	*a person from Marseille*

AVOID THE Blunder

✗ les suisses
✗ les lyonnais

- The names of historical periods are capitalized.

La Troisième République	*The Third Republic*
Le Siècle des Lumières	*The Enlightenment*

- To cite the title of a book or article, the most common usage in French is to capitalize the first word only.

« Le journal d'Anne Frank »	*The Diary of Anne Frank*
« L'armée des ombres »	*Army of Shadows*
« Les misérables »	*Les Misérables*

Words That Are Not Capitalized

■ The first-person pronoun *je* is never capitalized, unless it begins a sentence.

Il m'a demandé si je voulais sortir avec lui.	*He asked me if I wanted to go out with him.*

■ Adjectives referring to nationalities and the names of languages are not capitalized.

Il aime le vin italien.	*He likes Italian wine.*
Il existe environ 400 fromages français.	*There are about 400 French cheeses.*
L'italien n'est pas une langue facile.	*Italian is not an easy language.*
Parlez-vous anglais?	*Do you speak English?*
Nous apprenons le français.	*We are learning French.*
—Est-il français ou américain?	*"Is he French or American?"*
—C'est un Américain.	*"He is an American."*

AVOID THE Blunder

✗ Paul est Suisse.
✗ Nous parlons Anglais.

■ The names of religions and the nouns and adjectives derived from them are not capitalized, except for the word *l'Islam* "Islam."

le catholicisme	*Catholicism*
la religion catholique	*the Catholic religion*
un catholique	*a Catholic (person)*
le judaïsme	*Judaism*
la religion juive	*the Jewish religion*
les musulmans	*the Muslims*

■ Personal titles are not capitalized, unless the writer wants to indicate respect.

Monsieur le président Cartier	*President Cartier*
le professeur Duchemin	*Professor Duchemin*
le docteur Durand	*Doctor Durand*
la princesse Diana	*Princess Diana*

BUT

Madame la Directrice, je vous écris...	*Madame Director, I am writing to you . . .*

- The names of days of the week and months are not capitalized.

jeudi le 20 octobre	*Thursday, October 20*

AVOID THE Blunder

✗ le 20 Octobre
✗ le 1er Janvier

- Geographical terms, such as *lac, rue,* and *mer,* are not capitalized even if they are part of a place name.

la mer Méditerranée	*the Mediterranean Sea*
Le lac Travis est très agréable.	*Lake Travis is very pleasant.*
Notre hôtel se trouve place du Tertre.	*Our hotel is Place du Tertre.*
Ma mère habite rue des Lilas.	*My mother lives on Lilas Street.*
Il rêve d'escalader le mont Everest.	*He dreams of climbing Mount Everest.*

Exercise

A *Rewrite the following sentences, capitalizing the words in bold type where necessary.*

1. Nous sommes le 31 **octobre**.

   ____

2. Leur fille a double nationalité: elle est **canadienne** et **brésilienne**. Elle parle **français**, **anglais** et **portugais**.

   ____

   ____

3. Les **français** sont **catholiques**.

   ____

4. Sa maison se trouve 22 **place** du Tertre.

   ____

5. Si vous allez en **suisse**, vous verrez le **mont** Blanc et le **lac** Léman.

   ____

6. Les **suisses** sont très gentils. Ils parlent **français** aussi.

   ____

7. Quand vous y serez, essayez de parler **français** et achetez du chocolat **suisse**.

   ____

   ____

GRAMMAR

NOUNS

A noun is a word that names beings (persons and animals) and things (objects, concepts, and places). In French, a noun is either masculine or feminine. In dictionaries, a noun is followed by the designation for its gender, often expressed as *n.f.* for feminine nouns and *n.m.* for masculine nouns, whether the noun names a being or a thing.

When learning a new noun, memorize it with its definite article (masculine *le* or feminine *la*) to help you remember whether the noun is masculine or feminine.

Nouns Designating People and Animals

Most nouns that refer to male persons and male animals are masculine, and they have a feminine form to designate their female counterpart. Not all nouns that describe a male are masculine, however. For example, *une araignée* names a spider (male or female); *une mouche* names a fly (male or female).

AVOID THE Blunder

✗ un araignée
✗ un mouche

Following are some of the main rules for the formation of feminine nouns. (See also the unit on descriptive adjectives.)

- A feminine noun is most commonly formed by adding *-e* to a masculine noun.

un ami	*a male friend*
une amie	*a female friend*
un Français	*a Frenchman*
une Française	*a Frenchwoman*

□ If a masculine noun ends in a vowel, adding an *-e* to form the feminine does not affect its pronunciation. In such cases, both the masculine and feminine forms of the noun are pronounced the same (as in *ami* and *amie*).

In verbal communication, it is sometimes impossible to hear a difference between the masculine and the feminine forms of these nouns, especially if they begin with a vowel and, as a result, have no distinct form of determiner (*le* or *la*), but rather the ambiguous *l'*.

When you hear the following sentences, there are no clues to determine the gender of the "friend."

Je suis allé chez mon ami(e).	*I went to my friend's house.*
Je suis allé chez l'ami(e) de mon père.	*I went to my father's friend's house.*

The singular indefinite article is the only determiner that maintains the distinction between masculine and feminine, even before a vowel.

Je suis allé chez un ami / chez une amie.	*I went to a friend's house.*

However, the agreement of other determiners or adjectives can indicate gender.

J'ai des ami(e)s. (PLURAL INDEFINITE ARTICLE, NO CLUE)	*I have some friends.*
J'ai des amies intelligentes. (FEMININE ADJECTIVE)	*I have some smart female friends.*

□ If a masculine noun ends in a silent consonant, adding *-e* to form the feminine affects the pronunciation. In most cases, the silent consonant will be pronounced.

un chat	*a (male) cat*
une chatte (/t/ *pronounced*)	*a female cat*
un Français	*a Frenchman*
une Française (/z/ *pronounced*)	*a Frenchwoman*

■ About 30 masculine nouns that end in *-e* have a feminine form in *-esse*. Following are some common examples.

hôte	*host*
hôtesse	*hostess*
maitre	*master*
maitresse	*mistress*
prince	*prince*
princesse	*princess*

The main patterns for formation of feminine nouns from their masculine counterparts are given in the following chart.

MASCULINE NOUN ENDING		FEMININE NOUN ENDING	
-an	le gitan "gypsie"	-ane	la gitane
		(BUT le paysan, la paysanne "peasant")	
-at	le candidat "candidate"	-ate	la candidate
		(BUT le chat, la chatte "cat")	
-eau	le chameau "camel"	-elle	la chamelle
-el	le colonel "colonel"	-elle	la colonelle "colonel's wife"
-en	le Parisien "Parisian"	-enne	la Parisienne
-er	le sorcier "sorcerer"	-ère	la sorcière
-et	le cadet "youngest one"	-ette	la cadette
-eur	le voleur "thief"	-euse	la voleuse
-f	le veuf "widower"	-ve	la veuve "widow"
-in	l'orphelin "orphan"	-ine	l'orpheline
-on	le lion "lion"	-onne	la lionne "lioness"
		(BUT le démon, la démone "devil")	
-ot	l'idiot "idiot"	-ote	l'idiote "idiot"
		(BUT le sot, la sotte "silly person")	
-s/-x	l'époux "spouse"	-se	l'épouse
-teur	l'acteur "actor"	-trice	l'actrice "actress"

AVOID THE *Blunder*

Don't automatically add an *-e* to form the feminine counterpart of a masculine noun.

✗ bergere ✗ cadete

■ Some male-female noun pairs have one form for both the masculine and feminine. In dictionaries, such nouns are typically followed by an *n.* indicator (with no gender specified) or by *nmf.* Only a determiner can indicate if the noun refers to a male or a female.

un artiste une artiste	*an artist*
un malade une malade	*a sick person*
un secrétaire une secrétaire	*a secretary*
un touriste une touriste	*a tourist*

AVOID THE *Blunder*

Don't just change the ending of a noun to make it feminine. Use a feminine article to show its gender.

- Some male-female noun pairs have entirely different forms for the masculine and feminine.

un homme une femme	*a man* *a woman*
un garçon une fille	*a boy* *a girl*
un père une mère	*a father* *a mother*
un fils une fille	*a son* *a daughter*
un frère une sœur	*a brother* *a sister*
un oncle une tante	*an uncle* *an aunt*
un neveu une nièce	*a nephew* *a niece*
un parrain une marraine	*a godfather* *a godmother*
un roi une reine	*a king* *a queen*
un héros une héroïne	*a hero* *a heroine*
un taureau une vache	*a bull* *a cow*
un cheval une jument	*a (male) horse* *a mare*
un mâle une femelle	*a male* *a female*

AVOID THE *Blunder*

✗ une chevale
✗ une hérose
✗ une taurelle

■ Some nouns are used to name a person of a specific gender without a counterpart for the other gender. Following are some common examples.

une bonne	*a maid*
un évêque	*a bishop*
une fée	*a fairy*
le pontife	*the pontiff*
un ténor	*a tenor*

■ Some masculine nouns naming professions that are traditionally masculine do not have a lexical feminine form, even though there are females in those professions. As the number of women in those fields increases, masculine nouns are being adapted. The changes are slow and sometimes controversial, and euphemisms are often used, such as *une femme juge* "a woman judge," *une femme ingénieur* "a woman engineer," *une femme soldat* "a woman soldier," and *une femme peintre* "a woman painter."

Recently, the noun *une auteure* appears to have caught on as the feminine form of *un auteur* "an author." For the feminine noun *sagefemme* "midwife," however, the rarely used masculine form, *maïeuticien,* which is used to describe men now in that profession, is a completely unrelated word.

AVOID THE *Blunder*

Don't fabricate a feminine form for a noun naming a profession.

✗ une ingénieure
✗ une marine
✗ une soldate

- Some nouns have only one gender, even though they are used to refer to both males and females.

un bébé	*a baby* (male or female)
une connaissance	*an acquaintance* (male or female)
un mannequin	*a model* (male or female)
une personne	*a person* (male or female)
un professeur	*a professor* (male or female)
une recrue	*a recruit* (male or female)
une vedette	*a star* (male or female)
une victime	*a casualty* (male or female)

Adjectives modifying such nouns agree with those nouns in gender, even if the other gender is meant.

Votre fille est un beau bébé.	*Your daughter is a beautiful baby.*
Anna est un mannequin bien payé.	*Anna is a well-paid model.*

AVOID THE *Blunder*

✗ Raquel est un mannequin fascinante.
✗ Pierre est une personne très intéressant.

- If a single noun is used to refer to both the male and female of an animal species, the word *mâle* or *femelle* is used after the noun to indicate its gender.

une araignée mâle	*a male spider*
une araignée femelle	*a female spider*

Nouns Designating Things

Nouns that refer to things (instead of people or animals) are also either masculine or feminine. If a noun is unfamiliar to you and a dictionary is not available, there are some common spelling patterns that can help you determine the gender of the noun. Since things have a gender, they are designated by either the masculine pronoun *il* "he" or the feminine pronoun *elle* "she."

AVOID THE *Blunder*

Don't try to translate the English pronoun "it" into French; use *il* or *elle.*

Feminine Nouns

The following patterns identify feminine nouns. These patterns are generic, and each category has exceptions.

- Nouns ending in *-ade*

une limonade	*a lemon-flavored drink*
une promenade	*a walk*

- Nouns ending in *-ance* and *-ence*

la connaissance	*knowledge*
une séance	*a session*
la présidence	*the presidency*
une référence	*a reference*

- Nouns ending in *-ée*

l'arrivée	*the arrival*
une fusée	*a rocket*
la journée	*the day*
la soirée	*the evening*

There are, however, three exceptions:

un lycée	*a high school*
un musée	*a museum*
un trophée	*a trophy*

- Nouns ending in *-ette*

une allumette	*a match*
une navette	*a shuttle*
les toilettes	*the restrooms*

- Nouns ending in *-ie* that name a branch of science or a personal quality

l'astronomie	*astronomy*
la chimie	*chemistry*
la géographie	*geography*
la philosophie	*philosophy*
la psychiatrie	*psychiatry*
la modestie	*modesty*

AVOID THE Blunder

Don't use nouns with the French *-ie* ending to refer to people.

✗ la philosophie (when "the philosopher" is meant)

- Nouns ending in *-ique*

une boutique	*a boutique*
une clinique	*a clinic*
la république	*the republic*

- Nouns ending in *-ise* (often referring to a good or bad personal quality)

la bêtise	*stupidity*
la franchise	*honesty*

- Nouns ending in *-té*

la difficulté	*difficulty*
la méchanceté	*meanness*
la vérité	*truth*

- Nouns ending in *-sion* and *-tion* (often derived from a verb)

l'appréhension (appréhender)	*anxiety*
la dérision	*derision*
la fusion	*fusion*
une définition (définir)	*a definition*
l'éducation (éduquer)	*education*
la ponctuation (ponctuer)	*punctuation*
une punition (punir)	*a punishment*

- Geographical names that end in *-e*

la France
l'Italie
l'Océanie
la Seine

There are, however, five exceptions:

le Cambodge
le Mexique
le Danube
le Rhône
le Zaïre

AVOID THE *Blunder*

✗ la Cambodge
✗ la Mexique
✗ la Danube
✗ la Rhône
✗ la Zaïre

- Names of automobiles and motorcycles

une BMW
une Ford
une Peugeot

- Names of stores and businesses that end in *-erie*

une boulangerie	*a bakery*
une charcuterie	*a deli*
une épicerie	*a grocery store*
une poissonnerie	*a fish market*

Masculine Nouns

The following patterns identify masculine nouns. These patterns are generic, and each category has exceptions.

- Nouns ending in *-acle*

un réceptacle	*a receptacle*
un spectacle	*a show*

- Nouns ending in *-age*

le dressage	*training* (animals)
l'esclavage	*slavery*
un massage	*a massage*
le ménage	*housecleaning*
le recyclage	*recycling*

AVOID THE Blunder

Don't assume that a noun that ends in *-e* is a feminine noun. Check the gender of an unfamiliar noun in the dictionary.

✗ la massage
✗ la nuage

- Nouns ending in *-eau*

un anneau	*a ring*
le bureau	*the office*
un cadeau	*a gift*
un tableau	*a painting*
un vaisseau	*a ship*

- Nouns ending in *-et*

un robinet	*a faucet*
un tabouret	*a stool*

- Nouns ending in *-ier*

un amandier	*an almond tree*
un cahier	*a notebook*
un pompier	*a firefighter*

- Nouns ending in *-isme* (often referring to a theory, doctrine, or trade)

l'absolutisme	*absolutism*
le civisme	*civic duty*
le journalisme	*journalism*
le romantisme	*romanticism*
le tourisme	*tourism*

AVOID THE Blunder

Don't confuse the *-isme* and *-iste* endings. Words that end in *-iste* refer to people.

✗ un journalisme (when "a journalist" is meant)

- Nouns ending in *-ment* (often derived from a verb)

un enterrement (enterrer)	*a burial*
l'isolement (isoler)	*isolation*
le logement (loger)	*lodging*
un raisonnement (raisonner)	*a rationale*
le rangement (ranger)	*putting away, tidying up*

- Names of trees

un cerisier	*a cherry tree*
un chêne	*an oak tree*
un platane	*a plane tree*

- Names of metals

l'argent	*silver*
le bronze	*bronze*
l'or	*gold*

- Metric units

un gramme	*one gram*
un kilomètre	*one kilometer*
un litre	*one liter*
un mètre	*one meter*

There is, however, one exception:

une livre	*a pound*

- Nouns that refer to a period of time

le matin	*the morning*
le soir	*the evening*
un jour	*a day*
le lundi	*Monday*
un mois	*a month*
le printemps	*the spring*
l'hiver	*the winter*
un an	*a year*

Exceptions include the following:

une matinée	*a morning*
une soirée	*an evening*
une journée	*a day*
une semaine	*a week*
une année	*a year*

- Nouns of English origin

le football
le marketing
le parking
le stress

There is, however, one exception:

une interview

Nouns of Both Genders

Some nouns can be either masculine or feminine, depending on their meaning.

un boum	*a bang*
une boum	*a party for teenagers*
le capital	*money*
la capitale	*capital city*
le champagne	*champagne*
la Champagne	*the region of Champagne*
le chèvre	*goat cheese*
une chèvre	*a goat*

un livre	*a book*
une livre	*a pound*
le manche	*the handle*
la manche	*the sleeve*
la Manche	*the English Channel*
un mémoire	*a report*
la mémoire	*memory*
le mode	*the means*
la mode	*fashion*
le physique	*looks*
la physique	*physics*
un poste	*a post*
la poste	*the post office*
un pub	*a pub*
la pub	*advertising*
un somme	*a nap*
la somme	*the amount*
un tour	*a tour*
une tour	*a tower*
le vague	*vagueness*
une vague	*a wave*

Plurals of Nouns

There are several patterns for the formation of plural nouns in French; exceptions for each category below are noted.

- For nouns designating both beings and things, the most common marker of the plural is *-s*.

un album	*an album*
des albums	*albums*
un récit	*a narrative*
des récits	*narratives*
un rêve	*a dream*
des rêves	*dreams*

Adding *-s* does not affect the pronunciation of a noun, except in the following cases.

un bœuf (/f/ *pronounced*)	*a bull*
des bœufs (/f/ *silent*)	*bulls*

un œuf (/f/ *pronounced*)	*an egg*
des œufs (/f/ *silent*)	*eggs*

- Unlike English family names, French family names do not change in the plural, except for the name of a royal family, like *les Bourbons* or *les Capets*.

les Cartier	*the Cartiers*
les Cavallère	*the Cavallères*
les Judas	*the Judases*

- Nouns that end in *-al* change the ending to *-aux* in the plural.

un canal	*a canal*
des canaux	*canals*
un cheval	*a horse*
des chevaux	*horses*
un hôpital	*a hospital*
des hôpitaux	*hospitals*
un journal	*a newspaper*
des journaux	*newspapers*
un métal	*a metal*
des métaux	*metals*
un signal	*a signal*
des signaux	*signals*

Exceptions include the following:

un bal	*a ball*
des bals	*balls*
un carnaval	*a carnival*
des carnavals	*carnivals*
un festival	*a festival*
des festivals	*festivals*
un récital	*a recital*
des récitals	*recitals*
un régal	*a delight*
des régals	*delights*

AVOID THE Blunder

✗ des carnavaux
✗ des festivaux

- Nouns that end in *-au, -eau,* or *-eu* add *-x* to form the plural.

un bateau	*a boat*
des bateaux	*boats*
un bureau	*a desk; an office*
des bureaux	*desks; offices*
un oiseau	*a bird*
des oiseaux	*birds*
un cheveu	*a hair*
des cheveux	*hair*
un jeu	*a game*
des jeux	*games*
un neveu	*a nephew*
des neveux	*nephews*

There are, however, three exceptions:

un bleu	*a bruise*
des bleus	*bruises*
un landau	*a baby carriage*
des landaus	*baby carriages*
un pneu	*a tire*
des pneus	*tires*

- Seven nouns that end in *-ou* add *-x* to form the plural.

un bijou	*a jewel*
des bijoux	*jewels*
un caillou	*a pebble*
des cailloux	*pebbles*
un chou	*a cabbage*
des choux	*cabbages*
un genou	*a knee*
des genoux	*knees*
un hibou	*an owl*
des hiboux	*owls*
un joujou	*a toy*
des joujoux	*toys*
un pou	*a louse*
des poux	*lice*

All other nouns that end in *-ou* form their plural by adding *-s.*

un fou des fous	*a lunatic* *lunatics*
un trou des trous	*a hole* *holes*

- Nouns that end in *-ail* typically add *-s* to form the plural.

un détail des détails	*a detail* *details*
un éventail des éventails	*a fan* *fans*

The following seven nouns change the ending from *-ail* to *-aux* to form the plural.

un bail des baux	*a lease* *leases*
un corail des coraux	*a coral* *corals*
un émail des émaux	*an enamel* *enamels*
un soupirail des soupiraux	*a small window* *small windows*
un travail des travaux	*a job* *jobs*
un vantail des vantaux	*a door* *doors*
un vitrail des vitraux	*a stained glass window* *stained glass windows*

AVOID THE *Blunder*

Don't automatically add *-s* to form the plural of a noun, especially if it ends in *u* or *l*.

✗ des chous
✗ des corails

- Some nouns have irregular plural forms.

un bonhomme	*a fellow*
des bonshommes	*fellows*
le ciel	*the sky*
les cieux	*skies*
un gentilhomme (*archaic*)	*a gentleman*
des gentilshommes	*gentlemen*
madame	*lady; Mrs.*
mesdames	*Ladies*
mademoiselle	*Miss*
mesdemoiselles	*Misses*
monsieur	*Sir*
messieurs	*Gentlemen*
un œil	*an eye*
des yeux	*eyes*

- Foreign nouns follow the same pluralization rules as French nouns.

un match	*a game*
des matchs	*games*
une miss	*young lady; Miss*
des miss	*young ladies; Misses*

- Some nouns have different meanings in the singular and plural.

l'autorité	*authority*
les autorités	*the authorities*
la douceur	*sweetness*
des douceurs	*sweets*
l'économie	*economics*
les économies	*savings*
l'humanité	*humankind*
les humanités	*humanities*
le papier	*paper*
les papiers	*documentation*
la pâte	*dough*
les pâtes	*pasta*

- Singular nouns that end in *s, x,* or *z* do not change in the plural.

un fils	*a son*
des fils	*sons*

une fois des fois	*one time* *several times*
un Français des Français	*a Frenchman* *Frenchmen*
un sens les sens	*a sense* *senses*
un tapis des tapis	*a rug* *rugs*
un virus des virus	*a virus* *viruses*
un époux des époux	*a spouse* *spouses*
un prix des prix	*a prize* *prizes*
un gaz des gaz	*a gas* *gases*
un nez des nez	*a nose* *noses*

AVOID THE Blunder

✗ des nezs
✗ des voixs

■ Some nouns are plural in French, even though they are singular in English.

les fiançailles Les fiançailles ont lieu avant le mariage.	*engagement* *The engagement takes place before the wedding.*
les cheveux Elle se lave les cheveux le matin.	*hair* *She washes her hair in the morning.*
les ordures Après l'ouragan, il y avait des ordures partout.	*trash* *After the hurricane, there was trash everywhere.*
les vacances Mes vacances ont été formidables.	*vacation* *My vacation was wonderful.*

les funérailles	*funeral*
Le président a eu des funérailles nationales.	*The president had a state funeral.*

Following are other nouns that are plural in French but singular in English.

les céréales	*cereal*
les crevettes	*shrimp*
les ravages	*havoc*
les ténèbres	*the darkness*
les vivres	*food*

AVOID THE Blunder

✗ Ma vacance est formidable.
✗ Mon cheveu est mouillé.

■ Some nouns, such as those that refer to the sciences, school subjects, and some articles of clothing, are singular in French but plural in English.

l'économie	*economics*
la physique	*physics*
un pantalon	*pants*
un pyjama	*pajamas*

AVOID THE Blunder

✗ Les physiques sont difficiles.

■ When a group of nouns includes at least one masculine noun, the masculine plural is used for all dependent words.

un garçon et une fille heureux	*a happy boy and girl* (both are happy)
des étudiants et des étudiantes intelligents	*intelligent male and female students* (all are intelligent)
une robe et un manteau élégants	*an elegant dress and coat* (both are elegant)

AVOID THE *Blunder*

Don't automatically match an adjective to the noun it is closest to if it also describes another noun or nouns in the sentence.

✗ des étudiants et des étudiantes intelligentes

Compound Nouns

A compound noun is made up of two words. These two words can be nouns, adjectives, adverbs, prepositions, or nonconjugated verbs. Only the nouns and adjectives can take a plural form.

un chou-fleur des choux-fleurs	*a cauliflower* *cauliflowers*
un coffre-fort des coffres-forts	*a safe* *safes*
un couvre-lit des couvre-lits	*a bedspread* *bedspreads*
une demi-heure des demi-heures	*half an hour* *half hours*
un essuie-glace des essuie-glaces	*a windshield wiper* *windshield wipers*
un grand-père des grands-pères	*a grandfather* *grandfathers*

AVOID THE *Blunder*

Don't automatically add an *-s* to both parts of a compound noun to make it plural.

✗ des couvres-lits
✗ des essuies-glaces

Exercises

A *Write the feminine form of the following nouns. If no feminine form exists, write an* X.

1. un homme ________________
2. un Français ________________
3. un skieur ________________
4. un épicier ________________
5. un sportif ________________
6. un mannequin ________________
7. un réceptionniste ________________
8. un Canadien ________________
9. un hypocrite ________________
10. un cheval ________________
11. un chanteur ________________
12. un ingénieur ________________

B *Write the plural of the following nouns. If the plural form is the same as the singular, write an* X.

1. un banc des ________________
2. un animal des ________________
3. un jeu des ________________
4. un oiseau des ________________
5. un œil des ________________
6. un chou-fleur des ________________
7. un métal des ________________
8. un bijou des ________________
9. madame ________________
10. un travail des ________________
11. un prix des ________________
12. une chaise-longue des ________________

DESCRIPTIVE ADJECTIVES

In French, an adjective must agree in gender and number with the noun it describes. An adjective can therefore have four written forms: masculine singular, feminine singular, masculine plural, and feminine plural.

	SINGULAR	PLURAL
MASCULINE	petit	petits
FEMININE	petite	petites

AVOID THE Blunder

Don't forget to match the adjective to the noun(s) it describes.

The following chart shows the four forms of an adjective based on its masculine singular ending.

MASCULINE SINGULAR	MASCULINE PLURAL	FEMININE SINGULAR	FEMININE PLURAL
-[vowel]	-[vowel]s	-[vowel]e	-[vowel]es
-e	-es	-e	-es
-in	-ins	-ine	-ines
-ain	-ains	-aine	-aines
-un	-uns	-une	-unes
-an	-ans	-ane	-anes
-on	-ons	-onne	-onnes
-en/-ien	-ens/-iens	-enne/-ienne	-ennes/-iennes
-[consonant]	-[consonant]s	-[consonant]e	-[consonant]es
-er	-ers	-ère	-ères
-et	-ets	-ette	-ettes
-eur	-eurs	-euse	-euses
-teur	-teurs	-trice	-trices
-s	-s	-se	-ses
-x	-x	-se	-ses
-al	-aux	-ale	-ales
-f	-fs	-ve	-ves
-l	-ls	-lle	-lles
-g	-gs	-gue	-gues

- Some adjectives are invariable.
- An adjective describing a color when the adjective is also a noun

une veste marron (un marron = *a chestnut*)	*a brown jacket*
des chaussettes orange (une orange = *an orange*)	*orange socks*
une robe crème (la crème = *cream*)	*a cream-colored dress*

- An adjective describing a color when modified by another word

des cheveux bruns	*brown hair*
des cheveux brun clair	*light brown hair*
des cheveux blonds	*blonde hair*
des cheveux blond cendré	*ash blonde hair*

- The adjective *demi* before a noun

une demi-heure	*half an hour*
une demi-tasse	*half a cup*

- The adjectives *snob, chic,* and *bon marché*

une femme chic	*an elegant woman*
des magasins bon marché	*inexpensive stores*

Forming the Feminine of Adjectives

- The feminine of an adjective is most commonly formed by adding *-e* to the masculine form. If the masculine form ends in a silent consonant, adding *-e* makes the silent consonant pronounced in most cases. See the section on nasal sounds in the unit on pronunciation.

américain (*nasal*) américaine (/n/ *pronounced*)	*American*
brun (*nasal*) brune (/n/ *pronounced*)	*with dark hair*
court (/t/ *silent*) courte (/t/ *pronounced*)	*short*
fin (*nasal*) fine (/n/ *pronounced*)	*fine*
français (/s/ *silent*) française (/z/ *pronounced*)	*French*
petit (/t/ *silent*) petite (/t/ *pronounced*)	*little*

AVOID THE Blunder

Don't pronounce the last consonant of an adjective unless it is followed by *-e*.

✗ français (with an /s/ sound at the end)
✗ gentil (with an /l/ sound at the end)

☐ Adjectives that end in *-e* don't change in the feminine.

riche (*m. and f.*)	*rich*
facile (*m. and f.*)	*easy*
même (*m. and f.*)	*same*

AVOID THE Blunder

✗ facilee
✗ mêmee

☐ Most adjectives that end in *-x* form their feminine in *-se*.

amoureux amoureuse	*in love*
heureux heureuse	*happy*

☐ For a few adjectives, the final consonant must be doubled before adding *-e*.

bas basse	*low*
bon bonne	*good*
épais épaisse	*thick*
gentil gentille	*nice*
gras grasse	*fatty*
gros grosse	*fat*

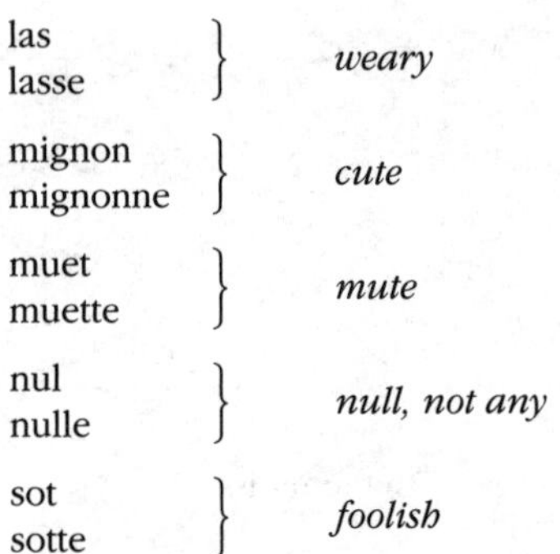

las lasse	*weary*
mignon mignonne	*cute*
muet muette	*mute*
nul nulle	*null, not any*
sot sotte	*foolish*

AVOID THE Blunder

✗ petitte
✗ grisse

■ The endings *-eur* and *-teur* usually form their feminine in *-euse* and *-trice*, respectively.

travailleur travailleuse	*hardworking*
provocateur provocatrice	*provocative*

AVOID THE Blunder

Don't confuse *-eur* and *-teur* endings when forming the feminine.

✗ créateuse

□ Some adjectives that end in *-eur* form their feminine simply by adding *-e*. Some common examples follow.

antérieur antérieure	*anterior*
extérieur extérieure	*exterior*
intérieur intérieure	*interior*

meilleur meilleure	*better, best*
supérieur supérieure	*superior*

- Some adjectives have irregular feminine forms. The most common ones follow.

beau belle	*beautiful*
blanc blanche	*white*
doux douce	*soft*
faux fausse	*false*
favori favorite	*favorite*
fou folle	*crazy*
frais fraiche	*fresh*
franc franche	*frank*
grec grecque	*Greek*
mou molle	*soft*
nouveau nouvelle	*new*
roux rousse	*redheaded*
sec sèche	*dry*
vieux vieille	*old*

Forming the Plural of Adjectives

- The plural of an adjective is usually formed by adding *-s*. The *-s* of the plural does not change the pronunciation of the adjective.

Elles sont grandes.	*They are tall.*
Nous sommes intelligents.	*We are smart.*

- Adjectives ending in *-s* and *-x* don't change in the plural.

Les fruits sont frais.	*The fruit is fresh.*
Nous sommes heureux.	*We are happy.*

AVOID THE Blunder

✗ Ils sont heureuxs.
✗ Vous êtes françaiss.

- Most masculine adjectives that end in *-al* change the ending to *-aux* in the plural. The feminine form of these adjectives is not irregular.

	MASCULINE	FEMININE	MASCULINE	FEMININE
SINGULAR	cardinal	cardinale	spécial	spéciale
PLURAL	cardinaux	cardinales	spéciaux	spéciales

Common exceptions include the following:

banal banals	*ordinary*
fatal fatals	*fatal*
final finals	*final*
glacial glacials	*icy*

AVOID THE Blunder

Don't assume that a masculine adjective with an irregular plural also has an irregular plural in the feminine.

✗ cardinauses
✗ spéciauses

Agreement with Several Nouns

■ When two or more nouns are of the same gender, the adjective is plural and of that gender.

une chemise et une veste élégantes	*an elegant shirt and jacket* (both are elegant)

■ When the nouns are of different genders, the adjective is masculine plural. As much as possible, the masculine noun should be closest to the adjective.

une robe et un chapeau violets	*a purple dress and hat* (both are purple)

AVOID THE Blunder

When the nouns are of different genders, try to avoid separating the adjective from the masculine noun.

✗ un chapeau et une robe violets

Position of the Adjective

■ An adjective can be placed next to (either before or after) the noun it describes, or after a verb like *être, sembler, avoir l'air,* etc.

La femme était grande et belle.	*The woman was tall and beautiful.*
Le prof semble fatigué.	*The professor seems tired.*
Ces livres ont l'air intéressants.	*Those books look interesting.*

AVOID THE Blunder

Don't forget to make the adjective agree with the noun, even when a verb separates them.

✗ Les immeubles étaient haut et délabré.
✗ L'actrice est joli.

■ The adjective *tout* "all/every" always precedes the article of the noun it modifies.

tout le monde	*everybody*
tous les jours	*every day*
toute la journée	*all day long*
toutes les filles	*all the girls*

AVOID THE Blunder

✗ les tous jours
✗ la toute journée

Note that *tout* is irregular in the masculine plural.

	SINGULAR	PLURAL
MASCULINE	tout	tous
FEMININE	toute	toutes

AVOID THE Blunder

✗ touts les jours

Adjective After the Noun

■ In French, unlike English, adjectives are usually placed after the noun they describe.

une voiture rouge	*a red car*
un enfant intelligent	*an intelligent child*

AVOID THE Blunder

Don't add *de* or *d'* between a noun and an adjective that follows it.

✗ un film d'étranger
✗ une fille de française

Don't use liaison between a noun and an adjective that follows it.

✗ un enfant‿intelligent
✗ un ballon‿orange

Adjective Before the Noun

■ The adjectives in the following groups must precede the nouns they describe.

- Ordinal adjectives

le premier jour	*the first day*
la troisième place	*the third place*
le vingtième siècle	*the twentieth century*

- Adjectives that describe a person's name

la belle Hélène	*beautiful Helen*
le Grand Condé	*the Great Condé*
la charmante Catherine	*charming Catherine*
le petit Nicolas	*little Nicolas*

- Certain short adjectives that are very common

Many of these short adjectives describe physical traits, such as beauty and size, and are often referred to as BAGS (**B**eauty, **A**ge, **G**oodness, **S**ize) adjectives.

B	beau	*beautiful*
	joli	*pretty*
	vilain	*ugly*
A	jeune	*young*
	nouveau	*new*
	vieux	*old*
G	bon	*good*
	gentil	*nice*
	meilleur	*better, best*
	mauvais	*bad*
S	bref	*short*
	grand	*tall*
	gros	*big*
	haut	*high*
	large	*broad*
	long	*long*
	petit	*small*
	vaste	*huge*

Other common short adjectives that always precede the noun are the following.

autre	*other*
faux	*false*
même	*same*
tel	*such*

une jolie femme	*a pretty woman*
une bonne tarte	*a good pie*
un bref discours	*a short speech*
une haute montagne	*a high mountain*
la même histoire	*the same story*
un faux témoignage	*a false testimony*

There are, however, some BAGS adjectives that usually follow the noun rather than precede it.

affreux	*very ugly*
âgé	*old*
laid	*ugly*
léger	*light*
méchant	*mean*

un homme âgé	*an old man*
un chien laid	*an ugly dog*
un enfant méchant	*a mean child*

■ A few adjectives have a fifth form when they precede a masculine singular noun beginning with a vowel or mute *h*.

beau	bel	*beautiful*
nouveau	nouvel	*new*
vieux	vieil	*old*
fou	fol	*crazy*
mou	mol	*soft*

un bel arbre	*a beautiful tree*
un nouvel élève	*a new student*
un vieil homme	*an old man*
un fol amour	*a mad love*

AVOID THE Blunder

✗ un vieux homme
✗ un beau appartement

However, if the adjective is separated from the noun, this fifth form is not used.

Cet homme est très beau.	*This man is very handsome.*

✗ Cet homme est bel.

■ When an adjective precedes a noun, liaison is used between the adjective and the noun whenever possible.

un faux‿ami ("faux" /z/ *pronounced*)
les mêmes‿idées ("mêmes" /z/ *pronounced*)
le premier‿homme ("premier" /r/ *pronounced*)

Change of Meaning Based on Position

Some adjectives have a different meaning depending on their position before or after a noun.

■ When placed before a noun, the following adjectives have an abstract sense; when placed after the noun, they have a more concrete sense.

ce cher enfant	*this dear child*
une robe chère	*an expensive dress*
C'est la même chose.	*It's the same thing.*
Il l'a fait lui-même.	*He did it himself.*
ta dernière chance	*your last chance*
l'année dernière	*last year*
un grand homme	*a great man*
un homme grand	*a tall man*
un pauvre homme	*a wretched man*
un homme pauvre	*a poor man*
son propre enfant	*his/her own child*
un enfant propre	*a clean child*
une sale affaire	*a bad business*
une chemise sale	*a dirty shirt*
un léger malentendu	*a slight misunderstanding*
un ballon léger	*a light ball*
Ce livre est nul.	*This book is worthless.*
Les résultats sont nuls.	*The results are invalid.*
une lourde peine	*a serious punishment*
Mon sac est lourd.	*My bag is heavy.*
son ancien professeur	*his former professor*
des livres anciens	*old books*

un simple "oui"	*a mere "yes"*
une histoire simple	*a simple story*
une fausse sortie	*a false exit*
une réponse fausse	*a wrong answer*
son seul ami	*his only friend*
un homme seul	*a lonely man*
une certaine chose	*some thing*
une chose certaine	*a sure thing*
pour différentes raisons	*for various reasons*
des raisons différentes des miennes	*reasons different from mine*
Diverses personnes sont venues.	*Various people came.*
des opinions diverses	*diverse opinions*
une brave femme	*a good woman*
un homme brave	*a brave man*
un sacré caractère	*a bad nature*
un lieu sacré	*a holy place*
un triste personnage	*a shady character*
un homme triste	*a sad man*

The abstract meaning of *brave, sacré,* and *triste* is only used in informal language.

AVOID THE Blunder

✗ Cette église est un sacré lieu.
✗ J'ai lavé ton sale linge.
✗ sa robe de mariée propre

■ Depending on their position in relation to the noun, the adjectives *prochain* "next" and *dernier* "last" are used to express different things.

When *prochain* and *dernier* are used in an expression of time, they follow the noun.

L'année prochaine, nous irons en vacances au Mexique.	*Next year, we will go on vacation to Mexico.*
Le mois dernier, il a beaucoup plu.	*Last month, it rained a lot.*

When *prochain* and *dernier* are used to express a sequence, they precede the noun.

La prochaine fois, tu seras puni.	*Next time, you will be punished.*
C'est ta dernière chance.	*It is your last chance.*

✗ le dernier hiver (when "last winter" is meant)

Phrases with Several Adjectives

- When more than one adjective describes a noun, each follows its own rule of placement.

Ma voisine est une vieille dame très aimable.	*My neighbor is a very charming old lady.*
La chambre a un vaste plafond blanc.	*The bedroom has a large white ceiling.*
une petite fille française	*a little French girl*

- When two adjectives precede the noun, no comma is used.

un bon gros gâteau	*a good, big cake*

- When two or more adjectives follow the noun, *et* "and" usually separates the last two adjectives.

une femme passionnante et généreuse	*a fascinating and generous woman*

Avoir l'air + Adjective

- When using *avoir l'air* "seems" to describe a person, you have the choice of keeping the adjective invariable or making it agree with the subject of *avoir l'air.*

Elle a l'air gentil. Elle a l'air gentille.	*She seems nice.*

When *avoir l'air* is used to describe a thing, the adjective must agree with the subject.

Ces bananes n'ont pas l'air mûres.	*Those bananas don't look ripe.*
Cette montre en or a l'air fausse.	*That gold watch looks fake.*

To avoid the possibility of error, always make the adjective agree with the subject of *avoir l'air,* whether you are describing a person or a thing.

Avoir l'air means "to seem," not "to look." *Avoir l'air* is used to make an educated guess about the appearance of someone or something. As an example, a person may seem to be under the weather, but you can't know for sure unless you see a doctor's note. Similarly, a fruit may appear ripe, but you won't know for sure until you cut it open.

Tu as l'air fatigué.	*You look tired.*
Ces enfants n'ont pas l'air heureux.	*Those kids don't look happy.*

Avoir l'air is not used to compliment someone on his or her physical appearance; the unintended meaning would be "it seems to me that you are beautiful."

Tu es très belle ce soir.	*You look beautiful tonight.*

AVOID THE Blunder

✗ Tu as l'air belle.

Exercises

A *Complete the following sentences with the correct form of the adjective in parentheses.*

1. Votre bébé sera un ________________ (beau) enfant.
2. Julie est ________________ (canadien).
3. C'est un ________________ (nouveau) élève.
4. Ces chats ne sont vraiment pas ________________ (beau).
5. Mes ________________ (vieux) amies et moi allons faire une grande fête de retrouvailles.
6. Il faut fêter la ________________ (nouveau) année.
7. Ce monsieur est un ________________ (vieux) ami de ma famille.
8. Cette fille est très ________________ (joli).

B *Write the feminine form of each masculine adjective.*

1. américain ________________
2. inoffensif ________________
3. heureux ________________
4. agaçant ________________
5. blanc ________________
6. bon ________________
7. jeune ________________
8. farceur ________________
9. beau ________________
10. brun ________________

C *Write the plural form of each singular adjective.*

1. beau ________________
2. gros ________________
3. principal ________________
4. affreux ________________
5. royal ________________
6. final ________________

D *Write the correct form of each adjective on the appropriate blank. Some sentences have two adjectives.*

1. Tu habites dans un ________________ appartement ________________? (nouveau)
2. C'est un ________________ arbre ________________! (beau)
3. J'ai des ________________ livres ________________ qui ont de la valeur. (ancien)
4. Marie est une ________________ fille ________________. (petit)
5. Ils habitent dans une ________________ maison ________________. (vieux)
6. C'est un ________________ livre ________________. (mauvais)
7. Tu as fait une ________________ tarte ________________. (très bon)
8. Il a une ________________ voiture ________________. (gros)
9. Mme Martin est une ________________ femme ________________. (laid)
10. Il a eu un ________________ entretien ________________ avec son patron. (bref)

DETERMINERS

French nouns are preceded by a determiner, which indicates the number and often the gender of the noun. There are several categories of determiners, including articles.

DEFINITE ARTICLES

le, la, l', les	*the*

INDEFINITE ARTICLES

un, une, des, (de)	*a, some*

PARTITIVE ARTICLES

du, de la, de l', (de)	*some, any*

EXPRESSIONS OF QUANTITY

beaucoup de	*a lot of*
un peu de	*a little of*
peu de	*little of*
trop de	*too much of*
(pas) assez de	*(not) enough of*
ne... plus de	*not any more of*
plus/moins de	*more/less of*
tant/tellement de	*so much/many of*
combien de	*how much/many*
quelques	*some, a few*
plusieurs	*several*
la plupart des	*most of*
une tranche de	*a slice of*
un morceau de	*a piece of*
une portion de	*a serving of*
une douzaine de	*a dozen of*
un kilo (un kg) de	*a kilo of*
une livre	*a pound of*
une bouteille de	*a bottle of*
un verre de	*a glass of*
un pot de	*a jar of*
un tube de	*a tube of*
un paquet de	*a package/bag of*

une cuillerée de	*a spoonful of*
une cannette de	*a can of* (drinks only)
une boite de	*a box/can of* (canned goods)
un rouleau de	*a roll*
un tas de	*a pile of*
une caisse de	*a case of*

POSSESSIVE ADJECTIVES (BEFORE A NOUN)

BEFORE A SINGULAR NOUN	BEFORE A PLURAL NOUN	
mon, ma	mes	*my*
ton, ta	tes	*your* (singular informal)
son, sa	ses	*his, her*
notre	nos	*our*
votre	vos	*your* (formal or plural informal)
leur	leurs	*their*

When a plural determiner precedes a noun that starts with a vowel or mute *h,* liaison is always used between the two.

ces‿enfants ("ces" /z/ *pronounced*)
les‿hommes ("les" /z/ *pronounced*)
des‿arbres ("des" /z/ *pronounced*)
quelques‿oiseaux ("quelques" /z/ *pronounced*)
leurs‿idées ("leurs" /z/ *pronounced*)
mes‿amis ("mes" /z/ *pronounced*)

DEMONSTRATIVE ADJECTIVES (BEFORE A NOUN)

ce (*before a masculine noun*) cet (*before a masculine noun beginning with a vowel*)	*this, that*
cette (*before a feminine noun*)	*this, that*
ces (*before a plural noun*)	*these, those*

Definite Articles

Review the forms of the definite article on page 71.

Le and *la* become *l'* in front of a vowel or mute *h,* with a few exceptions. For details on elision, see the unit on spelling.

L'arbre du jardin a perdu ses feuilles.	*The tree in the yard lost its leaves.*
L'avocate a gagné son procès.	*The lawyer won her case.*
C'est le héros de l'histoire.	*He is the hero of the story.*
l'homme en noir	*the man in black*

When used in a prepositional phrase with *à* or *de*, the definite article is contracted.

Il va au Portugal. (au = à + le)	*He is going to Portugal.*
Nous rentrons du Mexique. (du = de + le)	*We are coming back from Mexico.*
Il parle aux enfants. (aux = à + les)	*He talks to the kids.*
Ce rhum vient des Antilles. (des = de + les)	*This rum comes from the Antilles.*

Using the Definite Article

The definite article has three primary uses in French.

- To refer to something previously named
- To name concepts and things "in general"
- To express preferences

The definite article is not the most common article in French, however, and it should only be used for the specific usage described here.

The definite article is rarely used after *il y a* and the verb *avoir.*

AVOID THE Blunder

✗ Il y a l'ambiance ici!
✗ J'ai l'ordinateur.

■ Some uses of the definite article are similar in French and English.

□ The French definite article is used before a noun that refers to something previously mentioned or to something that is determined by what immediately follows.

Pierre est sorti avec la fille qu'il a rencontrée samedi dernier.	*Pierre went out with the girl he met last Saturday.*
Regarde le livre que je viens d'acheter!	*Look at the book I just bought!*
Ils ont acheté la maison de leurs rêves.	*They bought their dream house.*

AVOID THE *Blunder*

Don't use the definite article to refer to something that has not been mentioned previously or to something that is not determined by what immediately follows.

✗ Je suis allée dans une librairie pour acheter le livre.
✗ Philippe et Caroline viennent d'acheter la maison.

□ As in English, the definite article in French must be used in a superlative.

C'est le meilleur livre de l'année.	*It is the best book of the year.*
Paul est l'étudiant le plus sérieux de la classe.	*He is the most serious student in the class.*

□ When expressing a date, the number must be preceded by the definite article. English may or may not use the article in such situations.

Mon neveu est né le 7 juin.	*My nephew was born on the 7th of June.*
Noël est le 25 décembre.	*Christmas is on December 25.*

AVOID THE *Blunder*

✗ Noël est décembre 25.
✗ Ils se sont mariés mai 4.

■ There are some situations where French uses an article and English does not.

□ For nouns naming a class, a general category, or an abstraction, French uses the definite article. In English, the article is omitted.

Les enfants aiment jouer en plein air.	*Children like to play outside.*
La vie est douce.	*Life is sweet.*
le bien et le mal	*good and evil*
Le poisson est sain.	*Fish is healthy (food).*

AVOID THE *Blunder*

✗ Vie est belle.
✗ Art est nécessaire.
✗ Musique classique est relaxante.

However, when such nouns are the object of a verb (except a verb of preference), the partitive article must be used (see page 71).

Nous avons des enfants.	*We have children.*
Tu as mangé du poisson.	*You ate fish.*
J'écoute de la musique.	*I'm listening to music.*

AVOID THE Blunder

✗ Tu as mangé le poisson.
✗ J'écoute la musique classique.

□ The definite article must be used in French after a verb expressing a preference. In English, the article is not used in such cases.

aimer / ne pas aimer	*to like / to dislike*
aimer beaucoup / un peu	*to like a lot / a little*
préférer	*to prefer*
détester / ne pas détester	*to hate / to not hate*

Je n'aime pas le vin blanc.	*I don't like white wine.*
Aimez-vous les escargots?	*Do you like snails?*
Il préfère la viande.	*He prefers meat.*
Mon fils déteste le fromage.	*My son hates cheese.*

AVOID THE Blunder

Don't replace the definite article with *de* after a negative verb.

✗ Je n'aime pas de vin blanc.
✗ Vous n'avez pas aimé de dessert.

Note the difference between *aimer beaucoup* "to like a lot" + a definite article and *aimer beaucoup de* "to like a lot of . . ." + no article.

J'aime beaucoup les belles choses.	*I like beautiful things very much.*
J'aime beaucoup de belles choses.	*I like a lot of beautiful things.*

□ In French, the definite article must be used to name countries, as well as states and regions, continents, rivers and oceans, mountains, and compass points.

Nous avons visité l'Europe.	*We toured Europe.*
Il adore la Méditerranée.	*He loves the Mediterranean Sea.*
L'Himalaya est une montagne dangereuse.	*The Himalayas are a dangerous mountain range.*
Le soleil se lève à l'est.	*The sun rises in the east.*

AVOID THE *Blunder*

✗ France est un beau pays.
✗ Elle a visité Portugal.

☐ Names of languages must be preceded by the definite article in French, except after the prepositions *en* and *de* and the verb *parler*.

Le chinois est difficile.	*Chinese is hard.*
Elle voudrait apprendre l'allemand.	*She would like to learn German.*
Le texte est en espagnol.	*The text is in Spanish.*
Nous allons en cours de français.	*We are going to French class.*
Parlez-vous chinois?	*Do you speak Chinese?*

AVOID THE *Blunder*

✗ Parlez-vous le chinois?
✗ C'est écrit en l'anglais.
✗ un livre de l'espagnol

☐ The definite article must be used before people's titles in French. English does not use an article in such cases.

Le général Dupont va parler aux soldats.	*General Dupont will speak to the soldiers.*
Le président Chirac est allé en Allemagne.	*President Chirac went to Germany.*
C'est le bureau du professeur Martin. (du = de + le)	*This is the office of Professor Martin.*

However, when addressing a person directly, the definite article is *not* used with the title.

—Bonjour, professeur Martin.	*"Good morning, Professor Martin."*
—Comment allez-vous, docteur Cavallère?	*"How are you, Doctor Cavallère?"*

AVOID THE *Blunder*

✗ —Bonjour, le professeur Martin.

☐ Nouns describing parts of the body must be preceded by the definite article in French, particularly with reflexive verbs. English uses the possessive adjective instead.

Elle se brosse les cheveux.	*She is brushing her hair.*
Il s'est cassé la jambe.	*He broke his leg.*
J'ai mal aux yeux. (aux = à + les)	*My eyes hurt.*
Il a perdu la tête.	*He lost his head.*
Ouvre la bouche!	*Open your mouth!*

AVOID THE Blunder

✗ Ouvre ta bouche!
✗ Je me lave mes mains.
✗ J'ai mal à mon dos.

☐ Before the name of a day, the definite article is used to express a habitual action.

Le dimanche nous allons à la messe.	*On Sundays, we go to Mass.*
En France, on a cours le samedi matin.	*In France, you have class on Saturday mornings.*

AVOID THE Blunder

Don't use a definite article before the name of a day unless you are referring to a habitual action.

✗ Je te verrai le dimanche.
✗ Le lundi je suis allée au marché.

☐ The definite article is used to express a price per amount.

Les tomates coutent 2 euros le kilo.	*Tomatoes cost 2 euros a kilo.*
La chambre coute 250 euros la nuit.	*The room costs 250 euros per night.*

AVOID THE Blunder

✗ Les tomates coutent 2 euros par kilo.

■ Common expressions with the definite article follow.

à l'instant	*immediately*
à l'heure	*on time*
l'année dernière	*last year*
le mois dernier	*last month*
le mois prochain	*next month*
l'année prochaine	*next year*
à la maison	*at home*
à l'école	*at school*
au travail	*at work*
à la mode	*fashionable*
à la vanille / à la menthe / *etc.*	*flavored with vanilla/mint/*etc.
à l'ombre	*in the shade*
au soleil	*in the sun*
à la télé	*on TV*
à la radio	*on the radio*
prendre l'avion / le train / *etc.*	*to take the plane / the train /* etc.
faire le ménage	*to clean*
faire la vaisselle	*to do the dishes*
faire la lessive	*to do the laundry*
à la main	*by hand*
avoir mal à la tête / au dos / *etc.*	*to have a headache/backache/*etc.
hausser les épaules	*to shrug*
à l'encre	*in ink*
au crayon	*in pencil*
à la Picasso/Rubens/*etc.*	*in the style of Picasso/Rubens/*etc.

Overuse of the definite article is a very common mistake. Remember that the definite article is not the "default" article. When in doubt as to which article to use, it is better to use an indefinite article rather than a definite article.

Indefinite Articles

Review the forms of the indefinite article on page 71.

■ The following verbs often have an object preceded by the indefinite article.

avoir	*to have*
il y a	*there is / there are*
acheter	*to buy*

apporter	*to bring, to take*
boire	*to drink*
donner	*to give*
écrire	*to write*
entendre	*to hear*
faire	*to do*
lire	*to read*
manger	*to eat*
mettre	*to put*
offrir	*to offer*
prendre	*to take*
recevoir	*to receive, get*
regarder	*to look at*
tenir	*to hold*
voir	*to see*

J'ai un chat qui est très affectueux.	*I have a cat who is very affectionate.*
Il y a des fleurs partout.	*There are flowers everywhere.*
Écris une lettre à ta mère.	*Write a letter to your mother.*
Nous avons fait une erreur.	*We made a mistake.*
Si tu as faim, mange une banane.	*If you're hungry, eat a banana.*
Il m'a offert des fleurs.	*He gave me flowers.*

■ The French indefinite article is used before a noun that has not been mentioned before and before a nonspecific noun. It is the most commonly used article in French.

Je suis allée dans une librairie pour acheter un livre.	*I went to a bookstore to buy a book.*

■ In French, the plural indefinite article *des* is used before a nonspecific plural noun. English rarely uses an article in such cases.

J'ai acheté des magazines.	*I bought (some) magazines.*
Elle lui a apporté des biscuits.	*She brought him some cookies.*

AVOID THE Blunder

✗ Nous avons lu livres intéressants en classe.
✗ Elle a apporté biscuits.

Un and *une* can also mean "one."

J'ai un chat, pas deux.	*I have one cat, not two.*

- After verbs such as *se servir de, avoir besoin de, avoir envie de, manquer de,* and *changer de,* the partitive article (*du, de la, de l'*) and the plural indefinite article (*des*) are never used.

Je me sers de ciseaux pour couper.	*I use (some) scissors to cut.*
J'ai besoin d'aspirine.	*I need (some) aspirin.*
Il a envie de pizza.	*He wants some pizza.*

Note the distinction between *des* (the preposition *de* + the definite article *les*) and *des* (the indefinite article). The former denotes specific things, whereas the latter denotes an unspecified object.

Il a besoin des lunettes qui sont là. (des = de + les)	*He need those glasses there.*
Il a besoin de lunettes.	*He needs (some) glasses.*
Je parle des enfants. (des = de + les)	*I am talking about the* (= *our*) *kids.*
Je parle d'enfants.	*I am talking about (some) children.*
Je me souviens du conte que j'ai lu. (du = de + le)	*I remember the tale I read.*
Je me souviens d'histoires drôles.	*I remember (some) funny stories.*
J'ai besoin de l'aspirine qui est dans mon sac. (de l' = de + la)	*I need the aspirin that is in my purse.*
J'ai besoin d'aspirine.	*I need (some) aspirin.*

AVOID THE Blunder

✗ Nous avons besoin des lunettes. (when "We need (some) glasses" is meant)
✗ Je me souviens des histoires drôles. (when "I remember (some) funny stories" is meant)

- When a noun is preceded by an adjective, *de* replaces the plural indefinite article.

Vous avez de beaux enfants.	*You have beautiful children.*
Elle a de petits pieds.	*She has small feet.*

AVOID THE Blunder

✗ Ce sont des grands arbres.
✗ Ne me donnez pas des mauvais conseils.

However, if that adjective is an integral part of the meaning of the noun, *de* does not replace *des*.

des jeunes filles	*(some) young ladies*
des petits fours	*(some) petit fours*
des petits pois	*(some) peas*

The Indefinite Article After a Negative Verb

■ In a negative sentence (except with the verb *être*), *un, une,* and *des* become *de* or *d'*.

—As-tu des chats?	*"Do you have (any) cats?"*
—Non, je n'ai pas de chat.	*"No, I don't have cats."*
Il mange toujours une banane le matin.	*He always eats a banana in the morning.*
Elle ne mange jamais de banane.	*She never eats bananas.*
Dans mon bureau il y a des livres partout.	*In my office there are books everywhere.*
Dans votre bureau il n'y a pas de livre.	*In your office, there are no books.*

AVOID THE *Blunder*

✗ Il n'a pas des chats.
✗ Nous ne voulons pas un enfant.

However, after the verb *être, un, une,* and *des* are used.

Il n'y avait pas de tomates au marché.	*There weren't any tomatoes at the market.*
La tomate n'est pas un légume, c'est un fruit.	*A tomato is not a vegetable; it is a fruit.*
Je n'ai pas mangé de soupe.	*I did not eat any soup.*
Ce n'est pas de la soupe; c'est un ragout.	*This is not soup; it is a stew.*

Partitive Articles

Review the forms of the partitive article on page 71.

The French partitive article is used before nouns that refer to a partial amount, to part of a larger whole, or to something abstract that can't be counted. In English, the article is often omitted, although "some" and "any" can be used.

Il y a du vent aujourd'hui.	*It is windy today.*
J'ai pris de l'aspirine pour mon mal de tête.	*I took some aspirin for my headache.*

The partitive is commonly used before food-related nouns.

- The following verbs are often followed by the partitive: *avoir* and *il y a, boire, faire, manger,* and *prendre.*

Buvez de l'eau quand il fait chaud.	*Drink water when the weather is hot.*
Les enfants doivent manger de la soupe.	*Children must eat soup.*
Nous mangeons du poisson le vendredi.	*We eat fish on Fridays.*

- When an abstract noun is the object of a verb, the partitive article is used.

la chance (*naming the concept*)	*luck*
Il a de la chance.	*He has luck. (He is lucky.)*
le respect (*naming the concept*)	*respect*
Nous avons du respect pour nos parents.	*We have respect for our parents.*

AVOID THE Blunder

✗ Nous avons le respect.
✗ Il a la chance.

- In some cases, use of the partitive article reflects what the speaker has in mind.

J'ai pris un café a midi.	*I had one (cup of) coffee at lunchtime.*
Le matin je bois du café.	*In the morning, I drink coffee.*
Je mange souvent de la salade.	*I eat salad often.*
J'ai commandé une salade.	*I ordered a salad.*

- In a negative sentence (except with the verb *être*), the partitives *du, de la,* and *de l'* become *de* or *d'.*

Il n'y a pas d'eau dans la carafe.	*There is no water in the pitcher.*
Nous n'avons pas pris de café ce matin.	*We did not have any coffee this morning.*

AVOID THE *Blunder*

✗ Il n'y a pas de l'eau dans la carafe.

When to Use *de*: A Recap

- *De* replaces *des* and the partitive article after verbs such as *avoir besoin de* and *se servir de.*
- *De* replaces the indefinite and partitive articles in a negative sentence (except after the verb *être*).
- *De* replaces the plural indefinite article *des* before an adjective.

Expressions of Quantity

Review the expressions of quantity on pages 71–72.

Expressions of quantity are used *in place of* (not in addition to) another determiner. They are always followed by *de* except for numbers and the following expressions.

la plupart (+ des)	*most of*
plusieurs	*several*
quelques	*a few, some*
aucun(e)	*no*

The noun that follows an expressions of quantity can be either singular or plural.

J'ai beaucoup d'argent dans mon sac.	*I have a lot of money in my purse.*
Il a trop d'animaux.	*He has too many pets.*
Prenez un morceau de pain.	*Have a piece of bread.*
J'ai quelques bijoux anciens.	*I have a few antique jewelry pieces.*
Il n'a aucune chance, le pauvre!	*He has absolutely no luck, poor guy!*
Nous avons plusieurs chats.	*We have several cats.*
La plupart des gens aiment le chocolat.	*Most people like chocolate.*

AVOID THE *Blunder*

Don't combine an expression of quantity and an article.

✗ J'ai beaucoup de la chance.
✗ Il y a trois des chiens.
✗ Il gagne beaucoup de l'argent.
✗ J'ai plusieurs des amis australiens.

For numerical expressions, see the unit on numbers.

Omission of Articles

In English, a noun is not always preceded by an article. In some cases, the article is never used; in others, it is optional. In French, except in rare cases, a noun is always preceded by a determiner.

Nous aimons la musique classique.	*We like classical music.*
La viande est aussi bonne que le poisson.	*Meat is as good as fish.*
Nous avons des amis qui vivent en France.	*We have (some) friends who live in France.*
Elle n'a pas d'argent.	*She doesn't have (any) money.*

Following are the circumstances in which articles can be omitted in French.

- The article is omitted after the prepositions *sans* and *en*.

une enfance sans problème	*a childhood without a problem*
un café sans sucre	*a coffee without sugar*
Le film est en anglais.	*The film is in English.*
Ils voyagent en été.	*They travel in summer.*
C'est une bague en or.	*It is a gold ring.*

- The article is omitted after *être*, *devenir*, and *rester* + the name of a profession, unless the noun is qualified by an adjective or in the expression *c'est / ce sont*.

Elle est actrice.	*She is an actress.*
Il est devenu médecin.	*He became a doctor.*
Paul est un médecin très patient.	*Paul is a very patient doctor.*
Ce sont des acteurs.	*They are actors.*

AVOID THE *Blunder*

✗ Il est un avocat.
✗ Nous sommes des professeurs.

- The article is omitted after *quel* (in all its forms) in an exclamation.

Quelle bonne idée!	*What a good idea!*
Quel clown!	*What a clown!*
Quels enfants adorables!	*What adorable children!*

- The article is omitted after an expression of quantity.

un morceau de pain	*a piece of bread*
beaucoup d'argent	*a lot of money*
quelques bijoux	*a few pieces of jewelry*
plusieurs chats	*several cats*
aucune chance	*no luck*

AVOID THE *Blunder*

✗ beaucoup de l'argent
✗ plusieurs des chats
✗ quelques des bijoux

AVOID THE *Blunder*

Don't automatically omit articles in French in situations where English does not have them.

✗ Nous avons amis qui vivent en France.
✗ Vie est belle.

Possessive Adjectives

Review the forms of the possessive adjective on page 72.

In French, the possessive adjective reflects the gender and number of the object it modifies; it does not indicate the gender of the possessor of the object. (See the unit on constructions.)

ses amis	*his friends* OR *her friends*
son enfant	*his child* OR *her child*

AVOID THE *Blunder*

Don't try to infer the gender of an object's possessor from the possessive adjective.

Before a vowel or mute *h*, *ma*, *ta*, and *sa* change to *mon*, *ton*, and *son*.

Julia est mon amie.	*Julia is my girlfriend.*
Tu aimes ton école.	*You like your school.*
Il adore son auto.	*He loves his automobile.*

AVOID THE *Blunder*

✗ sa amie Catherine
✗ Le chat a bu ma eau!

Don't use elision with a possessive adjective followed by a noun that begins with a vowel or mute *h*.

✗ s'amie
✗ t'auto

The possessive adjective is not used with nouns that describe parts of the body; the definite article is used instead (see page 77).

Demonstrative Adjectives

Review the forms of the demonstrative adjective on page 72.

French does not have two sets of demonstrative adjectives like the English "this" and "that." To contrast two people or objects in French, the tags *-ci* "this one" and *-là* "that one" are attached to the noun in addition to use of the demonstrative adjective.

Voulez-vous cette place-ci ou cette place-là?	*Do you want this seat or that seat?*
J'aime cet artiste-ci, mais je n'aime pas du tout cet artiste-là.	*I like this artist, but I don't like that artist at all.*

There is no gender distinction in the plural of the demonstrative adjective.

AVOID THE Blunder

✗ cettes filles
✗ cettes maisons

Cet must be used instead of *ce* before a masculine singular noun that begins with a vowel or mute *h*. A demonstrative adjective is never elided.

cet homme	*this/that man*
cet arbre	*this/that tree*
cet étranger	*this/that stranger*

AVOID THE Blunder

✗ c'arbre
✗ c'homme

Don't use *cet* before a noun that begins with a consonant.

✗ cet parent
✗ cet rêve

Exercises

A *Fill in the blank with an appropriate expression of quantity, for example,* un morceau de. *There may be more than one correct answer for some items.*

1. ________________ vin
2. ________________ lait
3. ________________ jambon
4. ________________ fromage
5. ________________ tomates
6. ________________ confiture

B *Fill in the blanks with the correct form of the article. Choose from* le, la, l', les, de, du, de la, de l', des, un, *and* une. *If no article is needed, write an* X.

1. Il n'a pas ______ amis.
2. J'ai ______ argent dans mon portemonnaie.
3. —Avez-vous ______ sœurs? —Non, je n'ai pas ______ sœur.
4. Est-ce que ce chien est ______ chien de Marie?
5. J'ai ______ cousine américaine et ______ cousin brésilien.
6. Il y a ______ ambiance dans la classe.
7. Aimez-vous ______ livre de français?
8. Ils se sont mariés en ______ été.
9. En général, ______ poisson est meilleur pour la santé que ______ viande.
10. Nous mangeons ______ poisson ______ vendredi.
11. Est-ce que c'est ______ soupe, ou ______ ragout?

C *Write in the correct form of the possessive adjective in parentheses.*

1. ________________ sœurs (*his*)
2. ________________ amie (*her*)
3. ________________ animaux (*our*)
4. ________________ amis (*your* [formal])
5. ________________ livres (*my*)
6. ________________ mère (*our*)
7. ________________ vie (*their*)
8. ________________ oncle (*her*)

D *Fill in the blanks with the correct form of the demonstrative adjective. Choose from* ce, cet, cette, *and* ces.

1. ________________ hôtel est confortable.
2. Regarde ________________ avions!
3. Tu connais ________________ fille!
4. ________________ fruits ne sont pas mûrs.
5. ________________ idée est absurde.
6. ________________ article est intéressant.
7. On a tourné ________________ film en Russie.
8. ________________ voitures sont en panne.
9. ________________ amie n'est pas fidèle.

E *Choosing between* de *and* des, *fill in the blank with the correct word.*

1. Ils ont beaucoup ________ enfants.
   They have a lot of kids.
2. Il voudrait visiter ________ autres pays.
   He would like to visit other countries.
3. Cet enfant a peur ________ autres enfants de sa classe.
   This child is afraid of the other children in his class.
4. As-tu besoin ________ lunettes pour lire?
   Do you need glasses to read?
5. Mon chat n'a pas ________ puces!
   My cat does not have fleas!
6. Bébé a ________ petits pieds.
   Baby has little feet.
7. Nous mangerons du poulet avec ________ petits pois ce soir.
   We will have chicken and green peas for dinner.
8. Est-ce que tu te souviens ________ bêtises que nous faisions à 10 ans?
   Do you recall the silly things we used to do when we were 10?
9. Cet homme est coupable ________ crimes horribles.
   That man is guilty of horrible crimes.
10. La plupart ________ gens aiment le chocolat.
    Most people like chocolate.
11. Les chats ne sont pas ________ animaux bruyants.
    Cats are not noisy animals.
12. Elle se mêle toujours ________ affaires des autres.
    She always meddles into other people's business.

NUMBERS

Cardinal Numbers

This unit follows the recommendations of the spelling reform of 1990.

0 zéro
1 un/une
2 deux
3 trois
4 quatre
5 cinq
6 six
7 sept
8 huit
9 neuf
10 dix
11 onze
12 douze
13 treize
14 quatorze
15 quinze
16 seize
17 dix-sept
18 dix-huit
19 dix-neuf
20 vingt
21 vingt-et-un(e)
22 vingt-deux
23 vingt-trois
30 trente
31 trente-et-un(e)
32 trente-deux
33 trente-trois
40 quarante
41 quarante-et-un(e)
42 quarante-deux
43 quarante-trois
50 cinquante

51	cinquante-et-un(e)
52	cinquante-deux
53	cinquante-trois
60	soixante
61	soixante-et-un(e)
62	soixante-deux
63	soixante-trois
70	soixante-dix
71	soixante-et-onze
72	soixante-douze
73	soixante-treize
80	quatre-vingts
81	quatre-vingt-un(e)
82	quatre-vingt-deux
83	quatre-vingt-trois
90	quatre-vingt-dix
91	quatre-vingt-onze
92	quatre-vingt-douze
93	quatre-vingt-treize
99	quatre-vingt-dix-neuf
100	cent
101	cent-un(e)
102	cent-deux
103	cent-trois
110	cent-dix
111	cent-onze
112	cent-douze
120	cent-vingt
121	cent-vingt-et-un(e)
175	cent-soixante-quinze
180	cent-quatre-vingts
181	cent-quatre-vingt-un(e)
182	cent-quatre-vingt-deux
183	cent-quatre-vingt-trois
197	cent-quatre-vingt-dix-sept
200	deux-cents
201	deux-cent-un(e)
250	deux-cent-cinquante
280	deux-cent-quatre-vingts
281	deux-cent-quatre-vingt-un(e)
300	trois-cents
301	trois-cent-un(e)
1000	mille
1999	mille-neuf-cent-quatre-vingt-dix-neuf
10 000	dix-mille
10 005	dix-mille-cinq

AVOID THE *Blunder*

Don't say the letter *o* for the word *zéro* in French.

■ The numbers *1* and *7* are handwritten differently in French.

un	1	a one with a tail in the front
sept	7	a seven with a short line through its center

■ Numbers above 100 are never read out one digit at a time. In English, the number 360 can be read as "three sixty," but in French it must always be read *trois-cent-soixante.*

AVOID THE *Blunder*

✗ quarante-deux soixante-et-un (when 4261 is meant)
✗ trois soixante (when 360 is meant)

■ Numbers can describe plural quantities, but they cannot be plural themselves, with the exception of 80 and 100.

Il y a trente étudiants dans la classe.	*There are thirty students in the class.*
Ils ont cent-cinquante chevaux.	*They have a hundred and fifty horses.*

The numbers 80 (*quatre-vingts*) and 100 (*cent*) are pluralized (with *-s*) when they are not followed by another cardinal number.

SINGULAR FORM	PLURAL FORM
quatre-vingt-trois	quatre-vingts
cent-quatre-vingt-dix	cent-quatre-vingts
deux-cent-onze	deux-cents
trois-cent-deux	trois-cents

AVOID THE *Blunder*

✗ trentes étudiants
✗ cinquantes personnes
✗ deux-cent-onzes arbres

■ French never uses an article in front of *cent* "hundred" or *mille* "thousand," but it does use one before the following numerical expressions.

un millier	*a thousand*
un million	*a million*
un milliard	*a billion*
un billion	*a trillion*

J'ai mille euros.	*I have one thousand euros.*
un million d'habitants	*one million inhabitants*

AVOID THE Blunder

Don't use an article with *cent* and *mille.*

✗ un cent
✗ un mille

■ *Million* and *milliard* are not cardinal numbers; they are nouns used to express a quantity. As such, they can be preceded by an article or a cardinal number and can be pluralized (with *-s*).

six-cents millions d'habitants	*six hundred million inhabitants*
quatre-vingts milliards d'étoiles	*eighty billion stars*
un billion de dollars	*a trillion dollars*

■ The number *un* "one" and *un* in numbers above 20 become *une* before a feminine noun.

vingt-et-une filles	*twenty-one girls*
vingt-et-un garçons	*twenty-one boys*

■ Cardinal numbers are never preceded by an article, except when they represent a grade, a winning number (in games or gambling), or a date.

Il a eu un zéro.	*He got a zero.*
J'ai eu un 20 sur 20.	*I got 20/20.*

AVOID THE Blunder

✗ des 30 étudiants

■ When the definite article *le* precedes *un, huit,* or *onze* (which begin with either a vowel or a mute *h*), it is not elided.

le un	*the one*
le huit	*the eight*
le onze	*the eleven*

AVOID THE Blunder

✗ l'huit
✗ l'un

■ For 21, 31, 41, 51, 61, and 71 (as well as larger numbers ending with these numbers), *et* is inserted before the numbers *un* and *onze.*

51	cinquante-et-un
71	soixante-et-onze
161	cent-soixante-et-un
221	deux-cent-vingt-et-un
341	trois-cent-quarante-et-un

■ For 81, 91, and numbers in the hundreds or thousands ending in 01, *et* is not inserted before *un* or *onze.*

81	quatre-vingt-un
91	quatre-vingt-onze
281	deux-cent-quatre-vingt-un
801	huit-cent-un
3001	trois-mille-un

AVOID THE Blunder

✗ quatre-vingt-et-un
✗ cent-et-un
✗ deux-mille-et-un

■ In French, a decimal is marked by a comma. In English, a comma demarcates groups of thousands, not a decimal.

2,25
deux virgule vingt-cinq } *2.25*

AVOID THE *Blunder*

✗ sept mille neuf-cent cinquante-sept (when 7,957 is meant)

In French, thousands can be demarcated by a period, a space, or nothing at all.

2.225 = 2 225 = 2225 deux mille deux cent vingt-cinq	*2,225*

However, when a number does not represent a quantity, but instead represents a date, an address, etc., the digits are joined together.

chambre 3016	*room 3016*
en 1999	*in 1999*

To be sure that any number above 1000 is written correctly, always keep the digits together, with no intervening period or space.

- In an expression with both a cardinal number and *premier/première* or *dernier/dernière,* the cardinal number comes first. It is the opposite in English.

les cinq premiers candidats	*the first five candidates*
les vingt dernières minutes	*the last twenty minutes*

AVOID THE *Blunder*

✗ les premiers trois coureurs

Roman Numerals

I	1
V	5
X	10
L	50
C	100
D	500

The following categories of numbers are expressed in Roman numerals in French.

- Roman numerals are used for numbers after the names of kings, queens, and popes. Unlike spoken English, French does not use ordinal numbers for dynasties; instead, these expressions use cardinal numbers.

Henri IV	IS READ AS	Henri quatre	*Henry the Fourth*
Louis XVI	IS READ AS	Louis seize	*Louis the Sixteenth*
le pape Paul VI	IS READ AS	Paul six	*Paul the Sixth*
le pape Pie XII	IS READ AS	Pie douze	*Pius the Twelfth*

AVOID THE *Blunder*

✗ Louis le quatorzième

The only exception is for the first person in a lineage or succession. In this case, the ordinal *premier/première* "first" is placed after the noun, without the definite article.

François Ier	IS READ AS	François premier	*Francis the First*

■ Volumes of a literary work are expressed in Roman numerals, using the cardinal number designation.

« Les misérables », tome II	Les Misérables, *volume 2*

■ Political régimes, trade shows, and centuries are expressed in Roman numerals, using the ordinal number designation.

le IIIe Reich	*the Third Reich*
la Ve République	*the Fifth Republic*
XXXIIe Salon de l'automobile	*the 32nd Auto Show*
les XXVIIIe Jeux Olympiques	*the 28th Olympic Games*
le XLe « superbowl »	*Super Bowl XL*
le XXIe siècle	*the 21st century*

Using Cardinal Numbers

Expressing the Word "Number" in French

- chiffre

1 et 500 sont des chiffres arabes.	*1 and 500 are Arabic numerals.*
I et D sont des chiffres romains.	*I and D are Roman numerals.*
Il y a quatre chiffres dans mon code secret.	*My secret code has four numbers/ digits.*
C'est mon chiffre portebonheur.	*It's my lucky number.*

- nombre

Un grand nombre de personnes sont venues.	*A large number of people came.*
les nombres pairs	*even numbers*

- numéro

Quel est votre numéro de téléphone?	*What is your phone number?*
J'ai tiré le numéro gagnant!	*I drew the winning number!*
Nous sommes dans la chambre numéro 19.	*We are in room (number) 19.*
Je cherche le numéro de décembre.	*I'm looking for the December issue.*

Expressing the Date

Unlike English, French expresses all dates using cardinal numbers, except for the first day of a month, which uses the ordinal *le premier* "the first."

le 25 décembre	*December 25* OR *December 25th*
le 11 novembre	*November 11* OR *November 11th*
le 1er janvier	*January 1* OR *January 1st*

AVOID THE Blunder

✗ le 25ème de décembre

When writing a date using numbers, the first number indicates the day of the month, the second one indicates the month, and the third one indicates the year. The day and the month are usually reversed when writing the date in English.

3/7/05	*7/3/05*
le trois juillet deux-mille-cinq	*July 3, 2005*

AVOID THE Blunder

Don't abbreviate dates by writing the number of the month before the number of the day of the month.

✗ 7/3/05 (when July 3, 2005 is meant)
✗ 12/01/05 (when December 1, 2005 is meant)

There are two ways to express a year.

mille-neuf-cent-soixante dix-neuf-cent-soixante	*1960*

Expressing the Time of Day

French uses several words to translate "time." When telling time, the word *heure* is used.

Quelle heure est-il?	*What time is it?*

✗ Quelle temps fait-il? (when "What time is it?" is meant)

The response to the question *Quelle heure est-il?* always begins with *Il est....* In spoken French, however, sometimes the time is stated by itself.

Il est trois heures vingt-cinq.	*It is twenty-five past three.*
Il est huit heures moins dix.	*It is 10 to eight.*
Quatre heures vingt.	*Four twenty.*

To write a specific time, the letter *h* or a period can be used. The period is usually found in schedules, such as for trains and television.

4h30 4.30	*4:30 A.M.*
0h10 0.10	*12:10 A.M.*

AVOID THE Blunder

Don't use a colon when writing a specific time in French.

✗ 16:30

The word *heure* becomes *heures* when it names more than one hour.

une heure et quart	*1:15*
trois heures dix	*3:10*
sept heures et demie	*7:30*

The word *heure* is not used after *midi* "noon" and *minuit* "midnight."

Il est midi et quart.	*It is 12:15 P.M.*

AVOID THE *Blunder*

✗ Il est huit dix.
✗ Il est quatre cinq.
✗ Il est minuit heure trente.

The word *minute* "minute" is not used in stating a specific time.

AVOID THE *Blunder*

✗ Il est deux heures cinq minutes.
✗ Il est huit heures moins vingt minutes.

The word *demi* "half" is spelled *demie* after the feminine noun *heure(s)*. It is not pluralized.

deux heures et demie	*2:30*

AVOID THE *Blunder*

✗ deux heures et demies

The conjunction *et* "and" is added before *quart* and *demie*. Otherwise, the number of minutes directly follows the word *heure(s),* without *et*.

quatre heures vingt	*four twenty*
quatre heures et demie	*half past four*
six heures et quart	*a quarter past six*

When it is 1, 21, 31, 41, or 51 minutes past the hour, *une* is used instead of *un*.

minuit vingt-et-une	*12:21 A.M.*
dix-sept heures trente-et-une	*5:31 P.M.*

When subtracting minutes from the next hour, two constructions are used: *moins* + the number of minutes or *moins le quart* "a quarter of."

neuf heures moins le quart	*a quarter to nine*
onze heures moins vingt	*twenty to eleven*

24-Hour Clock vs. 12-Hour Clock

The 24-hour clock, or military clock, is used in most schedules (for instance, for trains, planes, television, cinemas, appointments, and business hours for stores, offices, and restaurants). To express the number of minutes between 1 and 9, *zéro* is inserted before the number.

3.01 trois heures zéro une	*3:01 A.M.*
1.05 une heure zéro cinq	*1:05 A.M.*
17.08 dix-sept heures zéro huit	*5:08 P.M.*

The expressions *et quart, moins le quart, et demie, midi,* and *minuit* are not used when telling time by the 24-hour clock.

14h15 quatorze heures quinze	*2:15 P.M.*
0h31 zéro heures trente-et-une	*12:31 A.M.*
12h30 douze heures trente	*12:30 P.M.*

AVOID THE Blunder

✗ quatorze heures et quart
✗ dix-huit heures et demie

In spoken French, the 12-hour clock is preferred, and the following expressions are added, if necessary.

du matin	*in the morning* OR *A.M.*
de l'après-midi	*in the afternoon* OR *P.M.*
du soir	*in the evening* OR *P.M.*

The word *nuit* is never used when telling time.

AVOID THE Blunder

✗ Il est neuf heures de la nuit.

The choice of using *du soir* or *de l'après-midi* is personal and may be influenced by the season and by the speaker's work schedule, usual mealtimes, or other habits. As a general rule, the cutoff time seems to be 5 P.M.: Starting at 5 P.M., it is perfectly acceptable to say *du soir.*

Expressing Telephone Numbers

Telephone numbers are usually given in a sequence of two- or three-digit groups of numbers, which are read as tens or hundreds, respectively. Phone numbers are never read aloud one number at a time, as they are in English.

0 11 334 91 64 12	zéro, onze, trois-cent-trente-quatre, quatre-vingt-onze, soixante-quatre, douze
81 02 18	quatre-vingt-un, zéro deux, dix-huit

AVOID THE *Blunder*

✗ huit-trois-un, quatre-deux, sept-cinq (when 831 42 75 is meant)

Expressing the Price

In French, written prices are expressed using a comma, with the currency symbol after the numbers. Although the currency symbol appears after the amount in written form, a price is read using the following pattern: whole number + currency name + decimal.

2,55 € deux euros cinquante-cinq	*two euros, fifty-five cents*
10,20 € dix euros vingt	*ten euros, twenty cents*
1000000 € un million d'euros	*one million euros*

AVOID THE *Blunder*

✗ € 2,55

Don't forget that *un milliard, un million,* etc., are numerical expressions, not numbers, and must therefore be followed by *de.*

✗ trois milliards dollars
✗ un million euros

Ordinal Numbers

An ordinal number indicates the place of a person or thing in an ordered sequence. Ordinal numbers are adjectives that agree in gender and number with the noun they describe.

1er / 1ers	premier/premiers	*first*
1ère / 1ères	première/premières	
2^{d} / 2^{ds}	second/seconds	*second*
2de / 2des	seconde/secondes	
2e / 2^{es}	deuxième/deuxièmes	*second*

The other ordinal numbers follow the pattern of *deuxième* for their feminine and plural forms.

3^{e}	troisième
4^{e}	quatrième
5^{e}	cinquième
6^{e}	sixième
9^{e}	neuvième
10^{e}	dixième
19^{e}	dix-neuvième
20^{e}	vingtième
21^{e}	vingt-et-unième
22^{e}	vingt-deuxième
70^{e}	soixante-dixième
71^{e}	soixante-et-onzième
72^{e}	soixante-douzième
80^{e}	quatre-vingtième
81^{e}	quatre-vingt-et-unième
82^{e}	quatre-vingt-deuxième
101^{e}	cent-unième

The *-x* at the end of cardinal numbers *six* and *dix* is pronounced /s/. In the corresponding ordinal numbers, the /s/ sound changes to /z/, but the spelling remains the same.

dix (*pronounced* /s/)	*ten*
dixième (*pronounced* /z/)	*tenth*

■ The definite article always precedes an ordinal number, except when naming the first person in a lineage or succession.

les trente-huitièmes Jeux Olympiques	*the 38th Olympic Games*
la onzième heure	*the eleventh hour*
la vingtième fois	*the twentieth time*

■ *Second* may be used instead of *deuxième* where the sequence of numbers stops at two. If the sequence of numbers continues, *deuxième* should be used. In *second* and *seconde,* the *c* is pronounced like the *g* in "gum."

Formation of Ordinal Numbers

■ Most ordinal numbers are formed by adding the suffix *-ième* to the corresponding cardinal number.

dix → dixième	*ten → tenth*
vingt → vingtième	*twenty → twentieth*

□ If the cardinal number ends in *-e,* the *-e* is dropped before the suffix *-ième.*

quatre → quatrième	*four → fourth*
trente → trentième	*thirty → thirtieth*

□ For *cinq* and its compounds, *-u* is inserted before the suffix *-ième.*

vingt-cinq → vingt-cinquième	*twenty-five → twenty-fifth*

□ For *neuf* and its compounds, *-f* is changed to *-v* before the suffix *-ième.*

neuf → neuvième	*nine → ninth*

AVOID THE Blunder

✗ neufième

Numerical Expressions

Instead of an exact number, a numerical expression can be used in French to indicate approximate numbers. A numerical expression has an article and can be plural. When used before a noun, it is followed by *de,* like an expression of quantity.

des centaines de manifestants	*hundreds of demonstrators*
un millier de personnes	*about one thousand people*
plusieurs milliers de personnes	*several thousands of people*
une moitié	*a half*
une dizaine	*about ten*
une douzaine	*a dozen*
une vingtaine	*about twenty*

une trentaine	*about thirty*
une quarantaine	*about forty*
une cinquantaine	*about fifty*
une soixantaine	*about sixty*
une centaine	*about a hundred*
des centaines	*hundreds*
un millier	*about a thousand*
des milliers	*thousands*
un million	*about a million*
des millions	*millions*
un milliard	*about a billion*
des milliards	*billions*

une moitié de pomme	*half an apple*
une douzaine d'œufs	*a dozen eggs*
deux millions d'euros	*two million euros*
un milliard d'étoiles	*a billion stars*

AVOID THE *Blunder*

✗ un milliard dollars
✗ un millier personnes

Fractions

As in English, fractions are formed in French by using the cardinal number as the numerator (upper number) and the ordinal number as the denominator (lower number). If the numerator is larger than one, the denominator must be plural.

$1/5$	un cinquième	*one fifth*
$4/5$	quatre cinquièmes	*four fifths*
$1/8$	un huitième	*one eighth*

Three fractions do not use the ordinal numbers for the denominator.

$1/4$	un quart	*one fourth*
$1/3$	un tiers	*one third*
$1/2$	un demi / une demie	*one half*

le quart	*the quarter*
le tiers	*the third*
la moitié	*the half*

AVOID THE *Blunder*

✗ un quatrième de litre

Except for *demi*, all fractions can be used as expressions of quantity. As such, they are always followed by *de*.

un quart de livre	*a quarter of a pound*
un tiers de litre de lait	*a third of a liter of milk*
une moitié de pomme	*half an apple*
trois quarts de litre	*three quarters of a liter*

Demi is used like an adjective, and as such it is placed between the article and noun. It is not used with *de*.

une demi-pomme	*half an apple*
un demi-kilo	*half a kilo*

AVOID THE *Blunder*

✗ une demie de pomme

Remember: Use *moitié* + *de* before a noun; use *demi* directly before a noun.

AVOID THE *Blunder*

✗ un demi de kilo
✗ une moitié de lune

Exercises

A *Write the French words for the following numbers.*

1. 101 ______
2. 71 ______
3. 80 ______
4. 1000 ______
5. 500 ______
6. 185 ______
7. 81 ______

B *Express the following in words.*

1. 21 filles ______
2. $3000000 ______
3. 0 euros ______
4. ½ kilo ______
5. 3/12/89 ______
6. 12:15 A.M. ______
7. James I ______
8. 9ème ______

SUBJECTS, OBJECTS, AND THEIR PRONOUNS

A pronoun is used in place of a noun or noun expression in order to avoid repeating it. The pronoun takes on the gender, number, and function (subject or object) of the noun or noun expression in the sentence.

SUBJECT PRONOUNS

je/j'	*I*	nous	*we*
tu	*you* (singular)	vous	*you* (plural OR formal)
il/elle/on	*he/she/one*	ils/elles	*they*

The subject pronoun *je* is not capitalized unless it begins a sentence.

STRESS PRONOUNS

moi	*me*	nous	*us*
toi	*you*	vous	*you*
lui	*him*	eux	*them* (masculine)
elle	*her*	elles	*them* (feminine)
soi	*oneself*		

OBJECT PRONOUNS

DIRECT OBJECT PRONOUNS

me	*me*	nous	*us*
te	*you*	vous	*you*
le	*him/it*	les	*them*
la	*her/it*		

Me, te, le, and *la* become *m', t', and l'* before a vowel or mute *h*.

There is no gender distinction in the third-person plural.

INDIRECT OBJECT PRONOUNS

me	*me*	nous	*us*
te	*you*	vous	*you*
lui	*him/her/it*	leur	*them*

Me and *te* become *m'* and *t'* before a vowel or mute *h*.

There is no gender distinction in the third-person singular or the third-person plural.

REFLEXIVE PRONOUNS

me	*myself*	nous	*ourselves / each other*
te	*yourself*	vous	*yourselves / each other*
se	*himself/herself*	se	*themselves / each other*

Me, te, and *se* become *m', t',* and *s'* before a vowel or mute *h*.

RELATIVE PRONOUNS

qui	*who/that/which*
que	*that/whom*
dont	*of whose/that/which*
lequel/laquelle/lesquels/lesquelles (*after a preposition*)	*which*
où	*where*

Subject Pronouns

In French, as in English, all conjugated verbs must have a subject expressed in the sentence. The subject can be a noun or a subject pronoun. Imperative forms are the only ones that do not have a subject expressed. The subject determines the ending of the conjugated form of the verb.

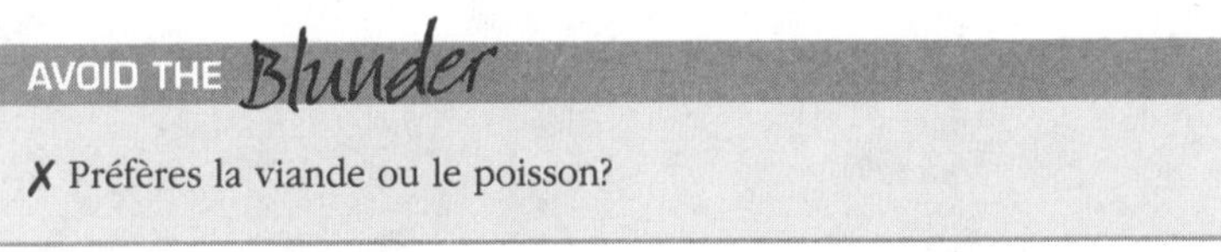

The subject must precede the verb, except when asking a question in inversion form.

STATEMENT		INVERSION	
Tu parles.	*You are speaking.*	Parles-tu?	*Are you speaking?*
Il écoute.	*He is listening.*	Écoute-t-il?	*Is he listening?*

When a noun is the subject of a verb, the subject pronoun is not used, except in inversion.

Alain aime danser.	*Alain likes to dance.*
Il aime danser.	*He likes to dance.*

✗ Alain, il aime danser.
✗ Les enfants, ils travaillent bien.

A noun subject cannot be inverted with its verb. If inversion is used, the verb will have two subjects: the noun and the subject pronoun. (See the unit on questions and answers.)

Alain danse-t-il?	*Does Alain dance?*
Les Martin sont-ils arrivés?	*Did the Martins arrive?*

Translating "It"

In French, there is no equivalent for "it" as a subject pronoun.

- "It" must be translated by *il* when it represents a noun that is masculine.

Ce fauteuil est confortable mais il est laid.	*This chair is comfortable, but it is ugly.*
J'ai un ordinateur et il est très petit.	*I have a computer and it is very small.*

- "It" is translated by *il* in an impersonal expression.

Il faut partir maintenant.	*It is necessary to leave now.*
Il a neigé hier.	*It snowed yesterday.*
Il fait chaud.	*The weather is hot.*
Il est important de bien manger.	*It is important to eat well.*

- "It" is translated by *elle* when it represents a noun that is feminine.

Regardez l'araignée! Elle est velue.	*Look at the spider! It is hairy.*
J'ai une belle voiture, mais elle tombe en panne souvent.	*I have a beautiful car, but it breaks down often.*

AVOID THE Blunder

✗ Regardez l'araignée! C'est velue.
✗ J'ai un chat. C'est noir et blanc.

- "It is" can be translated by *c'est / ce sont*, but the two expressions are not interchangeable.

☐ *C'est* + noun

C' or *ce* before a form of *être* is a demonstrative pronoun that introduces people or things. It is not a subject pronoun that names people or things in a description. In French, both people and things are described using *il/ils* or *elle/elles,* according to their gender.

Je vous présente Julie. C'est ma fille.	*Let me introduce Julie. She's my daughter.*

—Qu'est-ce que c'est?	*"What is it?"*
—C'est un grille-pain.	*"It is a toaster."*
C'est le meilleur professeur de l'école.	*He is the best professor in the school.*
Jack et Jane? Ce sont des acteurs célèbres.	*Jack and Jane? They are famous actors.*

AVOID THE Blunder

Don't confuse *c'est,* which simply introduces a person or thing, with *il/elle est,* in which the *il/elle* replaces a noun referring to a person or thing before the verb.

✗ Je vous présente Julie. Elle est ma fille ainée.
✗ Il est un grille-pain.

□ *C'est* + invariable adjective

C'est usually introduces a noun, but it can also introduce an adjective that expresses an emotional reaction to an event or object, rather than simply describing it.

Il y a eu un accident. C'est terrible.	*There's been an accident. It's terrible.*
C'est incroyable que tu ne comprennes pas!	*It is incredible that you don't understand.*
Je n'avais jamais vu la mer. C'est superbe!	*I had never seen the ocean. It's awesome!*

AVOID THE Blunder

Don't use *C'est* before a descriptive adjective unless you are expressing an emotional reaction.

✗ J'aime cette voiture. C'est belle.
✗ Je viens de finir ce livre. C'était intéressant.

The Subject Pronoun *on*

■ *on* = "one, people"

Grammatically, *on* is a singular subject that can be translated "one" or "people."

Quand on travaille bien, on est récompensé.	*When one works hard, one is rewarded.*
On ne doit pas courir au bord de la piscine.	*No running by the pool.*

- *on* = "we"

On can also have a plural meaning.

In everyday language, it is common to use *on* + a singular verb for *nous* + a plural verb. Adjectives that describe *on* are plural, and in a compound tense with *être*, the past participle is plural.

Quand il fait beau, on est tous contents.	*When the weather is nice, we're all happy.*
Dimanche on est allés au parc.	*On Sunday, we went to the park.*

AVOID THE Blunder

Don't use a first-person plural verb form with *on* when *on* means "we."

✗ On sommes allés au parc.

Don't use a singular past participle form when the participle refers to *on* meaning "we."

✗ Dimanche on est allé au parc.
(when "On Sunday, we went to the park" is meant)
✗ On s'est bien amusé chez toi.
(when "We had fun at your house" is meant)

Stress Pronouns

Stress pronouns, also called disjunctive pronouns, refer to people, not things.

AVOID THE Blunder

✗ Je parle d'elle. (when "elle" = ma voiture)

- A stress pronoun can be used to reinforce a subject, but it cannot be used instead of the subject.

Moi, je vais me reposer dimanche. Et toi?	***I** am going to rest on Sunday. And you?*

AVOID THE Blunder

✗ À qui parles-toi?
✗ Lui a de la chance.

- After most prepositions and after the expression *c'est,* the stress pronoun, rather than a subject (or other type of) pronoun, is used.

J'ai acheté ce livre pour toi.	*I bought this book for you.*
Êtes-vous sortis avec eux?	*Did you go out with them?*
Venez chez nous.	*Come to our house.*
C'est **toi** qui a fait ça?	*Did **you** do this?*

AVOID THE Blunder

✗ J'ai acheté ce livre pour tu.
✗ Êtes-vous sortis avec ils?

- When replacing a noun that is the object of certain transitive verbs + *de*, the stress pronoun must be used. Common verbs of this type follow.

avoir peur de	*to be afraid of*
être amoureux de	*to be in love with*
faire la connaissance de	*to make the acquaintance of*
s'occuper de	*to take care of*
parler de	*to talk about*
se souvenir de	*to remember*

When used as an object pronoun, the stress pronoun is placed after the verb.

Je parle de Julie.	*I am talking about Julie.*
Je parle d'elle.	*I am talking about her.*
Nous avons peur du nouveau prof.	*We are afraid of the new prof.*
Nous avons peur de lui.	*We are afraid of him.*

AVOID THE Blunder

✗ Je d'elle parle.
✗ Nous avons d'eux besoin.

After *de,* when the noun to be replaced by a pronoun describes a thing, the pronoun *en* is used.

Je parle des vacances.	*I am talking about vacation.*
J'en parle.	*I am talking about it.*
Nous avons peur des orages.	*We are afraid of storms.*
Nous en avons peur.	*We are afraid of them.*

- When replacing a noun that is the object of certain transitive verbs + *à,* the stress pronoun must be used instead of the indirect object pronoun. Common verbs of this type follow.

- Reflexive verbs + *à*: *s'habituer à* "to get used to," *s'intéresser à* "to be interested in"

Il s'intéresse à Julie.	*He is interested in Julie.*
Il s'intéresse à elle.	*He is interested in her.*

- Verbs like *penser à* "to think of," *tenir à* "to be fond of," *faire attention à* "to pay attention to," *être à* "to belong to"

Ma mère habite loin d'ici.	*My mother lives far away.*
Je pense souvent à elle.	*I think of her often.*
—C'est le livre de Julie?	*"Is this Julie's book?"*
—Oui, ce livre est à elle.	*"Yes, it is hers."*

It is helpful to memorize the few transitive verbs that take the stress pronoun instead of the indirect object pronoun after *à*.

AVOID THE Blunder

✗ Je lui pense.

After *à,* when the noun to be replaced by a pronoun describes a thing, the pronoun *y* is used.

Il s'intéresse à la politique.	*He is interested in politics.*
Il s'y intéresse.	*He is interested in it.*
Je pense aux vacances.	*I am thinking about vacation.*
J'y pense.	*I am thinking about it.*

Object Pronouns and *y* and *en*

An object pronoun is used to replace a noun that is the object of a verb and so avoid a repetition. In the form of a reflexive pronoun, it is used to reflect the action of the subject on itself.

In French, only transitive verbs can take an object. Before introducing an object in a sentence, it is important to know that the verb is transitive. For example, *partir* "to leave" is intransitive in French and therefore cannot take an object.

AVOID THE Blunder

✗ Je pars la maison.

Position of Object Pronouns

Unlike their English counterparts, French object pronouns are placed immediately before the verb, whether it is conjugated or an infinitive. As a rule of thumb, place the pronoun before the conjugated verb when there is no infinitive in the sentence. Place it before the infinitive when there is one. In a compound tense like the *passé composé*, the conjugated verb is a form of the auxiliary *être* or *avoir.*

Je dois aller au travail.	*I have to go to work.*
Je dois y aller.	*I have to go there.*
Nous allons voir Marie.	*We are going to see Marie.*
Nous allons la voir.	*We are going to see her.*

AVOID THE Blunder

✗ Tu y dois aller.
✗ Nous l'allons voir.

The following examples illustrate the various positions of the object pronoun.

Je mange ce gâteau.	*I am eating this cake.*
Je le mange.	*I am eating it.*
Je ne veux pas ce gâteau.	*I don't want this cake.*
Je ne le veux pas.	*I don't want it.*
Veux-tu ce gâteau?	*Do you want this cake?*
Le veux-tu?	*Do you want it?*
Je vais manger ce gâteau.	*I am going to eat this cake.*
Je vais le manger.	*I am going to eat it.*

Je ne vais pas manger ce gâteau. Je ne vais pas le manger.	*I am not going to eat this cake.* *I am not going to eat it.*
J'ai mangé le gâteau. Je l'ai mangé.	*I have eaten the cake.* *I have eaten it.*
Je n'ai pas mangé le gâteau. Je ne l'ai pas mangé.	*I have not eaten the cake.* *I have not eaten it.*
Mange ce gâteau! Mange-le!	*Eat this cake!* *Eat it!*
Ne mange pas ce gâteau! Ne le mange pas!	*Don't eat this cake!* *Don't eat it!*

When positioning the pronoun, do not confuse the past participle (for example, *mangé*) with the infinitive (for example, *manger*). The pronoun may go before the infinitive, but never before the past participle.

AVOID THE Blunder

✗ Il a le mangé.
✗ Tu es y allé.

■ In an affirmative command, the pronoun is placed after the verb and joined to it with a hyphen.

Mange tes légumes! Mange-les!	*Eat your vegetables!* *Eat them!*
Parle à ta sœur. Parle-lui.	*Speak to your sister.* *Speak to her.*

AVOID THE Blunder

✗ Les mange!
✗ Lui parle!

□ In the *tu* form of the imperative, the *-s* of the present tense forms in *-es,* as well as the *-s* of the *tu* imperative form of *aller,* is dropped. However, if the pronoun that follows the verb is *y* or *en*, the *-s* is restored.

Va au lit tout de suite! Vas-y!	*Go to bed at once!* *Go there!*
Mange des légumes! Manges-en!	*Eat some vegetables!* *Eat some!*

AVOID THE Blunder

✗ Va-y!
✗ Mange-en!

□ Negative commands, however, are like regular negative sentences, and the pronoun is placed before the conjugated verb.

Ne mange pas ce gâteau!	*Don't eat this cake!*
Ne le mange pas!	*Don't eat it!*

AVOID THE Blunder

✗ Ne mange-le pas!
✗ Ne parlez-leur pas!

■ One verb may have two pronouns as objects. The pronouns may be indirect object, reflexive, direct object, or *y* or *en,* in several combinations.

□ For all verb forms, except in the affirmative command

- If the second pronoun is a direct object

me			
te	le		
se	la	+	*verb*
nous	les		
vous			

Tu nous la prépare.	*You prepare it for us.*
Il me les donne.	*He gives them to me.*

- If the second pronoun is an indirect object

le			
la	lui/leur	+	*verb*
les			

Je le lui ai donné.	*I gave it to him.*
Il la lui chante.	*He sings it to her.*

- If the second pronoun is *y* or *en*

m' t' s' l' (for *le* and *la*) nous vous les lui leur	y/en	+	*verb*

Elle m'y a invité.	*She invited me there.*
Je vous y rejoindrai.	*I will meet you there.*
Je leur en ai acheté.	*I bought them some.*
Elle les en informe.	*She informs them about it.*
Il y en a beaucoup.	*There are a lot.*

- For verb forms in the affirmative command

- If the second pronoun is an indirect object

verb	+	*hyphen*	+	le- la- les-	+	moi toi lui nous vous leur

Passe-le-moi.	*Give it to me.*
Donne-la-leur.	*Give it to them.*
Offre-la-toi.	*Buy it for yourself.*

- If the second pronoun is *y* or *en*

verb	+	*hyphen*	+	m' t' lui- nous- vous- leur-	+	y/en

Donne-m'en.	*Give me some.*
Parle-leur-en.	*Talk to them about it.*

The Direct Object Pronoun

VERB + DIRECT OBJECT

The direct object pronoun replaces a noun that refers to a person or thing. The noun being replaced must be preceded by a specific determiner: a demonstrative adjective ("this"), a possessive adjective ("my"), or a definite article ("the"). (By contrast, a nonspecific determiner is an expression of quantity, an indefinite article, or a partitive article.)

Common verbs followed by a direct object include *acheter* "to buy," *aimer* "to love," *boire* "to drink," *écouter* "to listen to," *manger* "to eat," *regarder* "to look at," *trouver* "to find," and *voir* "to see."

Ils écoutent leurs parents.	*They listen to their parents.*
Ils les écoutent.	*They listen to them.*
Regarde cette voiture!	*Look at this car!*
Regarde-la!	*Look at it!*
Aimez-vous les escargots?	*Do you like the snails?*
Les aimez-vous?	*Do you like them?*

AVOID THE Blunder

Don't use the direct object pronoun to replace an expression introduced by a nonspecific determiner.

✗ Il le mange. (when "Il mange un gâteau" is meant)
✗ Elle les a. (when "Elle a des chats" is meant)
✗ Ils les ont. (when "Ils ont beaucoup de problèmes" is meant)

■ Some verbs take a direct object in French, even though the corresponding English verbs do not. "To enter" and "to leave" are transitive in English, but intransitive in French. For details on transitive and intransitive verbs, see the unit on verb types.

AVOID THE Blunder

✗ Il l'a entré.
✗ Nous l'avons parti.

■ Agreement of the past participle with *avoir*

When *avoir* is the auxiliary in a compound tense, the past participle must agree in gender and number with the object of the verb if that object is placed before *avoir*. Since pronouns are always placed before *avoir*, the agreement always occurs with a direct object pronoun. For details, see page 177 in the unit on the *passé composé*.

Il a mangé la tarte.	*He ate the pie.*
Il l'a mangée.	*He ate it.*
Tu as vu les enfants.	*You saw the children.*
Tu les as vus.	*You saw them.*

AVOID THE Blunder

Don't make the past participle agree with the subject if the auxiliary verb is *avoir*.

✗ Ils l'ont mangés.
✗ Elle les a regardée.

The final consonant of a past participle is usually silent. If the past participle agrees with a feminine object, *-e/-es* is added and the final consonant is pronounced.

Il a écrit cette lettre. ("écrit" /t/ *silent*)	*He wrote this letter.*
Il l'a écrite. ("écrite" /t/ *pronounced*)	*He wrote it.*
Il a pris les chaises. ("pris" /s/ *silent*)	*He took the chairs.*
Il les a prises. ("prises" /z/ *pronounced*)	*He took them.*

The Indirect Object Pronoun

VERB + *à* + HUMAN INDIRECT OBJECT

The indirect object is always introduced by the preposition *à*. It can only refer to people.

■ There is no gender distinction for the indirect object pronoun in the third-person singular. *Lui* refers to a male as well as to a female indirect object, and without a context, there is no way to infer the gender.

Elle lui parle.	{ *She speaks to him.* *She speaks to her.*

■ If the object of the preposition *à* is a thing or if *à* is an indication of place, the pronoun *y* is used instead of the indirect object pronoun.

Je parle à ma mère. (PERSON)	*I speak to my mother.*
Je lui parle.	*I speak to her.*

Je réponds au professeur. (PERSON)	*I answer the professor.*
Je lui réponds.	*I answer him/her.*

BUT

Je réponds à la question. (THING)	*I answer the question.*
J'y réponds.	*I answer it.*
Je vais à l'école. (PLACE)	*I go to school.*
J'y vais.	*I go there.*

It is important to look at the context before replacing the *à* + noun construction with an indirect object pronoun.

AVOID THE Blunder

✗ Je leur réponds. (when "Je réponds aux questions" is meant)

■ There is no agreement between an indirect object pronoun and a past participle.

AVOID THE Blunder

✗ Elle leur a donnés des bonbons.

■ Some verbs that require the preposition *à* may have English equivalents that do not require any preposition.

J'ai demandé à Julie. (PREPOSITION)	*I asked Julie.* (NO PREPOSITION)
Ils obéissent à leur parents. (PREPOSITION)	*They obey their parents.* (NO PREPOSITION)

Check the construction of a verb in a dictionary to learn whether or not to use an indirect object pronoun.

AVOID THE Blunder

✗ J'obéis mes parents.
✗ J'ai demandé Julie.

When using an indirect object pronoun, remember that the preposition *à* disappears from the sentence and that the pronoun goes before the verb.

AVOID THE Blunder

✗ Je parle à lui.
✗ Je demande à elle.

■ Some verbs that are followed by the *à* + human object construction do not allow the phrase to be replaced by an indirect object pronoun and placed before the verb. Instead, the preposition remains in the sentence and is followed by a stress pronoun.

Compare the following examples.

Je parle à Pierre.	*I speak to Pierre.*
Je lui parle.	*I speak to him.*
Je pense à Pierre.	*I think about Pierre.*
Je pense à lui.	*I think about him.*

It is helpful to memorize the verbs that take the stress pronoun instead of the indirect object pronoun after *à*. See page 113 in this unit.

AVOID THE Blunder

✗ Je lui pense.
✗ Elle leur tient.

The Pronoun *y*

The pronoun *y* is invariable and cannot replace nouns referring to a person.

■ *Y* is an indication of location when it replaces a prepositional phrase introduced by any preposition of place other than *de*.

Nous allons en France.	*We are going to France.*
Nous y allons.	*We are going there.*
Tu es dans ton lit.	*You are in your bed.*
Tu y es.	*You are there.*
Regarde sur le toit!	*Look on the roof!*
Regardes-y!	*Look there!*

The verb *visiter* "to visit" takes a direct object that names a place. However, even though *y* indicates location, *y* is never used as the object pronoun for *visiter*.

AVOID THE *Blunder*

✗ J'y ai visité.

■ *Y* is an indirect object when it replaces an *à* + thing construction with verbs like *jouer à* "to play," *s'intéresser à* "to be interested in," *penser à* "to think about," and *répondre à* "to answer."

Je pense à nos dernières vacances.	*I think about our last vacation.*
J'y pense.	*I think about it.*
Elle ne s'intéresse pas à la politique.	*She is not interested in politics.*
Elle ne s'y intéresse pas.	*She is not interested in it.*

Be sure to make the distinction between the *à* + person construction, which is replaced by the indirect object pronoun, and the *à* + thing construction, which is replaced by the pronoun *y*.

AVOID THE *Blunder*

✗ Je leur pense. (when "Je pense à nos vacances" is meant)

The Pronoun *en*

■ The pronoun *en* is invariable and can replace nouns introduced by an expression of quantity or a prepositional phrase with *de*.

J'ai deux chats. (QUANTITY)	*I have two cats.*
J'en ai deux.	*I have two of them.*
Il y a beaucoup d'étudiants. (QUANTITY)	*There are a lot of students.*
Il y en a beaucoup.	*There are a lot of them.*
Nous arrivons de Londres. (PREPOSITIONAL PHRASE)	*We are arriving from London.*
Nous en arrivons.	*We are arriving from there.*

When replacing a prepositional phrase that indicates location, remember that *y* is not the only pronoun that can be used.

AVOID THE *Blunder*

✗ J'y viens. (when "Je viens de Londres" is meant)

■ Specific expressions of quantity like *deux, beaucoup,* and *un peu* must remain in the sentence, even if the noun they describe is replaced by *en*.

J'ai deux chats.	*I have two cats.*
J'en ai deux.	*I have two of them.*
Il y avait beaucoup de gens.	*There were lots of people.*
Il y en avait beaucoup.	*There were lots of them.*

AVOID THE *Blunder*

✗ J'en ai. (when "J'ai deux chats" is meant)
✗ Il y en a. (when "Il y avait beaucoup de gens" is meant)

Reflexive Pronouns

■ A reflexive pronoun reflects the action of the subject on itself. In English, it is translated by "myself," "yourself," etc., but the English verb equivalent of a French pronominal verb does not always include a "-self" word. See the section on pronominal verbs in the unit on types of verbs.

Je me regarde dans le miroir.	*I look at myself in the mirror.*
Il se lève tôt.	*He gets up early.*
S'habille-t-il vite?	*Does he get dressed fast?*

■ A pronominal verb in the plural often indicates reciprocal action and is translated by "(to) each other."

Nous nous parlons.	*We are talking to each other.*
Ils s'aiment.	*They love each other.*

AVOID THE Blunder

Don't assume that *ils s'aiment* means "they love themselves." It is more likely to mean "they like each other." If there is no context, choose the reciprocal sense "they like each other."

■ The reflexive pronoun and the subject pronoun must refer to the same person(s).

REFLEXIVE PRONOUN	OBJECT PRONOUN
Je me regarde. *I look at myself.*	Je te regarde. *I look at you.*
Nous nous parlons. *We talk to each other.*	Nous vous parlons. *We talk to you.*
Ils se parlent. *They talk to each other.*	Ils leur parlent. *They talk to them.*
Il va se laver. *He is going to wash (himself).*	Il va le laver. *He is going to wash him/it.*

The reflexive pronoun must always refer to the same person(s) as the subject, even if the pronominal verb is an infinitive.

AVOID THE Blunder

✗ Je vais s'habiller.
✗ Nous voulons s'amuser.

■ The rules of placement for reflexive pronouns are the same as for other pronouns. In the affirmative command, with the pronoun after the verb, *te* becomes *toi.*

Dépêche-toi!	*Hurry up!*
Amusons-nous!	*Let's have fun!*

Do not confuse the inversion of a nonpronominal verb and the imperative of a pronominal verb—some forms look almost the same. A question mark usually indicates that the verb is not reflexive.

Regardes-tu? (NONPRONOMINAL)	*Are you looking?*
Regarde-toi! (PRONOMINAL)	*Look at yourself!*
Parlez-vous anglais? (NONPRONOMINAL)	*Do you speak English?*
Parlez-vous? (NONPRONOMINAL)	*Are you talking?*
Parlez-vous! (PRONOMINAL)	*Talk to each other!*

Summary of Object Pronouns

VERB CONSTRUCTION	CHOICE OF PRONOUN
■ verb + person or thing object	Use the direct object pronoun.
Il aime ses parents. Il les aime.	*He loves his parents.* *He loves them.*
Nous regardons la télé. Nous la regardons.	*We watch TV.* *We watch it.*
■ verb + *à* + person object	Use the indirect object pronoun.
Je parle à Pierre. Je lui parle.	*I speak to Pierre.* *I speak to him.*
■ exception verb + *à* + person object	Use the stress pronoun.
Je pense à ma mère. Je pense à elle.	*I think about my mother.* *I think about her.*
■ verb + *à* + thing object	Use *y*.
Il pense à l'examen. Il y pense.	*He thinks about the exam.* *He thinks about it.*
Je m'intéresse aux oiseaux. Je m'y intéresse.	*I am interested in birds.* *I am interested in them.*
■ verb + prepositional phrase of place object (any preposition other than *de*)	Use *y*.
Je vais au cinéma. J'y vais.	*I am going to the movies.* *I am going (there).*
Il habite sur la lune. Il y habite.	*He lives on the moon.* *He lives there.*
■ verb + *de* + person object	Use the stress pronoun.
Le bébé a besoin de ses parents. Il a besoin d'eux.	*The baby needs his parents.* *He needs them.*
Nous parlons du prof. Nous parlons de lui/d'elle.	*We talk about the professor.* *We talk about him/her.*
■ verb + *de* + thing or place object	Use *en*.
Il ne parle jamais de ses problèmes. Il n'en parle jamais.	*He never talks about his problems.* *He never talks about them.*

VERB CONSTRUCTION	CHOICE OF PRONOUN
Il vient de son bureau.	*He comes from his office.*
Il en vient.	*He comes from there.*
Il a beaucoup d'oranges.	*He has a lot of oranges.*
Il en a beaucoup.	*He has a lot of them.*

Relative Pronouns

Unlike the other pronouns, a relative pronoun does not "replace" a noun. It introduces a relative clause that describes the noun. The clause must immediately follow the noun it describes.

Le livre que tu lis semble intéressant.	*The book (that) you are reading seems interesting.*
Ils ont un chien que je déteste.	*They have a dog (that) I cannot stand.*

AVOID THE Blunder

Don't separate a relative clause from the noun it describes.

✗ Le livre est intéressant que tu lis.
✗ Le bruit vient du jardin que tu as entendu.

■ In English, the relative pronoun can sometimes be omitted, but the relative pronoun in French may never be omitted.

Où sont les livres dont j'ai besoin?	*Where are the books (that) I need?*
Le bruit que tu as entendu vient d'ici.	*The noise (that) you heard is coming from here.*

AVOID THE Blunder

✗ Le livre tu lis semble intéressant.
✗ J'ai un chat j'adore.

■ The form of the relative pronoun depends on its grammatical function in its clause: It can be the subject of the verb, the object of the verb, or the object of a preposition.

- Relative pronoun as subject

Julie est une fille qui s'ennuie partout.	*Julie is a girl who gets bored everywhere.*

- Relative pronoun as object

J'ai un chat que j'adore.	*I have a cat (that) I adore.*

- Relative pronoun as object of a preposition

la raquette avec laquelle je joue le mieux	*the racket with which I play best*

Object of the Verb: *que*

If the relative pronoun is an object of the verb in its clause, *que* is used. *Que,* which can refer to both persons and things, is followed by the subject and verb of the relative clause.

Les Martin sont des gens que je n'aime pas.	*The Martins are people (that) I don't like.*
C'est un film que nous avons vu ensemble.	*It's a movie (that) we saw together.*

Note that the gender of the noun described does not affect the form of the relative pronoun.

AVOID THE Blunder

Don't use *qui* simply because the noun described refers to people.

✗ Les Martin sont des gens qui je n'aime pas.

Before a vowel, *que* becomes *qu'*.

C'est une voiture qu'il aime beaucoup.	*It's a car he likes a lot.*

Subject of the Verb: *qui*

If the relative pronoun is the subject of the verb in its clause, *qui* is used. *Qui,* which can refer to both persons and things, is immediately followed by the conjugated verb of the relative clause.

Mon ordinateur est une chose qui est très utile.	*My computer is a thing that is very useful.*
C'est un enfant qui aime les bonbons.	*This is a child who likes candy.*
Les Martin sont des gens qui aiment l'art.	*The Martins are people who like art.*

Qui is not elided because the distinction between *que* and *qui* would become impossible.

AVOID THE *Blunder*

✗ des enfants qu'aiment le chocolat
✗ une fille qu'est souvent triste
✗ la personne à qu'il s'intéresse

AVOID THE *Blunder*

Don't change *qui* to *que* because the noun described is a thing.

✗ une moto que fait du bruit

- In a relative clause, adjectives and verbs must agree in gender and number with the *last* noun that precedes the relative pronoun.

Anne est un professeur qui est très passionnant.	*Anne is a professor who is very exciting.*
Les Martin sont un couple qui est sympathique.	*The Martins are a friendly couple.*

AVOID THE *Blunder*

✗ Anne est un professeur qui est très passionnante.
✗ Les Martin sont un couple qui sont sympathiques.

Object of a Preposition: *dont, qui,* or *lequel*

With a verb that requires a preposition, the rules that determine the form of the relative pronoun change.

With Verbs Requiring the Preposition *de*

- Preposition *de* + person or thing = *dont*

If the verb of the relative clause requires the preposition *de*, the relative pronoun is *dont,* regardless of the gender of the noun described by the relative clause.

Common verbs that take the preposition *de* follow.

avoir peur de	*to be afraid of*
avoir besoin de	*to need*
avoir envie de	*to want*
être amoureux de	*to be in love with*
faire la connaissance de	*to make the acquaintance of*
s'occuper de	*to take care of*
parler de	*to talk about*
rêver de	*to dream about*
se souvenir de	*to remember*

J'ai besoin des livres.	*I need the books.*
Où sont les livres dont j'ai besoin?	*Where are the books that I need?*
Marc est amoureux de Julie.	*Marc is in love with Julie.*
Julie est la fille dont Marc est amoureux.	*Julie is the girl Marc is in love with.*
Je m'occupe d'enfants.	*I take care of children.*
Les enfants dont je m'occupe sont mignons.	*The children I take care of are cute.*
Il rêve d'une voiture.	*He dreams about a car.*
La voiture dont il rêve est une Miata bleue.	*The car he dreams about is a blue Miata.*
Il se souvient d'une maison en France.	*He remembers a house in France.*
La maison dont il se souvient est en France.	*The house (that) he remembers is in France.*

AVOID THE Blunder

✗ C'est la maison que je me souviens.
✗ Voilà les livres que j'avais besoin.

☐ In rare cases, the *de* + *lequel* form is used instead of *dont*. See page 130 in this unit for the four forms of the relative pronoun *lequel*. *De* + *lequel* contracts as follows: *duquel, desquels,* and *desquelles*.

With Verbs Requiring a Preposition Other Than *de*

■ Preposition + person = preposition + *qui*

Anne est une fille pour qui j'ai de l'affection.	*Anne is a girl I have feelings for.*
La fille à qui je pense s'appelle Julie.	*The girl I think about is named Julie.*

- Preposition + thing = preposition + *lequel*

The relative pronoun *lequel* has four forms: *lequel* (masculine singular), *laquelle* (feminine singular), *lesquels* (masculine plural), and *lesquelles* (feminine plural).

With the preposition *à, lequel, lesquels,* and *lesquelles* contract as follows.

à + lequel	=	auquel
à + lesquels	=	auxquels
à + lesquelles	=	auxquelles

Un stylo est un objet avec lequel on écrit.	*A pen is an object one writes with.*
La compagnie pour laquelle tu travailles s'appelle IBM.	*The company you work for is IBM.*
Le restaurant dans lequel nous avons diné était cher.	*The restaurant in which we had dinner was expensive.*
Les choses auxquelles il s'intéresse sont bizarres.	*The things he is interested in are strange.*
Le livre auquel je pense est à la bibliothèque.	*The book that I am thinking about is in the library.*

AVOID THE Blunder

Don't use *que* after a preposition introducing a relative clause; use *lequel* instead.

✗ C'est un objet avec que on écrit.

The Relative Pronoun *où*

- A relative clause introduced by *où* describes a place when no specific preposition is required.

Voici la maison où j'ai grandi.	*This is the house where I grew up.*
Voici la maison dans laquelle j'ai grandi.	*This is the house in which I grew up.*

Sometimes a sentence with *où* is ambiguous, however, and a more specific construction, preposition + *lequel,* must be used.

Voici le bureau où je travaille.	{ *This is the desk where I work.* *This is the office where I work.*

Voici le bureau dans lequel je travaille.	*This is the office in which I work.*
Voici le bureau sur lequel je travaille.	*This is the desk at which I work.*

- The relative pronoun *où* may also express "when."

le jour où je l'ai rencontré	*the day (when) I met him*
l'année où Katrina a frappé	*the year (when) Katrina hit*

AVOID THE Blunder

Don't use *quand* as a relative pronoun.

✗ le jour quand je l'ai rencontré

Rules for Determining the Correct Relative Pronoun

First, bracket the relative clause and find its verb. Then ask yourself the following questions, in order.

1. Does the verb have a subject?

   If *no,* use *qui.*

Une personne [qui est généreuse] a beaucoup d'amis.	*Someone who is generous has a lot of friends.*

   If *yes,* go to Question 2.

2. Does the verb require a preposition (like *avec, de,* or *pour*)?

   If *no,* use *que* (or *où* if it refers to a time or place).

Une personne [que je connais] m'a raconté cette histoire.	*Someone I know told me this story.*
La maison [où je suis né] est bleue et blanche.	*The house where I was born is blue and white.*

   If *yes,* go to Question 3.

3. Is the preposition *de*?

   If *yes,* use *dont.*

Les gens [dont je parle] habitent à coté. (parler de)	*The people I am talking about live next door.*

   If *no,* go to Question 4.

4. Is the object of the preposition a person or a thing?

   If *a person,* use the preposition + *qui.*

Jeanne est une collègue à qui je parle souvent.	*Jeanne is a colleague that I often talk to.*

   If *a thing,* use the preposition + *lequel/laquelle/lesquels/lesquelles.*

C'est un objet avec lequel nous écrivons.	*It is an object that we write with.*

Exercises

A *Rewrite each of the following sentences, changing the direct object in bold type to a direct object pronoun. Pay attention to the agreement of the past participle.*

1. Ils veulent **cette voiture.**

    ____

2. Nous n'allons pas vendre **notre maison.**

    ____

3. Elle a acheté **la voiture de ses rêves.**

    ____

4. Ils vont voir **ce film.**

    ____

5. Ils aiment **leurs parents.**

    ____

6. Allez-vous faire **ce travail**?

    ____

7. Entendez-vous **le professeur**?

    ____

8. Etienne a invité **Caroline.**

    ____

9. Bois **ton café**!

    ____

10. Fais **tes devoirs**!

    ____

11. Il a écrit **ses cartes de Noël.**

    ____

B *Rewrite each of the following sentences, changing the indirect object in bold type to an indirect object pronoun.*

1. Nous n'avons pas pu parler **au prof.**

    ____

2. Tu as écrit **à tes cousins.**

    ____

3. Il va donner des roses **à sa femme**.

____

4. Le professeur a donné un livre **à la jeune fille**.

____

5. Prête ton livre **à Paul**!

____

6. Parles-tu souvent **à tes parents**?

____

C *Answer each of the following questions in both the affirmative and negative, changing the phrase in bold type to the appropriate pronoun (direct object, indirect object, or stress pronoun, or* y *or* en*).*

1. Es-tu déjà allé **au Maroc**?

____

____

2. As-tu **des enfants**?

____

____

3. Voudrais-tu avoir **des enfants**?

____

____

4. Les végétariens mangent-ils **de la viande**?

____

[*negative answer only*]

5. Est-ce que vous avez vu **vos parents** récemment?

____

____

6. Fais-tu souvent **du sport**?

____

____

7. As-tu visité **la France**?

____

____

8. Est-ce que tu aimes parler **de tes problèmes**?

9. Penses-tu souvent **aux vacances**?

10. Allez-vous apprendre **cette leçon**?

11. As-tu peur **des orages violents**?

12. Téléphones-tu souvent **à tes professeurs**?

13. Pensez-vous souvent **à vos parents**?

D *Answer the following questions in both the affirmative and negative, using* **two** *appropriate pronouns (direct object or indirect object pronouns,* y, *or* en*).*

1. Est-ce que le professeur vous a invités au café? [*Note the plural.*]

2. Allez-vous apporter des chocolats à vos professeurs?

3. Avez-vous acheté vos livres à la Coop?

4. Est-ce que vous voulez me parler de vos problèmes?

5. Avez-vous donné des bonbons aux enfants pour Halloween?

____

____

6. Peux-tu me prêter un peu d'argent?

____

____

7. A-t-il offert beaucoup de fleurs à sa femme?

____

____

E *Fill in the blanks with the correct form of the relative pronoun. Hint: Determine if the verb of the relative clause (after the blank) requires a preposition.*

1. Nomme la personne pour ______________ tu as le plus d'antipathie.
2. Comment s'appelle la fille ______________ nous avons fait connaissance samedi soir?
3. Le film ______________ je te parle va gagner un Oscar.
4. Un stylo est un objet avec ______________ on écrit.
5. Je ne trouve jamais les choses ______________ j'ai besoin!
6. Le livre ______________ tu m'as donné est excellent.
7. Ma mère est une personne sur ______________ je compte beaucoup.
8. Une discothèque est un endroit ______________ on rencontre beaucoup de gens.
9. La France est un pays ______________ nous aimerions visiter.
10. Mes parents sont des gens ______________ aiment l'art abstrait.

VERBS
types of verbs

Word order is very important in French. The verb is crucial in determining the construction of a sentence and the placement of all its components. When you write a French sentence, focus first on the verb. Knowing if a verb is transitive (takes an object) or intransitive (cannot take an object) sets you on the right path to correct sentence structure. The verb's dictionary listing indicates this, typically with an abbreviation like *v.t.* for a transitive verb and *v.i.* for an intransitive verb.

Transitive Verbs

Transitive verbs express a relationship between the subject and one or several direct objects. To recognize a transitive verb, ask the question *quoi?* "what?" or *qui?* "who?" after the verb. If you can answer the question, the verb is transitive. If you cannot answer the question, the verb is intransitive.

Il dort.	—Il dort quoi?	NO ANSWER	INTRANSITIVE VERB
Il mange.	—Il mange quoi?	—Une pomme.	TRANSITIVE VERB

Keep in mind that the English equivalent of a French transitive verb is not necessarily transitive itself. That is why you should ask the questions above in French, not in English.

For example, *quitter* is transitive and must have an object expressed, but its English equivalent "to leave" can be used without an object as well as with one.

Il quitte la maison. *He leaves the house.*

When "to leave" is used without an object, the French equivalent must be an intransitive verb, such as *partir.*

Il part. *He leaves.*

AVOID THE Blunder

✗ Elle quitte à huit heures.

Direct Transitive Verb

VERB + OBJECT = DIRECT TRANSITIVE VERB

Some transitive verbs, called direct transitive verbs, are directly followed by an object: They must have the object expressed in the sentence in order to have meaning. Other transitive verbs do not absolutely require an object to have meaning.

MUST HAVE OBJECT EXPRESSED

Nous donnons. (INCOMPLETE MEANING)	*We give.*
Nous donnons une pomme au professeur. (COMPLETE MEANING)	*We give an apple to the professor.*

MAY OR MAY NOT HAVE OBJECT EXPRESSED

Je mange. (COMPLETE MEANING)	*I'm eating.*
Je mange une pomme. (COMPLETE MEANING)	*I'm eating an apple.*

Some common direct transitive verbs include the following.

apprendre	*to learn*
attendre	*to wait*
chercher	*to look for*
dire	*to say*
écouter	*to listen to*
faire	*to do*
quitter	*to leave*
regarder	*to look at*
savoir	*to know*
vouloir	*to want*

Nous apprenons la leçon.	*We are learning the lesson.*
Elle quitte la maison à 8 heures tous les jours.	*She leaves the house at 8 o'clock every day.*
Ils savent la vérité.	*They know the truth.*

To determine if a transitive verb must have its object expressed, check the dictionary. The examples above illustrate the various constructions in which a verb can be used.

English verbs and their French equivalents do not necessarily have the same construction. For example, *écouter* is a direct transitive verb in French. Its equivalent in English, "to listen to," requires a preposition before the object, and is therefore an indirect transitive verb.

AVOID THE *Blunder*

✗ J'écoute à la musique.

When you learn a new verb, be sure to memorize any preposition(s) that may accompany it.

Indirect Transitive Verb

VERB + PREPOSITION + OBJECT = INDIRECT TRANSITIVE VERB

If a transitive verb is followed by a preposition, it is indirect. In the following examples, note that the English equivalents of the French verbs may have a direct or indirect object.

avoir peur de quelqu'un	*to be afraid of someone*
obéir à quelqu'un	*to obey someone*
parler à quelqu'un	*to talk to someone*
Il écrit à sa mère.	*He writes to his mother.*
Parlez au professeur.	*Talk to the professor.*

To recognize an indirect transitive verb, ask the question *quoi?* "what?" or *qui?* "who?" after the verb. If you need to add a preposition in order to answer the question, the verb has an indirect construction. If you cannot answer the question at all, the verb is not transitive.

Il mange.	—Il mange quoi?	—Une pomme.	DIRECT TRANSITIVE VERB
Il parle.	—Il parle quoi/qui?	—**À** sa mère.	INDIRECT TRANSITIVE VERB

Transitive Verbs with Two Objects

Some transitive verbs can have two objects, usually a direct object and an indirect object. The indirect object always refers to a person. Following are some common verbs of this type.

apprendre quelque chose à quelqu'un	*to teach someone something*
demander quelque chose à quelqu'un	*to ask someone something*
dire quelque chose à quelqu'un	*to tell someone something*
donner quelque chose à quelqu'un	*to give someone something*
écrire quelque chose à quelqu'un	*to write someone something*
envoyer quelque chose à quelqu'un	*to send someone something*
montrer quelque chose à quelqu'un	*to show someone something*
raconter quelque chose à quelqu'un	*to tell someone something*
répondre quelque chose à quelqu'un	*to answer someone something*

Ils écrivent une lettre au Père Noël.	*They write a letter to Santa.*
Elle raconte une histoire à ses enfants.	*She tells a story to her children.*
Il apprend la grammaire aux étudiants.	*He teaches the students grammar.*

■ In French, the direct object must be closer to the verb, followed by the indirect object. In English, the order of the two objects can vary.

Il donne une pomme au professeur.	*He gives an apple to the teacher.* *He gives the teacher an apple.*

AVOID THE Blunder

✗ Il donne au professeur une pomme.
✗ Elle raconte aux enfants une histoire.

Intransitive Verbs

Intransitive verbs do not take an object, and their meaning is complete without one. Examples of common intransitive verbs include: *arriver* "to arrive," *bavarder* "to chat," *courir* "to run," *crier* "to shout," *dormir* "to sleep," *entrer* "to enter," *être* "to be," *mourir* "to die," *naitre* "to be born," *partir* "to leave," *rester* "to stay," and *venir* "to come." Most verbs expressing movement are intransitive.

Les enfants dorment.	*The children are sleeping.*
Nous sommes arrivés.	*We have arrived.*

The English equivalents of some of these intransitive verbs are transitive, like "to enter (a room)" and "to leave (a house)."

AVOID THE Blunder

✗ Elle entre la maison. (entrer, *v.i.*)
✗ Ils sont partis le bureau. (partir, *v.i.*)

Some transitive verbs can be used intransitively, and their meaning may change according to their use.

passer (*v.i.*)	*to pass by*
passer (*v.t.*)	*to hand over something*
patiner (*v.i.*)	*to skate*
patiner (*v.t.*)	*to give a sheen to something*

plonger (*v.i.*)	*to dive*
plonger (*v.t.*)	*to dip something*

Pronominal Verbs

Pronominal verbs are listed in the dictionary with the pronoun *se,* for example, *se lever* and *se souvenir.* See also the unit on subjects, objects, and their pronouns.

Form of Pronominal Verbs

The pronoun *se* cannot be detached from the verb in any form, even in commands, and it has the same person and number as the subject of the verb, even when the verb itself remains unconjugated and has an implied subject.

SUBJECT	REFLEXIVE PRONOUN
je	me/m'
tu	te/t'
	toi (*after the verb in affirmative commands*)
il/elle	se/s'
nous	nous
vous	vous
ils/elles	se/s'

Me, te, and *se* become *m', t',* and *s'* before a vowel or mute *h.*

Nous nous promenons.	*We are taking a walk.*
Nous aimons nous reposer.	*We like to rest.*
Tu te coiffes.	*You are fixing your hair.*
Lève-toi!	*Get up!*
Ils s'aiment.	*They love each other.*

AVOID THE Blunder

✗ Vous se promenez.
✗ Tu vas se reposer.

Position of Reflexive Pronouns

Like other pronouns, the reflexive pronoun must immediately precede the verb, except in affirmative commands, where it follows the verb. With an infinitive in the sentence, the reflexive pronoun precedes the infinitive, and in a compound tense, it precedes the conjugated form of the auxiliary *être* (see the unit on subjects, objects, and their pronouns). Note the position of the reflexive pronouns below.

Tu te souviens.	*You remember.*
Tu ne te souviens pas.	*You do not remember.*
Tu t'es souvenu(e).	*You remembered.*
Tu ne t'es pas souvenu(e).	*You did not remember.*
Tu vas te souvenir.	*You are going to remember.*
Tu ne vas pas te souvenir.	*You are not going to remember.*
Souviens-toi!	*Remember!*
Ne te souviens pas!	*Don't remember!*
Te souviens-tu?	*Do you remember?*
T'es-tu souvenu(e)?	*Did you remember?*
Vas-tu te souvenir?	*Are you going to remember?*

Pronominal Verbs in Compound Tenses

In compound tenses like the *passé composé*, the auxiliary of a pronominal verb is always *être*.

AVOID THE Blunder

Don't use *avoir* to form the compound tenses of a pronominal verb.

✗ Je m'ai amusé.
✗ Nous nous avons réveillés.

- As with any verb conjugated with *être,* the past participle of a pronominal verb must agree in gender and number with the subject.

Il s'est blessé.	*He hurt himself.*
Elle s'est coiffée.	*She did her hair.*
Nous nous sommes amusés.	*We had fun.*

AVOID THE Blunder

✗ Elle s'est coiffé.
✗ Nous nous sommes amusé.

In fact, the agreement is between the reflexive pronoun (which reflects the subject) and the past participle. For the sake of simplicity, however, and to make the rule easier to remember, we call it "agreement with the subject."

■ In some cases, the past participle of a pronominal verb remains invariable.

□ If a direct object is expressed after the verb, there is no agreement between the past participle and the subject.

Elle s'est lavée. (AGREEMENT WITH THE SUBJECT)	*She washed (herself).*
Elle s'est lavé les mains. (NO AGREEMENT)	*She washed her hands.*

This frequently happens with verbs that describe daily routines or injuries, when the object is a part of the body (*les dents, les cheveux, les mains, la cheville, le bras,* etc.).

Ils se sont brossé les dents.	*They brushed their teeth.*
Elle s'est brossé les cheveux.	*She brushed her hair.*
Nous nous sommes lavé les mains.	*We washed our hands.*
Elle s'est cassé le bras.	*She broke her arm.*
Elle s'est offert un bijou.	*She bought herself a piece of jewelry.*

AVOID THE Blunder

✗ Ils se sont brossés les dents.
✗ Elle s'est cassée la jambe.

□ If the object (for example, *les mains* or *le bras*) is replaced by a direct object pronoun (*les* or *le*), the past participle must agree with that pronoun. This occurs infrequently.

Elle s'est lavé les mains.	*She washed her hands.*
Elle se les est lavées.	*She washed them.*
Ils se sont brossé les dents.	*They brushed their teeth.*
Ils se les sont brossées.	*They brushed them.*

AVOID THE Blunder

✗ Elle se les est lavée. (when "She washed them" is meant)
✗ Ils se la sont offerts. (when "They bought it for themselves" is meant)

☐ If a pronominal verb has a nonpronominal form that takes *à*, no agreement occurs.

Some common verbs of this type, in their nonpronominal form, include the following.

demander	*to ask*
dire	*to tell*
donner	*to give*
écrire	*to write*
envoyer	*to send*
montrer	*to show*
raconter	*to tell*
rendre	*to give back*
téléphoner	*to phone*

Ils se sont parlé longuement.	*They talked (to each other) for a long time.*
Ils se sont donné rendez-vous.	*They made a date.*

To identify a pronominal verb of this type, ask the question *qui?* or *à qui?* of its nonpronominal form. If you identify it as an indirect transitive verb (verb + *à* + object), the past participle should remain invariable.

AVOID THE Blunder

✗ Ils se sont parlés.
✗ Elles se sont écrites.

Agreement of the Past Participle of Pronominal Verbs: A Summary

■ In general, the past participle agrees in gender and number with the subject of the verb.

Elle s'est levée.	*She got up.*
Ils se sont souvenus.	*They remembered.*

■ If the verb is indirect transitive (takes an indirect object) in its nonpronominal form, there is no agreement.

Ils se sont parlé. (NONPRONOMINAL FORM = parler à quelqu'un) — *They talked (to each other).*

■ If the verb has a direct object that is expressed in the sentence and the direct object follows the conjugated form of *être,* there is no agreement with the subject or with the object.

Elle s'est lavé les mains. — *She washed her hands.*

■ If the direct object of the verb is replaced by a direct object pronoun that precedes the conjugated form of *être,* the past participle agrees with the direct object (though this is rare).

Elle se les est lavées. — *She washed them.*

■ The past participle of *se rendre compte* is always invariable.

Elle s'est rendu compte qu'elle n'avait pas tout vu. — *She realized she had not seen everything.*

Types of Pronominal Verbs

Pronominal verbs can be divided into three categories: reflexive verbs, "idiomatic" reflexive verbs, and reciprocal verbs.

■ Reflexive verbs express an action performed by the subject on himself, herself, or themselves. If used without the pronoun *se*, the verb is usually transitive.

REFLEXIVE	Elle se réveille tôt.	*She wakes up early.*
NONREFLEXIVE	Elle réveille les enfants.	*She wakes the children up.*

AVOID THE Blunder

Don't add *moi-même* to a pronominal verb to express "myself."

✗ Je me regarde moi-même. (when "I look at myself" is meant)

Common reflexive verbs and their nonpronominal counterparts follow.

s'habiller	*to get dressed*	habiller	*to dress (someone)*
se laver	*to wash (oneself)*	laver	*to wash (something)*
se raser	*to shave (oneself)*	raser	*to shave (someone)*
se regarder	*to look at oneself*	regarder	*to look at (someone)*

□ To translate a French reflexive verb, you may not need to add "oneself" to the basic English verb. Some English verbs have an implied reflexive meaning, but French verbs never do.

se regarder	*to look at oneself* (*oneself* required)
s'habiller	*to get dressed* (implied reflexive meaning)

Ils se sont rencontrés au cinéma.	*They met at the movies.*
Est-ce que tu t'es lavé?	*Did you wash?*
Elle se lève à 8 heures.	*She gets up at 8:00.*

Most French verbs dealing with daily routine are pronominal.

se réveiller	*to wake up*
se lever	*to get up*
se préparer	*to get ready*
se laver	*to wash (oneself)*
se raser	*to shave (oneself)*
se maquiller	*to put makeup on*
se brosser (les dents/cheveux)	*to brush (one's teeth/hair)*
s'habiller	*to get dressed*
se reposer	*to rest*
se déshabiller	*to undress*
se coucher	*to go to bed*
s'endormir	*to fall asleep*

A French reflexive verb may have an English equivalent that is not reflexive. As a general rule, if you can add "(to) oneself" or "(to) each other" to the English verb, use a pronominal verb in French.

Est-ce que tu t'es lavé?	*Did you wash (yourself)?*
Est-ce que tu t'es reposé?	*Did you rest (yourself)?*

■ "Idiomatic" reflexive verbs are those for which the pronoun does not actually reflect anything—certainly not the subject. Many of these verbs are never used without a reflexive pronoun, while others have a different meaning when used without one.

Common "idiomatic" reflexive verbs and their nonpronominal counterparts (if a verb has one) follow.

s'adresser à	*to talk to*	adresser	*to send*
s'appeler	*to be named*	appeler	*to call*
s'attendre à	*to expect*	attendre	*to wait*
se dépêcher	*to hurry*	—	
se douter de	*to suspect*	douter	*to doubt*
s'entendre	*to get along*	entendre	*to hear*
se moquer	*to make fun*	—	
se plaindre	*to complain*	plaindre	*to pity*
se rappeler	*to remember*	rappeler	*to call back*
se reposer	*to rest*	reposer	*to put back*
se servir de	*to use*	servir	*to serve*
se souvenir	*to remember*	—	
se tromper	*to make an error*	tromper	*to mislead*
se trouver	*to be located*	trouver	*to find*

Idiomatic reflexive verbs follow the same rules of formation and use as other reflexive verbs. The pronoun must agree in person and number with the subject, even though they don't reflect each other in meaning.

In the *passé composé*, the past participle agrees with the subject.

Elle s'est souvenue.	*She remembered.*
Ils se sont reposés.	*They rested.*

■ Reciprocal verbs are pronominal verbs in the plural that indicate that the action goes back and forth between the subjects. In English, these verbs are translated by verb + "(to) one another / each other."

Pierre et Marie se regardent.	*Pierre and Marie are looking at each other.*
Vous vous téléphonez souvent.	*You call each other often.*

AVOID THE Blunder

Don't add an expression like *l'un l'autre* to a plural pronominal verb to translate "(to) one another."

✗ Ils s'aiment l'un l'autre.
✗ Nous nous regardons l'un l'autre.

Many verbs, especially those expressing communication between people, can become reciprocal verbs. Examples of such reciprocal verbs and their indirect transitive nonreciprocal forms follow.

s'aimer	*to love each other*	aimer	*to love*
se détester	*to hate each other*	détester	*to hate*
se dire	*to tell each other*	dire	*to tell*
s'écrire	*to write to each other*	écrire	*to write*
se parler	*to talk to each other*	parler	*to talk*
se téléphoner	*to phone each other*	téléphoner	*to phone*

Some verbs however, cannot be pronominal. For these verbs, *ensemble* "together" must be used.

Ils jouent ensemble.	*They play together.*
Nous dinons ensemble.	*We have dinner together.*

AVOID THE Blunder

Don't use a pronominal verb in French if "together" can be added to the English verb (instead of "each other").

✗ Nous nous mangeons. (when "We eat together" is meant)
✗ Les enfants se dorment. (when "The kids sleep together" is meant)

Exercises

A *Express the following in English.*

1. Les enfants se moquent de toi.

 ____

2. Déjeunons ensemble samedi.

 ____

3. Qu'est-ce que tu écoutes?

 ____

4. Tu te brosses les dents trois fois par jour.

 ____

5. Il ne s'est pas souvenu de mon anniversaire.

 ____

6. Regarde-toi!

 ____

7. Hier soir, nous nous sommes parlé deux heures au téléphone.

 ____

B *Express the following in French, using pronominal verbs. Pay attention to the agreement of the past participle.*

1. *They love each other.*

 ____

2. *They don't speak to each other anymore.*

 ____

3. *We visit each other frequently.*

 ____

4. *They helped each other.*

 ____

5. *They met at the park.*

 ____

6. *Did you wash your hands, Janine?*

 ____

7. *She got up at 8 A.M.*

 ____

VERBS
the infinitive

The infinitive is the nonconjugated form of a verb as it is found in the dictionary. Unlike the English infinitive, which consists of two words ("to" + verb), the French infinitive is a single word. Its ending of *-er, -ir,* or *-re* indicates which conjugation pattern the verb follows when it is conjugated.

A typical dictionary entry as shown below provides basic information about the verb.

parler (*v.i.*)	*Parler* is an *-er* verb, and it is intransitive.
souvenir (se)	*Se souvenir* is an *-ir* verb, and it is pronominal (with the pronoun *se*).

For more information, see the unit on types of verbs.

Some verbs may not be listed in a conjugation table, since they are compounds of a verb that is listed.

venir	*to come*
prévenir	*to warn*
revenir	*to come back*
devenir	*to become*
prendre	*to take*
reprendre	*to take again*
apprendre	*to learn*
tenir	*to hold*
obtenir	*to obtain*

■ In a negative sentence, both negative words are placed before an infinitive. Exceptions are *personne, nulle part, ni,* and *aucun.*

Le dimanche nous aimons ne rien faire.	*On Sundays we like to do nothing.*
Il vaut mieux ne pas réveiller un ours qui dort.	*It is better to not wake up a sleeping bear.*
Nous préférons n'inviter personne.	*We would rather not invite anybody.*
Il préfère n'avoir aucun problème.	*He would rather not have any problem.*

■ The infinitive is typically used after a conjugated verb when all verbs have the same (implied) subject.

Elle voudrait aller danser.	*She would like to go dancing.*
Je préfère partir maintenant.	*I prefer to leave now.*
Tu dois finir ton travail.	*You must finish your work.*
Nous allons commencer.	*We are going to start.*
Veux-tu sortir ce soir?	*Do you want to go out tonight?*
Julie apprend à skier.	*Julie is learning to ski.*
Votre fils semble grandir rapidement.	*Your son seems to grow quickly.*
Il aime lire.	*He likes to read.*
Cet enfant sait déjà lire et écrire.	*This child can already read and write.*

AVOID THE Blunder

✗ Je préfère je pars maintenant.

□ In the case of a generic subject, the sentence becomes a proverbial saying.

Il faut manger pour vivre.	*It is necessary to eat, in order to live.*
Il faut travailler.	*It is necessary to work.*

□ After a conjugated verb, English may use a gerund (verb + "-ing") instead of an infinitive. In French, however, the verb that follows the conjugated verb must be an infinitive.

Il aime regarder la télé.	*He likes watching TV.*
Ils vont danser.	*They go dancing.*
Nous préférons faire du yoga.	*We prefer practicing yoga.*

AVOID THE Blunder

✗ Il aime regardant la télé.
✗ Ils vont dansant.

□ If the subject of the verb in a dependent clause is different from the subject of the verb in the main clause, the subjunctive is used in French, even though the infinitive is used in English. (See the unit on the subjunctive mood.)

Le professeur veut que ses étudiants réussissent.	*The professor wants his students to succeed.*
Je voudrais que tu m'écoutes.	*I would like you to listen to me.*

AVOID THE *Blunder*

✗ Le prof veut ses étudiants réussir.
✗ Les enfants aiment leur mère faire un bon dessert.

Using the Infinitive

The Infinitive as a Command

The French infinitive can replace an imperative. This use is generally limited to notices and written instructions.

Ne pas courir au bord de la piscine.	*Do not run by the pool.*
Ajouter du sel.	*Add salt.*

"To" in the English Infinitive

In English, "to" always precedes an infinitive. "To" is not a preposition in this case, and it should not be translated into French.

AVOID THE *Blunder*

✗ Il préfère à boire de l'eau.
✗ Elle veut à dormir.

If you can replace the "to" of the English infinitive by "in order to," you must use the French word *pour* before the infinitive in French.

Il aime lire.	*He likes to read.*
Il lit pour apprendre.	*He reads to (in order to) learn.*

AVOID THE *Blunder*

✗ Il lit apprendre.

The Prepositions *à* and *de* and the Infinitive

Many French verbs are followed by the prepositions *à* or *de,* which may affect the structure of the sentence. If *à* or *de* introduces a noun, the noun is an indirect object. However, when *à* or *de* introduces an infinitive, it has no effect on the sentence. For this reason, it can be difficult to remember which verbs may be followed by *à* or *de* and which ones may not.

J'apprends à skier.	*I am learning to ski.*
J'obéis à mes parents.	*I obey my parents.*
Il m'aide à me préparer.	*He helps me get ready.*
Arrête de pleurer.	*Quit crying.*

AVOID THE Blunder

Don't assume that a French verb imitates the structure of its English equivalent.

✗ J'écoute à la radio.

■ Some common French verbs followed directly by an infinitive, without a preposition, include most verbs of perception, like the following.

écouter	*to listen to*
entendre	*to hear*
regarder	*to look at*
sentir	*to feel*
voir	*to see*

Other common verbs followed directly by an infinitive include the following.

aimer	*to like to*
aller	*to be going to*
devoir	*to have to*
envoyer	*to send to*
espérer	*to hope to*
faillir	*to almost* (as a qualifier for the following infinitive)
faire	*to make*
falloir	*to be necessary to* (impersonal verb)
laisser	*to let*
penser	*to consider (_____ing)*
pouvoir	*to be able to*
préférer	*to prefer to*
savoir	*to know how to*
sembler	*to seem to*
vouloir	*to want to*

Il aime danser.	*He likes to dance.*
Nous voulons sortir.	*We want to go out.*
J'ai failli tomber.	*I almost fell.*
Elle semble dormir.	*She seems to be sleeping.*

■ The following are examples of French verbs that require the preposition *à* when followed by an infinitive.

aider à	*to help (to)*
apprendre à	*to learn (how) to*
arriver à	*to manage to*
commencer à	*to begin to*
continuer à	*to continue (____ing)*
s'habituer à	*to get used to (____ing)*
inviter à	*to invite to*
se mettre à	*to start to*
obliger à	*to force to*
penser à	*to remember to*
réussir à	*to succeed in (____ing)*

■ The following are examples of French verbs that require the preposition *de* when followed by an infinitive.

accepter de	*to agree to*
arrêter de	*to stop (____ing)*
choisir de	*to choose to*
décider de	*to decide to*
défendre de	*to forbid to*
essayer de	*to try to*
être + *adjective* + de	*to be* + adjective + *to*
être obligé de	*to have to*
finir de	*to stop (____ing)*
oublier de	*to forget to*
refuser de	*to refuse to*
regretter de	*to regret to*
se souvenir de	*to remember to*

Note that the English equivalents of these verbs do not require a preposition.

Il a essayé de venir.	*He tried to come.*
Ils ont décidé d'arrêter.	*They decided to stop.*

AVOID THE Blunder

Don't forget, when translating from English to French, to check whether the French verb requires a preposition.

✗ J'obéis mes parents.
✗ J'écoute à la radio.

■ Many of the verbs that require a preposition when followed by an infinitive do not require the preposition when followed by a noun. For example, *aider* takes *à* before an infinitive, but no preposition before a noun (*aider quelqu'un à faire...*). Similarly, *finir* takes *de* before an infinitive, but no preposition before a noun (*finir ses devoirs*).

Le chat essaie de monter sur la fenêtre.	*The cat tries to climb on the window.*
Elle essaie une nouvelle jupe.	*She tries on a new skirt.*
Il a choisi de continuer.	*He chose to continue.*
Il a choisi un ballon rouge.	*He chose a red balloon.*

AVOID THE Blunder

✗ Nous apprenons à la leçon.
✗ Il a invité à Julie.
✗ Tu as oublié de notre rendez-vous.

■ These common English verbs take a preposition, even though their French equivalents never do.

attendre quelqu'un	*to wait for someone*
chercher quelque chose	*to look for something*
écouter quelque chose	*to listen to something*
regarder quelque chose	*to look at something*
payer quelque chose	*to pay for something*

AVOID THE Blunder

✗ J'attends pour ma mère.
✗ Je cherche pour mes clés.
✗ Il écoute à la musique.

The Immediate Future

When an infinitive follows *aller,* the construction is usually considered a verb tense, called the "immediate future," much like the English construction "to be going to" + infinitive. *Aller* can be conjugated in the present or *imparfait*. See the unit on the future.

Elle allait avoir un bébé.	*She was going to have a baby.*
Il va y avoir un orage.	*There is going to be a storm.*

However, *aller* + infinitive does not always indicate the immediate future.

Le dimanche nous allons danser.	*On Sundays, we go dancing.*
Dimanche soir nous allons aller danser.	*Sunday night, we are going to go dancing.*
Elle va voir sa grand-mère souvent.	*She goes to visit her grandmother often.*
Jeudi elle va aller voir sa grand-mère.	*On Thursday, she is going to visit her grandmother.*

In French, the context must guide you. In English, the ambiguity can be avoided by using the gerund for the latter use.

Nous allons danser.	*We are going dancing.* *We are going to dance (right now).*

The Recent Past

The verb *venir* means "to come," but when it is followed by *de* + an infinitive, it expresses the notion that something "has just happened." *Venir* can be conjugated in the present or in the *imparfait,* but it should not be conjugated in the *passé composé* for this usage.

Ils viennent d'acheter une maison.	*They just bought a house.*
Je venais d'arriver.	*I had just arrived.*
Le cours vient de commencer.	*Class has just begun.*

AVOID THE Blunder

✗ Nous sommes venus d'acheter une maison.
(when "We just bought a house" is meant)

Venir de + a noun expresses origin in the sense of "from."

Ils viennent de loin.	*They come from far away.*
Elle vient de Paris.	*She is from Paris.*
D'où viens-tu?	*Where do you come from?*

Exercise

A *Express the following in French, using an infinitive construction.*

1. *It is starting to rain.*

   ____

2. *Are you* (tu) *happy to go on vacation?*

   ____

3. *She would like to go shopping.*

   ____

4. *He can leave now.*

   ____

5. *She has just left.*

   ____

6. *They are learning to dance the tango.*

   ____

7. *I prefer to leave early.*

   ____

VERBS
the conjugated form

The Conjugation Types

The infinitive ending (*-er*, *-ir*, or *-re*) determines how a verb is conjugated. Each of these endings corresponds to a regular conjugation pattern. Most textbooks include conjugation tables based on these three patterns, and you should use these tables rather than memorize each individual conjugation. For other infinitive endings, it is best to check their conjugation in a book of verbs.

-Er Verbs

- Ninety percent of French verbs are *-er* verbs; they form what is referred to as the "first group." *Aller*, even though it ends in *-er*, is not included in this group. Examples of *-er* verbs are *aimer* "to like / to love," *danser* "to dance," *donner* "to give," *parler* "to speak," and *travailler* "to work."

AVOID THE Blunder

Don't try to conjugate *aller* like an *-er* verb.

✗ J'alle.

-Ir Verbs

There are two types of *-ir* verbs.

- About 300 regular *-ir* verbs form the "second group," which adds *-iss-* before the ending in some tenses. Examples of these verbs are *agir* "to act," *choisir* "to choose," *punir* "to punish," *réfléchir* "to think," and *réussir* "to succeed."

This book does not include units on advanced or rare verb forms such as the *passé simple*, the past anterior, the imperfect subjunctive, and the pluperfect subjunctive.

Many *-ir* verbs of the second group are based on an adjective, for example, *rougir* from *rouge*, *blanchir* from *blanc*, and *grandir* from *grand*. Several *-ir* verbs with English counterparts ending in *-ish* also belong to this group: *accomplir* "to accomplish," *enrichir* "to enrich," *finir* "to finish," and *nourrir* "to nourish."

■ Thirty short *-ir* verbs, including *dormir* "to sleep," *mentir* "to lie," and *partir* "to leave," belong to the "third group." These verbs are called "short *-ir* verbs" because they do not add *-iss-* before the ending in their conjugations.

Before conjugating an *-ir* verb, it is important to determine whether it belongs to the second group (long *-ir* verbs) or to the third group (short *-ir* verbs).

AVOID THE Blunder

✗ Nous finons.
✗ Vous partissez.

-Re Verbs and Other Infinitives

■ There are about 100 *-re* verbs like *descendre* "to go down," *entendre* "to hear," *répondre* "to answer," and *vendre* "to sell." They are included in the third group, along with the short *-ir* verbs and all the verbs that do not belong to the other two groups, such as the *-oir* verbs. This third group has about 350 verbs, and most of them are considered irregular.

Examples of some of the most common verbs from the third group include *aller* "to go," *avoir* "to have," *boire* "to drink," *devoir* "must," *être* "to be," *mourir* "to die," *offrir* "to offer," *ouvrir* "to open," *pouvoir* "can," *prendre* "to take," *sentir* "to feel," *tenir* "to hold," *venir* "to come," *voir* "to see," and *vouloir* "to want."

Useful Reminders

■ In spite of the different conjugation patterns, all verbs share some common characteristics.

□ Depending on the conjugation, a first- or second-person form can end in *-s,* but never the third-person form.

□ The second-person singular ends in *-s* in all groups. In English, the third-person form ends in *-s* in the present tense (as in "she speaks").

AVOID THE *Blunder*

✗ Il joues.
✗ Tu parle.

□ For all verbs, with three exceptions, and in all tenses except the *passé simple,* the *nous* form ends in *-ons,* the *vous* form in *-ez,* and the third-person plural form in *-nt.*

nous dormirons (FUTURE)	*we will sleep*
que vous dormiez (SUBJUNCTIVE)	*that you are sleeping*
elles dormaient (IMPARFAIT)	*they were sleeping*
ils ont (PRESENT)	*they have*
nous aurions (CONDITIONAL)	*we would have*

Exceptions for the *vous* form are the verbs *dire* (and its compounds), *être,* and *faire.*

vous dites	*you say*
vous êtes	*you are*
vous faites	*you do*

■ In French, the conjugated form of a verb is marked in two ways: by the subject and by the ending. As in English, the subject must be expressed, except in the imperative (commands).

Nous parlons.	*We talk.*
Vous êtes.	*You are.*
Je dors.	*I am sleeping.*
Parlons!	*Let's talk!*
Partez!	*Leave!*

AVOID THE *Blunder*

Don't use the subject pronoun in the imperative.

✗ Dors-tu!
✗ Partez-vous!

■ If all the verbs in a clause have the same subject, only the first verb is conjugated.

Elle voudrait aller danser.	*She would like to go dancing.*
Allons nous amuser!	*Let's go have fun!*

AVOID THE Blunder

✗ Elle voudrait va danser.
✗ Allons s'amusons.
✗ J'ai fais mes devoirs.

■ *Être* and *avoir* are never followed by an infinitive. The only verbal form that can follow *être* and *avoir* is the past participle.

AVOID THE Blunder

✗ Je suis faire mes devoirs.
(when "I am doing my homework" is meant)
✗ J'ai faire mes devoirs.
(when "I have to do my homework" is meant)

Simple and Compound Tenses

French and English conjugated forms are rarely equivalent word for word. A French single-verb form like the *imparfait* can have an English equivalent that is a multiple-verb form. In the interrogative and the negative, English always uses a multiple-verb form, whereas French keeps the form that the verb had in an affirmative statement. See the charts on page 164.

Que **fait**-il?	*What **does** he **do**?*
(ONE VERB)	(TWO VERBS)
Il n'**aime** pas danser.	*He **does** not **like** to dance.*
(ONE VERB)	(TWO VERBS)

AVOID THE Blunder

Unlike English, French does not use an auxiliary verb to form the negative and interrogative.

✗ Il ne fait pas aimer danser.
✗ Il sera faire son travail.
✗ Je n'aurais pas été venu.
✗ Est-ce qu'il fait aimer danser?

Simple Tenses

In French, the present, *imparfait, passé simple,* future, present subjunctive, and present conditional tenses have one-word forms and are called simple tenses. The tense is marked by the ending of the verb (without an auxiliary verb), even in the negative and interrogative forms.

Nous **parlons**.	*We talk. / We are talking.*
Elle **dansait**.	*She danced. / She was dancing.*
Elle **dansera**.	*She will dance. / She will be dancing.*
Nous **sortirions**.	*We would go out.*

AVOID THE *Blunder*

There is no French word-for-word equivalent for the English "to be + _____ing" forms.

✗ Il était danser.
✗ Nous sommes dormons.

Compound Tenses

French compound tenses are composed of two parts: a conjugated auxiliary verb (*être* or *avoir*) and the past participle of the main verb.

The *passé composé,* pluperfect, future perfect, past subjunctive, and past conditional are compound tenses. All are past tenses.

AVOID THE *Blunder*

Don't use the past participle by itself.

✗ J'allé au cinéma hier soir.
✗ Ils mangé une pomme.

CONJUGATED VERB FORM PATTERNS

être or *avoir* in a simple conjugated form + past participle = a past tense
être or *avoir* in the present + past participle = *passé composé*
être or *avoir* in the *imparfait* + past participle = pluperfect
être or *avoir* in the future + past participle = future perfect
être or *avoir* in the conditional + past participle = past conditional
être or *avoir* in the subjunctive + past participle = past subjunctive

Elle avait déjà fini.	*She had already finished.*
J'aurais aimé rencontrer tes parents.	*I would have liked to meet your parents.*
Il aurait fallu les écouter.	*It would have been necessary to listen to them.*
Elle aura fini à huit heures.	*She will be finished by 8 o'clock.*

■ In negative sentences, the two negative words go on either side of the auxiliary verb. In questions using inversion, the auxiliary verb is inverted, not the main verb.

Tu n'avais pas pensé à cette solution.	*You had not thought about this solution.*
Êtes-vous allé au cinéma hier soir?	*Did you go to the movies last night?*

AVOID THE Blunder

In a negative sentence, don't put the second negative word after the past participle.

✗ Je n'ai fini pas.
✗ Ils ne sont allés jamais au Maroc.

Don't invert the subject pronoun and the main verb in questions using inversion.

✗ Êtes allés-vous au Maroc?
✗ As fini-tu ton travail?

■ The charts below contrast French tenses with their English equivalents. For example, the French future is a simple tense (*je partirai*), whereas the English future requires an auxiliary ("I will leave").

□ In the following tenses, the French and English verb forms have the same number of words.

The following French one-word forms have a one-word equivalent form in English.

PRESENT	PRESENT
je **parle**	***I speak***
IMPARFAIT	PRETERIT
je **parlais**	***I spoke***

The following French two-word forms have a two-word equivalent form in English.

PASSÉ COMPOSÉ	PRESENT PERFECT
j'ai parlé	***I have spoken***
PLUPERFECT	PLUPERFECT
j'avais parlé	***I had spoken***

□ In the tenses that follow, the verb forms in French have a different number of words than the verb forms in English.

The following French one-word forms have a two-word equivalent form in English.

FUTURE	FUTURE
je **parlerai**	***I will talk***
CONDITIONAL	CONDITIONAL
je **parlerais**	***I would talk***

The following French two-word forms have a three-word equivalent form in English.

FUTURE PERFECT	FUTURE PERFECT
j'aurai parlé	***I will have talked***
PAST CONDITIONAL	PAST CONDITIONAL
j'aurais parlé	***I would have talked***

Exercise

A *Without translating the following sentences, write the name of the English verb tense, then decide whether the equivalent French verb form would be a simple tense or a compound tense and circle the correct answer.*

1. *I would have liked to go with you.*

   ____________________ simple tense | compound tense

2. *They are dancing.*

   ____________________ simple tense | compound tense

3. *He will come if it does not rain.*

   ____________________ simple tense | compound tense

   ____________________ simple tense | compound tense

4. *They are having a good time.*

   ____________________ simple tense | compound tense

5. *She would go if she could.*

   ____________________ simple tense | compound tense

   ____________________ simple tense | compound tense

6. *She would have gone if she had had the time.*

   ____________________ simple tense | compound tense

   ____________________ simple tense | compound tense

VERBS
the present tense

Tense Formation

Regular French verbs are grouped in three main categories: *-er* verbs like *parler*, long *-ir* verbs like *finir* (with plural forms in *-iss-*), and *-re* verbs like *vendre*. All other verbs are considered irregular; a book of verb conjugations is the best tool for learning them.

Endings for *-er* Verbs

je	-e	nous	-ons
tu	-es	vous	-ez
il/elle/on	-e	ils/elles	-ent

parler

je parle	nous parlons
tu parles	vous parlez
il parle	ils parlent

■ A few *-er* verbs have spelling changes in certain forms of the present.

The main purpose of spelling changes is to maintain a similar pronunciation of the verb stem throughout the conjugation.

□ For verbs that end in *-ger*, the *-g* of the stem changes to *-ge* in the *nous* form. Adding the *-e* maintains the sound of the *g* in the infinitive. Without it, the *nous* form would have the /g/ sound of English "gum." Common verbs of this type are *bouger* "to move," *exiger* "to demand," *loger* "to dwell," *manger* "to eat," and *plonger* "to dive."

manger

je mange	nous mangeons
tu manges	vous mangez
il mange	ils mangent

□ For verbs that end in *-cer*, the *-c* of the stem changes to *-ç* in the *nous* form. Adding the cedilla maintains the /s/ sound. Without it, the *nous* form would have a /k/ sound, as in English "cup." Common verbs of this type are *avancer* "to move forward," *commencer* "to begin," *glacer* "to ice," and *tracer* "to draw."

glacer

je glace	nous glaçons
tu glaces	vous glacez
il glace	ils glacent

□ For verbs that end in *-yer,* the *-y* of the stem changes to *-i* in all but the *nous* and *vous* forms.

The *-y* occurs only in the forms that do not have a silent ending. The *je, tu, il,* and *ils* forms have a silent ending. Common verbs of this type are *employer* "to use," *s'ennuyer* "to be bored," *envoyer* "to send," *essayer* "to try," and *payer* "to pay."

employer

j'emploie	nous employons
tu emploies	vous employez
il emploie	ils emploient

□ For verbs that end in *-e-* or *-é-* + a consonant + *-er,* the *-e-* or *-é-* of the stem becomes *-è-* in all but the *nous* and *vous* forms. The stem of the *nous* and *vous* forms is spelled like that of the infinitive. Common verbs of this type are *acheter* "to buy," *espérer* "to hope," *exagérer* "to exaggerate," *geler* "to freeze," *harceler* "to harass," *se lever* "to get up," and *semer* "to sow."

espérer

j'espère	nous espérons
tu espères	vous espérerez
il espère	ils espèrent

Appeler and *jeter,* along with most verbs ending in *-eler* and *-eter,* do not follow this rule. Instead, the final consonant of the stem is doubled in all but the *nous* and *vous* forms. Common verbs that follow this pattern are *épeler* "to spell out," *étinceler* "to sparkle," *renouveler* "to renew," and *feuilleter* "to turn pages."

jeter

je jette	nous jetons
tu jettes	vous jetez
il jette	ils jettent

AVOID THE Blunder

✗ Je jète.
✗ Ils appèlent.

Endings for Long *-ir* Verbs

je	-is	nous	-issons
tu	-is	vous	-issez
il/elle/on	-it	ils/elles	-issent

finir

je finis	nous finissons
tu finis	vous finissez
il finit	ils finissent

AVOID THE *Blunder*

Don't confuse the conjugation patterns of long *-ir* verbs (regular) with the patterns of short *-ir* verbs (irregular).

✗ Nous partissons.
✗ Nous finons.

Endings for *-re* Verbs

je	-s	nous	-ons
tu	-s	vous	-ez
il/elle/on	–	ils/elles	-ent

vendre

je vends	nous vendons
tu vends	vous vendez
il vend	ils vendent

-Re verbs have the same endings as short *-ir* verbs, except that they have no *-t* on the third-person singular. Note that for the many *-re* verbs that are actually *-dre* verbs, the conjugated forms end in *-ds, -ds, -d, -dons, -dez, -dent.*

Common verbs of this type are *attendre* "to wait for," *descendre* "to go down," *entendre* "to hear," *rendre* "to return," and *vendre* "to sell."

Prendre, a very common verb, is irregular and does not follow the *-re* verb pattern.

prendre

je prends	nous prenons
tu prends	vous prenez
il prend	ils prennent

Endings for Short *-ir* Verbs

je	-s	nous	-ons
tu	-s	vous	-ez
il/elle/on	-t	ils/elles	-ent

partir

je pars	nous partons
tu pars	vous partez
il part	ils partent

dormir

je dors	nous dormons
tu dors	vous dormez
il dors	ils dorment

Note that for short *-ir* verbs, the endings are consistent with the pattern above but the stem varies within the same conjugation.

Irregular Verbs

Irregular verbs belong to the same group as *-re* verbs and short *-ir* verbs. The endings of these verbs are the same, but the stems can alternate in as many as three ways within the same conjugation. Since there is no way to guess which alternations apply to an individual verb, it is a good idea to check the conjugation of unfamiliar verbs that do not end in *-er*.

AVOID THE Blunder

Don't try to follow a conjugation pattern for a verb in the third group. Knowing the ending of the verb is not enough to conjugate it correctly.

✗ Nous prendons. (prendre)
✗ Nous parons. (partir)

■ Following are some common third-group verbs with spelling changes.

□ For verbs that end in *-cevoir*, the *-c* of the stem changes to *-ç* in all but the *nous* and *vous* forms. Without the cedilla, the *-c* before the *-o* would have a /k/ sound, as in English "cocoa."

Common verbs of this type are *apercevoir* "to notice," *concevoir* "to imagine," *décevoir* "to disappoint," *percevoir* "to understand," and *recevoir* "to receive."

recevoir

je reçois	nous recevons
tu reçois	vous recevez
il reçoit	ils reçoivent

□ *Tenir* "to hold," *venir* "to come," and their compounds (for example, *appartenir* "to belong," *contenir* "to contain," *obtenir* "to obtain," *devenir* "to become," *prévenir* "to warn," and *se souvenir* "to remember") alternate between two different stems. The *je, tu, il,* and *ils* forms share one stem, and the *nous* and *vous* forms share another.

tenir

je tiens	nous tenons
tu tiens	vous tenez
il tient	ils tiennent

venir

je viens	nous venons
tu viens	vous venez
il vient	ils viennent

□ A few *-ir* verbs are conjugated like *-er* verbs. They are *accueillir* "to welcome," *couvrir* "to cover," *cueillir* "to pick" (vegetables), *découvrir* "to discover," *offrir* "to offer," *ouvrir* "to open," and *souffrir* "to suffer."

souffrir

je souffre	nous souffrons
tu souffres	vous souffrez
il souffre	ils souffrent

Uses of the Present Tense

Similarities with the English Present Tense

■ As in English, the present tense in French states current facts and general truths.

Nous sommes lundi.	*Today is Monday.*
Il fait beau.	*The weather is nice.*
Le chocolat est bon.	*Chocolate is good.*
2 et 2 font 4.	*2 plus 2 equals 4.*

As in English, the present tense in French is used to express habitual action.

Il se lève à 7 heures chaque matin.	*He gets up at 7 o'clock every morning.*
Ils vont au Mexique tous les étés.	*They go to Mexico every summer.*

Certain expressions of time are commonly used with the present tense to express habitual action.

- **chaque + *expression of time in the singular***

chaque mois	*each month*
chaque année	*each year*
chaque jour	*each day*

- **tous/toutes + *expression of time in the plural***

tous les mois	*every/each month*
tous les jours	*every/each day*
toutes les années	*every/each year*

- ***definite article + day of the week / time of day***

le lundi	*on Mondays*
le matin	*in the morning*

Differences with the English Present Tense

To state current facts or actions in English, it is common to use the progressive present ("to be + _____ing"). This construction does not exist in French. The only way to express the present is to conjugate the verb in the present tense, with the proper endings and without an auxiliary.

Je mange une pomme.	*I am eating an apple.*
Nous sortons.	*We are going out.*
Qu'est-ce que tu fais?	*What are you doing?*

AVOID THE Blunder

Do not translate "to be + _____ing" by *être* + infinitive.

✗ Il était écrire.
✗ Nous sommes partir maintenant.
✗ Qu'est-ce que tu es faire?
✗ Nous sommes sortir.

□ When "to be + _____ing" emphasizes the ongoing aspect of an action, *être en train de* + an infinitive can be used in French, instead of the present tense.

Je suis en train de travailler.	*I am (in the middle of) working.*
Nous sommes en train de diner.	*We are (in the middle of) having dinner.*

■ In expressions of time with "for" and "since," English uses the present perfect tense to indicate that an action that started in the past extends up to the present moment. French uses the following constructions with the present tense.

- **depuis + *a date*** (to express "since")

Elle fait du yoga depuis janvier.	*She has been practicing yoga since January.*

- **depuis + *a period of time*** (to express "for")

Nous sommes mariés depuis cinq ans.	*We have been married for five years.*

See also the unit on constructions.

AVOID THE Blunder

✗ Nous avons été mariés depuis cinq ans.
✗ Ça fait deux semestres que nous avons étudié le français.

AVOID THE Blunder

Don't forget that a verb in the present tense can have three forms in English: "I speak," "I am speaking," and "I do speak." All are translated in French as *je parle*.

✗ Je suis parle.
✗ Je fais parle.

Exercises

A *Express the following in French.*

1. *We're eating an apple.*

   ____

2. *They have lived in this house for ten years.*

   ____

3. *On Sundays and Thursdays, we go to the gym.*

   ____

4. *My cat is being very loving these days.*

   ____

5. *It is raining.*

   ____

6. *Snow is white.*

   ____

7. *We have worked here since 1989.*

   ____

B *Complete the following sentences with the correct present tense form of the verb in parentheses.*

1. Nous ____________ (commencer) toujours à l'heure.
2. Pourquoi est-ce que tu ne ____________ (s'amuser) pas avec tes jouets?
3. Les magasins ____________ (ouvrir) en général à 10 heures.
4. Cet enfant ne ____________ (décevoir) jamais ses parents.
5. À quelle heure ____________-nous (partir)?
6. Il ____________ (attendre) depuis plus d'une heure!
7. En vacances, nous ____________ (loger) chez ma sœur.
8. Elle ne ____________ (se sentir) pas bien aujourd'hui.
9. Vous ne ____________ (dormir) pas assez.
10. Je ____________ (se lever) à 9 heures le dimanche.
11. Ils ne ____________ (réfléchir) pas assez avant de parler.
12. Il ____________ (appeler) sa mère tous les dimanches.
13. J'____________ (espérer) que tout ira bien.

VERBS
the *passé composé*

Tense Formation

Present tense of *avoir* or *être* + past participle

The *passé composé* is similar to the English present perfect in form (auxiliary + past participle). However, the uses of the two tenses are not equivalent. If the *passé composé* has an equivalent in English, it is the preterit ("he went," "she did").

Formation of the Past Participle

- For *-er* verbs: Drop the *-er* infinitive ending and replace it with *-é*.

parler	parlé
chanter	chanté

AVOID THE Blunder

Don't forget the acute accent over the *e* (*-é*) on the past participle of *-er* verbs.

✗ Nous avons danse.
✗ Elle a parle avec son professeur.

- For long and short *-ir* verbs: drop the *-ir* infinitive ending and replace it with *-i*.

sortir	sorti
finir	fini

- For *-re* verbs: drop the *-re* infinitive ending and replace it with *-u*.

rendre	rendu
mordre	mordu
répondre	répondu

- A number of past participles do not follow these rules of formation.

asseoir	assis
avoir	eu
boire	bu
conduire	conduit
connaitre	connu
croire	cru
devoir	dû
dire (*and compounds*)	dit
écrire	écrit
être	été
faire	fait
falloir	fallu
lire	lu
mettre (*and compounds*)	mis
mourir	mort
naitre	né
ouvrir	ouvert
paraitre	paru
plaire	plu
pleuvoir	plu
pouvoir	pu
prendre (*and compounds*)	pris
recevoir (*and* -cevoir *verbs*)	reçu
savoir	su
suivre	suivi
tenir (*and compounds*)	tenu
venir (*and compounds*)	venu
vivre	vécu
voir	vu
vouloir	voulu

Word Placement in the *passé composé*

The Negative

Ne and *pas* are placed around the auxiliary verb. If the sentence has an object pronoun, it comes between *ne* and the auxiliary verb.

Il n'a pas aimé le dessert.	*He did not like dessert.*
Je ne lui ai pas parlé.	*I did not talk to him/her.*

AVOID THE Blunder

✗ Il n'a diné pas. ✗ Nous n'avons pu pas finir.

All of the second negative words (*pas, rien, jamais, plus,* etc.) follow the auxiliary verb, except *personne* "nobody," *nulle part* "nowhere," *aucun/aucune* "no, none," and *ni* "nor," which follow the past participle.

Je n'ai jamais fait de ski.	*I never skied.*
Il n'a rien dit.	*He said nothing.*
Il n'a vu personne.	*He saw no one.*
Il n'est allé nulle part en vacances.	*He went nowhere for his vacation.*
Nous n'avons eu aucune nouvelle.	*We got no news.*
Tu n'as pris ni ton chapeau, ni tes gants.	*You took neither your hat nor your gloves.*

AVOID THE Blunder

✗ Il n'a personne vu.
✗ Il n'est nulle part allé en vacances.
✗ Je n'ai ni bu le lait ni l'eau.

Inversion

In questions using the *passé composé*, inversion occurs between the auxiliary verb and the subject pronoun.

As-tu fini?	*Have you finished?*
Est-il arrivé?	*Has he arrived?*
Êtes-vous allés au Canada?	*Did you go to Canada?*

AVOID THE Blunder

Don't invert the subject and the past participle.

✗ As fini-tu?
✗ Combien de jours resté-tu es?
✗ Êtes allés-vous au Canada?

Pronominal Verbs in the *passé composé*

As with any object pronoun, the reflexive pronoun precedes the auxiliary.

Tu t'es amusé.	*You had fun.*
T'es-tu amusé?	*Did you have fun?*
Tu ne t'es pas amusé.	*You did not have fun.*

AVOID THE *Blunder*

✗ Tu es t'amusé.
✗ Es-tu t'amusé?

The Auxiliary *avoir*

The *passé composé* of the following verbs is formed with the auxiliary *avoir.*

- *Être* and *avoir*

il a été	*he was*
nous avons eu	*we had*

- All transitive verbs and most intransitive verbs

tu as fini	*you finished*
elles ont écouté	*they listened (to)*
vous avez dansé	*you danced*
j'ai dormi	*I slept*

- Impersonal verbs such as *pleuvoir* and *falloir*

il a plu	*it rained*
il a fallu	*it was necessary*

Agreement of the Past Participle with *avoir*

■ In most cases when the auxiliary is *avoir*, the past participle is invariable.

Elle a lu ses livres de classe.	*She read her textbooks.*
Ils ont regardé la télé.	*They watched television.*

■ If the verb has a direct object that is placed before the auxiliary, however, the past participle agrees in gender and number with that object.

□ The direct object most often precedes the auxiliary when it is a pronoun (an object pronoun or a relative pronoun).

- If the direct object is a pronoun, the past participle changes to agree with the pronoun as follows.

la	*feminine singular*
les	*masculine plural or feminine plural*
me, te (*referring to a female*)	*feminine singular*
nous, vous (*referring to males*)	*masculine plural*
nous, vous (*referring to females*)	*feminine plural*

Elle a lu ses livres de classe.	*She read her textbooks.*
Elle les a lus.	*She read them.*
Ils ont regardé la télé.	*They watched TV.*
Ils l'ont regardée.	*They watched it.*

Direct object and indirect object pronouns have the same forms in the first and second persons: *me, te, nous,* and *vous*. Since the past participle does not agree with an indirect object, it is important to know whether the object pronoun is direct or indirect.

AVOID THE *Blunder*

✗ Il leur a donnés un chat.

To determine whether *me, te, nous,* or *vous* is a direct object pronoun, rewrite the sentence without the pronoun to discover if the verb takes a preposition or not.

Il nous a **donné** des chocolats.
QUESTION —Il a donné des chocolats... —Qui? / —À qui?
ANSWER —Il a donné des chocolats à...

The verb *donner* is indirect transitive (it takes *à*), so *nous* is an indirect object pronoun and there is no agreement.

Il vous a **aidé**.
QUESTION —Il a aidé... —Qui? / —À qui?
ANSWER —Il a aidé quelqu'un...

The verb *aider* is direct transitive (it takes no preposition), so *vous* is a direct object pronoun and there is agreement: *Il vous a aidés.*

- If the direct object is the relative pronoun *que,* the past participle agrees with it if it has a feminine or a plural antecedent (the noun it describes).

J'aime la robe que tu m'as prêtée.	*I like the dress (that) you loaned me.*
J'ai lu les livres que tu m'as donnés.	*I read the books (that) you gave me.*

The Auxiliary *être*

The *passé composé* of the following verbs is formed with the auxiliary *être*.

- All pronominal verbs

Je me suis levé.	*I got up.*
Vous vous êtes réveillés.	*You* (plural) *woke up.*

- Intransitive verbs expressing motion

aller	*to go*	venir	*to come*
arriver	*to arrive*	partir	*to leave*
entrer	*to enter*	sortir	*to go out of*
monter	*to go up*	descendre	*to go down*
naitre	*to be born*	mourir	*to die*
retourner	*to return*	passer (à/par/chez)	*to pass by*
tomber	*to fall*	rester	*to stay*

Compounds of these verbs also form the *passé composé* with *être.*

The intransitive verbs *descendre, monter, passer, rentrer,* and *sortir* can be used transitively (verb + direct object), in which case they are conjugated with *avoir.*

Papa a descendu la valise de grand-mère.	*Dad took Grandmother's suitcase downstairs.*
Il a passé le sel à son voisin de table.	*He passed the salt to the person sitting next to him.*
Elle a rentré les plantes avant le gel.	*She brought the plants in before the freeze.*

AVOID THE Blunder

✗ Papa est descendu la valise.
✗ Elle est rentrée les plantes.

The verb *passer* is used transitively more often than it is intransitively, especially in expressions about spending time. When used transitively, its *passé composé* is formed with *avoir,* not *être.*

J'ai passé la soirée à jouer avec mon chat.	*I spent the evening playing with my cat.*
Combien de temps as-tu passé à Paris?	*How long did you stay in Paris?*

AVOID THE *Blunder*

✗ Je suis passé la soirée seul.

Agreement of the Past Participle with *être*

■ When the auxiliary is *être,* the past participle must agree in gender and number with the subject of the verb.

Julie est née à Paris.	*Julie was born in Paris.*
Ils sont allés au cinéma.	*They went to the movies.*
Nous nous sommes amusés.	*We had fun.*

AVOID THE *Blunder*

✗ Ils sont parti.
✗ Elle est sorti.
✗ Elle s'est levé.
✗ Nous nous sommes amusé.

■ The past participle of a pronominal verb does not show agreement with the subject of the verb in the following cases.

- If a direct object is expressed

Elle s'est lavée. (NO DIRECT OBJECT IS EXPRESSED)	*She washed (herself).*
Elle s'est lavé la figure. (DIRECT OBJECT IS EXPRESSED—NO AGREEMENT)	*She washed her face.*

- If the verb takes an indirect object in its nonpronominal form

se parler	*to talk (to each other)*	parler à	*to talk to*
se dire	*to say (to each other)*	dire à	*to say to*
se donner	*to exchange*	donner à	*to give to*
s'écrire	*to write (each other)*	écrire à	*to write to*
se téléphoner	*to phone (each other)*	téléphoner à	*to phone*

Often these pronominal verbs express communication between two people.

Ils se sont parlé longuement.	*They spoke to each other for a long time.*

Nous nous sommes donné rendez-vous.	*We made a date.*
Elles se sont écrit.	*They wrote to each other.*

See the section on pronominal verbs in the unit on types of verbs.

AVOID THE Blunder

Don't automatically make the past participle of pronominal verbs agree with the subject of the verb.

✗ Elles se sont parlées.

Uses of the *passé composé*

The *passé composé* expresses a past action with reference to its completion rather than its unfolding. The action occurred at a specific moment in the past or was completed within a defined period of time. The important point is the action's completed aspect, not its duration.

Nous nous sommes bien amusés à ton anniversaire.	*We had fun at your birthday party.*
Nous avons passé une semaine à Aspen.	*We spent a week in Aspen.*
Hier il a plu.	*Yesterday it rained.*

An Isolated Action

The *passé composé* expresses an action that was isolated, accidental, or happened only one time.

J'ai sauté en parachute une fois dans ma vie.	*I skydived once in my life.*
Le professeur est tombé de sa chaise.	*The professor fell from his chair.*

AVOID THE Blunder

Don't use the *passé composé* to express actions that were in progress or to translate "used to."

✗ Elle a regardé la télé quand tu as sonné.
✗ Elle a nagé tous les matins.

An Action in a Sequence

The *passé composé* expresses a sequence of past actions.

D'abord, elle s'est brossé les dents, puis elle s'est maquillée. — *First she brushed her teeth, then she put her makeup on.*

Pierre a téléphoné à sa mère trois fois. — *Pierre called his mother three times.*

An Action with Ties to the Present

The *passé composé* can express actions or events that started in the past and still have ties with the present. English uses the present perfect in this situation.

J'ai toujours aimé *Autant en emporte le vent.* — *I have always liked* Gone with the Wind. *(and I still do)*

Quand j'étais petite, j'aimais les contes de fées. — *When I was little, I used to like fairy tales. (but I don't anymore)*

AVOID THE Blunder

Don't use the *imparfait* if the words "always" or "never" are used with a verb in the present perfect.

✗ Je trouvais toujours ce monument intéressant.
(when "I have always found this monument interesting" is meant)

A Change of State

The *passé composé* expresses a change of state caused by a previous action.

Quand j'ai appris la nouvelle, j'ai été ravie. — *When I found out, I was (became) delighted.*

Tout était calme et j'ai pu m'endormir. — *All was quiet, and I was able to go to sleep.*

Quand il a vu sa note, il a été content. — *When he saw his grade, he was (became) happy.*

AVOID THE *Blunder*

Don't use the *imparfait* to express the result of another action, even for verbs that usually express a state of being; use the *passé composé* instead.

✗ Quand il a vu sa note, il était content.

Expressions of Time

The following expressions of time are often associated with the *passé composé*. They imply that an action has occurred suddenly or has been completed.

un jour	*one day*
le 2 juillet (*or any specific date*)	*on July 2*
soudain	*suddenly*
tout à coup	*all of a sudden*
tout de suite	*immediately*
aussitôt que	*as soon as*
à ce moment-là	*at that moment*
au moment où	*at the very moment*
d'abord	*first*
ensuite	*then*
enfin	*finally*
une fois	*once*
il y a	*ago*
lundi/mardi/mercredi dernier	*last Monday/Tuesday/Wednesday*
l'an dernier	*last year*
le mois dernier	*last month*

Exercises

A *Rewrite the following sentences in the* passé composé. *Pay attention to the agreement of the past participle.*

1. Ils viennent de Lyon.

____

2. Elles ne vont pas en Europe.

____

3. Prenez-vous le bus?

____

4. Tu n'entends rien?

____

5. —Fais-tu la vaisselle? —Oui, je la fais.

____

6. Vous allez au cinéma, ou vous restez chez vous?

____

7. Cette fillette ne tombe jamais.

____

8. Ils n'aiment pas les bonbons.

____

9. Nous ne regardons personne.

____

B *Rewrite the following sentences in the* passé composé. *Pay attention to the agreement of the past participle.*

1. Ils s'aiment.

____

2. Ils se téléphonent.

____

3. Vous (*m. pl.*) ne vous réconciliez pas.

____

4. Elles se lavent les mains.

____

5. Nous nous ennuyons.

   ____

6. Ils s'écrivent.

   ____

7. Pierre et Annie se retrouvent au café.

   ____

8. Ils se lèvent.

   ____

9. Elle se brosse les dents.

   ____

VERBS
the *imparfait*

Tense Formation

The *imparfait* is a one-word past tense.

■ For all verb types, the *imparfait* is formed by dropping *-ons* from the *nous* form of the present tense and replacing it with the *imparfait* endings: *-ais, -ais,- ait, -ions, -iez, -aient.*

parlons	parl-	parlions
finissons	finiss-	finissions
prenons	pren-	prenions

Impersonal verbs form the *imparfait* as shown in the examples below.

pleuvoir → il pleuvait
falloir → il fallait

For verbs that end in *-ier,* like *étudier* "to study," *se marier* "to get married," and *prier* "to pray," the *i* of the ending of the *nous* and *vous* forms is doubled.

Nous étudiions.	*We were studying.*
Vous étudiiez.	*You were studying.*

■ Verbs that end in *-yer,* like *payer* "to pay," have *-yi-* in the *nous* and *vous* forms.

Nous payions.	*We were paying.*
Vous payiez.	*You were paying.*

■ *Être* is the only verb that has an irregular conjugation in the *imparfait.*

j'étais	nous étions
tu étais	vous étiez
il était	ils étaient

Verbs with a Spelling Change

■ For verbs that end in *-cer,* like *avancer* "to move forward" and *commencer* "to begin," the *-c* of the stem changes to *-ç* in all but the *nous* and *vous* forms.

je commençais	nous commencions
tu commençais	vous commenciez
il commençait	ils commençaient

■ For verbs that end in *-ger*, like *bouger* "to move," *manger* "to eat," *nager* "to swim," and *voyager* "to travel," the *-g* of the stem changes to *-ge* in all but the *nous* and *vous* forms.

je nageais	nous nagions
tu nageais	vous nagiez
il nageait	ils nageaient

AVOID THE *Blunder*

✗ Tu mangais.
✗ Il avancait.

Uses of the *imparfait*

The *imparfait* expresses a past action or event with reference to its ongoing and descriptive aspect, rather than to its completed aspect.

AVOID THE *Blunder*

Don't assume that the French *imparfait* is equivalent to the English preterit. Their usages are very different.

✗ Il sortait. (when "He went out" is meant)
✗ Il faisait ça. (when "He did it" is meant)

Reminiscing

The *imparfait* is used to express a past event without emphasis on its exact date.

□ The *imparfait* is used to reminisce about how things used to be (descriptions) and what people used to do (habitual past actions). In this sense, the *imparfait* is equivalent to English "used to."

Tous les étés nous allions chez ma grand-mère. { *Every summer, we used to go to my grandmother's.* / *Every summer, we went to my grandmother's.* }

Quand il était petit, il jouait du violon.	*When he was little, he used to play the violin.* *When he was little, he played the violin.*

AVOID THE Blunder

Don't use the *imparfait* with an expression of time that refers to a precise date or a one-time occurrence.

✗ Un jour, j'allais chez ma grand-mère.
✗ Le 2 juillet il passait un examen.

☐ The following expressions of time emphasize ongoing or habitual actions and are often used with the *imparfait*.

- Expressions that indicate habitual action

tous les jours/mois/ans	*every day/month/year*
chaque jour/mois/année	*each day/month/year*
le lundi/mardi	*on Mondays/Tuesdays*

- Expressions of frequency

tout le temps	*all the time*
d'habitude	*usually*
souvent	*often*
comme (*at the beginning of a sentence*)	*as*
pendant que	*while*
autrefois	*formerly*
rarement	*rarely*

AVOID THE Blunder

Don't automatically use the *imparfait* for any action in the past; for example, don't use the *imparfait* to tell what you did at a specific time in the past.

✗ Samedi dernier, j'allais diner avec mes amis. Ensuite, nous allions au ciné.

Describing

The *imparfait* expresses an action as it was happening, rather than expressing it as a past fact. This is the equivalent of a "was/were + ______ing" construction in English.

Ce matin dans le bus, des gens lisaient le journal, et d'autres dormaient. | *This morning on the bus, some people were reading the paper, others were sleeping.* / *This morning on the bus, some people read the paper, others slept.*

AVOID THE Blunder

Don't use the *passé composé* as an equivalent for the "was/were _____ing" construction in English.

✗ Il a plu. (when "It was raining" is meant)
✗ Il a mangé. (when "He was eating" is meant)

The *imparfait* is used to provide background information for a narrative in which the other verbs can be in the *passé composé*.

Le jour de notre mariage, il faisait beau.	*The day of our wedding, the weather was nice.*
Il pleuvait quand je me suis levé ce matin.	*It was raining when I got up this morning.*
Comme il faisait froid, j'ai pris mon manteau.	*As it was cold, I took my coat.*

Hypothesizing

The *imparfait* is used to indicate a hypothesis in an "if"-clause introduced by *si* in French. In this construction, the *imparfait* expresses a hypothetical situation that does not (yet) exist.

Si Paul n'avait pas de voiture, il prendrait le bus.	*If Paul did not have a car, he would ride the bus.*

For more information about the *imparfait* in "if"-clauses, see page 212 in the unit on the conditional.

State of Mind/State of Being

In a past tense, verbs describing opinions, desires, and states of being are usually in the *imparfait*. These verbs include *aimer* "to like," *avoir envie de* "to want," *croire* "to believe," *devoir* "must," *être* "to be," *penser* "to think," *pouvoir* "can," *se sentir* "to feel," and *vouloir* "to want."

Nous n'avions pas envie de sortir.	*We did not feel like going out.*
Il se sentait mal et ne pouvait pas travailler.	*He was not feeling well and could not work.*

With these verbs in the *imparfait,* the outcome of a situation is unclear. The *passé composé* is used to resolve the situation.

Hier soir Pierre voulait aller au cinéma, mais Julie ne voulait pas. (NO RESOLUTION)	*Last night, Pierre wanted to go to the movies, but Julie did not want to.*
Hier soir Pierre voulait aller au cinéma, mais Julie n'a pas voulu. (RESOLUTION)	*Last night, Pierre wanted to go to the movies, but Julie refused to.*

The first sentence (with the *imparfait*) indicates two opposing states of mind, with no decision being made. In the second sentence, using *vouloir* in the *passé composé* is equivalent to naming an action, as the English translation "she refused to" makes clear.

English uses the preterit for verbs describing a state of being, as well as for verbs naming actions. In French, using the *passé composé* can change the meaning of a verb describing a state of being. (See the unit on the *passé composé* versus the *imparfait.*)

Exercises

A *Complete the following sentences with the correct form of the* imparfait, *using the verb in parentheses.*

1. Elle ______________ (écrire) beaucoup de lettres.
2. Nous ne ______________ (habiter) pas loin de leur maison.
3. Son mari et elle ______________ (faire) des promenades.
4. Ils ______________ (prendre) toujours leurs deux chiens.
5. Ils ______________ (commencer) à l'heure.
6. Vous ______________ (jouer) souvent au foot.
7. Tu ______________ (être) souvent en retard à l'école.
8. Elle ______________ (voir) souvent ses amis.
9. Je ______________ (voyager) toujours en première classe quand j'______________ (aller) voir ma grand-mère.
10. Vous ______________ (étudier) toujours à la bibliothèque.
11. Leurs amis ______________ (venir) les voir en été.
12. Nous ______________ (avoir) des cours difficiles.

B *Express the following sentences in French.*

1. *Did you* (tu) *always help your mother when you were 12?*

   ____

2. *When he was little, he wanted to be a firefighter.*

   ____

3. *What did you* (tu) *do on Sundays when you were in high school?*

   ____

4. *Last year, I got up at 6* A.M. *every day.*

   ____

5. *We were studying when you* (tu) *called.*

   ____

6. *Every morning she drank a cup of coffee.*

   ____

VERBS
the *passé composé* versus the *imparfait*

A common error in French is to use the *imparfait* to translate every instance of the English preterit. In English, the preterit can be used to express a past routine as well as a one-time occurrence. French uses different tenses for these two situations.

The following examples contrast the *imparfait* and *passé composé*. Note that the English preterit is used to translate both.

Quand j'étais petit, j'allais voir ma grand-mère tous les jeudis.	*When I was little, I visited my grandmother every Thursday.*
Un jeudi, je ne suis pas allé chez elle.	*One Thursday, I did not go to her house.*
—Hier soir je n'avais pas mes clés.	*"Last night, I didn't have my keys."*
—Alors qu'est-ce que tu as fait?	*"What did you do then?"*

AVOID THE Blunder

Don't always use an English translation to help you choose between the *imparfait* and *passé composé* in French.

The following sections explain how to choose the correct past tense in French. You may also wish to consult the individual units on the *imparfait* and *passé composé*.

Single-Verb Sentence

"Was/were + ____ing" into French

If the English expression is "was/were + ____ing," the *imparfait* is used in French.

Il se réveillait.	*He was waking up.*

AVOID THE *Blunder*

Never use *passé composé* if the English sentence has "was/were + ____ing."

✗ Il s'est réveillé. (when "He was waking up" is meant)

"Used to" + Infinitive into French

If the English preterit can be replaced with "used to" + the infinitive, the *imparfait* is used in French.

J'allais voir ma grand-mère tous les jeudis.	*I visited my grandmother every Thursday.* *I used to visit my grandmother every Thursday.*

Expressions of Time in the Past

Some expressions of time are clear indicators of the tense to use.

- With the following expressions, the *passé composé* is used.

le 2 juillet (*or any specific date*)	*on July 2*
tout à coup / soudain	*all of a sudden*
tout de suite	*immediately*
d'abord	*first*
ensuite	*then*
enfin	*finally*
une fois	*once*

AVOID THE *Blunder*

✗ J'allais en France une fois. (when "I went to France once" is meant)
✗ Tout à coup, il commençait à pleuvoir. (when "Suddenly it began to rain" is meant)

- With the following expressions, the *imparfait* is used.

tous les jours/mois/ans	*every day/month/year*
chaque jour/mois/année	*each day/month/year*
le lundi/mardi	*on Mondays/Tuesdays*
tout le temps	*all the time*
d'habitude	*usually*
rarement	*rarely*
comme (*at the beginning of a sentence*)	*as*

pendant que	*while*
autrefois	*formerly*

AVOID THE Blunder

✗ Le lundi, j'ai fait des courses.
(when "On Monday I ran errands" is meant)
✗ D'habitude, il a fait ses devoirs vite.
(when "Usually he did his homework quickly" is meant)

Description or Fact?

Instead of resorting to an English translation, consider the aspect of the action. Is the action presented as a fact or piece of information, or is it presented as a description of action unfolding before your eyes?

FACT

Hier matin j'ai lu le journal.	*Yesterday morning, I read the paper.*
(Ils ont commencé à se disputer.) Ça a été affreux.	*(They started to argue.) It was awful.*

DESCRIPTION

Hier matin, j'étais installé dans mon lit et je lisais le journal.	*Yesterday morning, I was in my bed and reading the paper.*
(Ils ont commencé à se disputer.) C'était affreux.	*(They started to argue.) It was awful.*

Actions presented as fact are expressed with the *passé compose*. Descriptions of unfolding action are expressed with the *imparfait*.

Multiple-Verb Sentence

In a narrative, the different actions in a sentence are not necessarily presented in the same way, and a single past tense may not be enough. In order to choose the correct tense for each verb in the sentence, it is essential to understand how the actions relate to one another. The following section illustrates the various possibilities.

- The *passé composé* names events (*d'abord, ensuite* "first, then"), and the *imparfait* describes the context in which those events took place. Verbs commonly used in the *imparfait* are *avoir* "to have," *être* "to be," *regarder* "to watch," *savoir* "to know," *sembler* "to seem," and *vouloir* "to want." Verbs commonly used in the *passé composé* are *attendre* "to wait for," *commencer* "to begin," *comprendre* "to understand," *décider* "to decide," *dire* "to say," *entendre* "to hear," *finir* "to finish," *oublier* "to forget," and *voir* "to see."

Le voleur est entré pendant que tout le monde dormait.	*The thief came in while everyone was asleep.*
Le jour où nous nous sommes mariés, il faisait chaud et il y avait du soleil.	*The day we got married, it was sunny and hot.*

■ One verb describes an ongoing action (in the *imparfait*) that was suddenly interrupted by another event (in the *passé composé*).

Je lisais quand le facteur a sonné.	*I was reading when the mailman rang the bell.*

■ When all the actions are presented under the same aspect, all the verbs must be in the same tense.

Il a plu quand nous sommes sortis du cinéma.	*It rained (started to rain) as we got out of the movie theater.*
Il pleuvait quand nous sommes sortis du cinéma.	*It was (already) raining when we got out of the movie theater.*

□ When all the verbs in the sentence describe habitual past occurrences or ongoing actions in the past, the *imparfait* is used for all the verbs.

Quand j'étais petit, je faisais mes devoirs à la cuisine, puis j'allais jouer dans ma chambre.	*When I was little, I used to do my homework in the kitchen, and then I would go play in my room.*
Quand j'étais au lycée, le dimanche matin nous allions à la messe en famille, puis nous rendions visite à mes grands-parents.	*When I was in high school, on Sunday morning my family and I would go to Mass, and then we would visit my grandparents.*

AVOID THE Blunder

Don't switch tenses within a sentence if all the actions are presented under the same aspect.

✗ Quand j'étais petit, j'ai fait mes devoirs à la cuisine, puis j'allais jouer dans ma chambre.

☐ When all the verbs in the sentence describe a succession of past actions, the *passé composé* is used for all the verbs.

Il a mis son manteau et il est sorti.	*He put on his coat and went out.*
Dimanche dernier, je suis allée à la messe, puis je suis rentrée chez moi et j'ai déjeuné.	*Last Sunday, I went to Mass, then I went home and had lunch.*

Meaning Dependent on the Verb Tense

■ Some verbs, especially state-of-being verbs like *être* "to be," *paraitre* "to appear," and *sembler* "to seem," do not express an action and so are rarely found in the *passé composé*. When they are used in the *passé composé*, their meaning changes.

The following pairs of examples contrast the meanings of common verbs in the *imparfait* and *passé composé*.

Quand je suis arrivé sur la route, il y avait un accident.	*When I got on the road, there was (already) an accident.*
Quand je suis arrivé sur la route, il y a eu un accident.	*When I got on the road, an accident occurred.*
Sa mère avait deux filles.	*His mother (already) had two daughters.*
Sa mère a eu deux filles.	*His mother gave birth to two daughters.*
Quand il a vu sa note, il était content.	*When he saw his grade, he was (already) happy.*
Quand il a vu sa note, il a été content.	*When he saw his grade, he was (became) happy.*
J'avais mal aux pieds. Je ne voulais pas sortir.	*My feet were hurting. I did not want to go out.*
J'avais mal aux pieds. Je n'ai pas voulu sortir.	*My feet were hurting. I refused to go out.*
Après son examen il voulait faire la fête.	*After his exam, he intended to go party.*
Après son examen il a voulu faire la fête.	*After his exam, he wanted to go party. (and he did)*
Je savais que c'était toi.	*I knew it was you.*
J'ai su que c'était toi.	*I found out that it was you.*
Quand je suis arrivé, je ne connaissais personne.	*When I first arrived, I did not know anyone.*
Quand je suis arrivé, j'ai connu Pierre.	*When I first arrived, I met Pierre.*

Il ne pouvait pas réparer ma théière.	*He could not (even attempt to) fix my teapot.*
Il n'a pas pu réparer ma théière.	*He failed to fix my teapot. (although he tried)*

AVOID THE Blunder

Don't forget that some verbs usually conjugated in the *imparfait* change meaning when they are conjugated in the *passé composé.*

Exercises

A *Complete the following sentences with the correct form of the verb in parentheses, choosing between the* imparfait *and the* passé composé.

Hier, Paul (1) ______________ (décider) d'aller à la plage avec Julie parce qu'il (2) ______________ (faire) beau. Ils (3) ______________ (prendre) leurs vélos, et ils (4) ______________ (partir). La mer (5) ______________ (être) splendide et ils (6) ______________ (décider) de nager. Ils (7) ______________ (être) dans l'eau quand soudain, la pluie (8) ______________ (commencer) à tomber! Vite, ils (9) ______________ (courir) vers une grotte sur la plage et ils (10) ______________ (entrer). Dans la grotte, il (11) ______________ (faire) humide, mais au moins, les deux jeunes gens (12) ______________ (ne plus être) sous la pluie. Ils (13) ______________ (attendre) comme ça vingt minutes, puis ils (14) ______________ (mettre) le nez dehors. Il ne (15) ______________ (pleuvoir) plus et le soleil (16) ______________ (briller) à nouveau! Quelle chance!

B *Express the following in French.*

1. *When I left this morning, it was raining.*

   ____

2. *When I was ten, I used to ride my bike every day. One day, I broke my bike.*

   ____

3. *Yesterday, I went out. When I got home, I was tired.*

____

____

4. *I was doing my homework when the teacher entered the classroom.*

____

5. *She has always taken the bus to work. Why change?*

____

6. *The kids wanted to go outside, but their mother did not want them to, so they stayed inside.*

____

____

7. *We had fun during our trip last winter.*

____

8. *When she opened his door, she was already scared.*

____

C *Complete the following sentences with the correct form of the verb in parentheses, choosing between the* passé composé *and the* imparfait.

1. Le jour où nous ____________________ (se marier), il ____________________ (faire) chaud et il y ____________________ (avoir) du soleil.
2. Le voleur est entré pendant que tout le monde ____________________ (dormir).
3. Je ____________________ (lire) quand le téléphone a sonné.
4. Hier soir, Marie ____________________ (avoir) envie de sortir, mais son mari ____________________ (avoir) mal à la tête, et il ____________________ (ne pas vouloir). Alors ils sont restés à la maison, et ils ____________________ (regarder) un film.
5. Hier soir, quand je ____________________ (arriver) chez moi, je ____________________ (ne pas pouvoir) trouver ma clé! Alors je suis resté devant la porte jusqu'à ce que ma femme arrive!

D *The following English sentences are in the past tense. For each verb in bold type, indicate the appropriate French tense by circling* passé composé, imparfait, *or* can't tell.

1. *Yesterday, I* ***did not wash*** *the dishes!*

   passé composé | imparfait | can't tell

2. *Last Saturday, I* ***wanted*** *to work in the yard.*

   passé composé | imparfait | can't tell

3. *Last year, I* ***read*** *the paper every morning.*

   passé composé | imparfait | can't tell

4. *When I was little, I* ***visited*** *my grandmother on Thursdays.*

   passé composé | imparfait | can't tell

5. *The day Louis* (a) ***was born,*** *it* (b) ***was*** *a Thursday.*

   a. passé composé | imparfait | can't tell

   b. passé composé | imparfait | can't tell

6. *Yesterday, I* (a) ***went*** *out. I* (b) ***was*** *tired when I* (c) ***got*** *home.*

   a. passé composé | imparfait | can't tell

   b. passé composé | imparfait | can't tell

   c. passé composé | imparfait | can't tell

7. *When I was ten, I* ***broke*** *my bike.*

   passé composé | imparfait | can't tell

8. ***Have you ever taken*** *a yoga class?*

   passé composé | imparfait | can't tell

9. *I* (a) ***came*** *to your house but you* (b) ***were*** *not there.*

   a. passé composé | imparfait | can't tell

   b. passé composé | imparfait | can't tell

VERBS
the pluperfect

Tense Formation

Imparfait of *avoir* or *être* + past participle

The pluperfect is formed by using the *imparfait* forms of the auxiliary verb *avoir* or *être* plus the past participle.

j'avais parlé	nous avions parlé
tu avais parlé	vous aviez parlé
il/elle avait parlé	ils/elles avaient parlé
j'étais allé(e)	nous étions allé(e)s
tu étais allé(e)	vous étiez allé(e)(s)
il/elle était allé(e)	ils/elles étaient allé(e)s

See the unit on the *passé composé* for formation of the past participle, determination of which auxiliary to use with a specific verb, and agreement of the past participle with a subject or object.

Uses of the Pluperfect

- Like the English pluperfect, the French *plus-que-parfait* is used to describe pre-past actions, or actions that occurred in the past prior to the main action.

J'avais faim ce matin en classe parce que je n'avais pas pris de petit-déjeuner.	*I was hungry this morning in class, because I had not had breakfast.*
En sortant, j'ai remarqué que je n'avais pas éteint la lumière.	*Upon going out, I noticed that I had not turned the lights off.*

In English, the distinction between the pre-past action and the past action is often not made. In French, a pre-past action must be indicated by using the pluperfect.

Tu as réussi à ton examen parce que tu avais beaucoup étudié.	*You passed your exam because you studied a lot.*

AVOID THE Blunder

Don't use the *imparfait* or *passé composé* for pre-past actions.

✗ J'avais faim ce matin en classe parce que je n'ai pas pris de petit-déjeuner.

✗ Tu as réussi ton examen parce que tu as beaucoup étudié.

- The expressions *pas encore* "not yet" and *déjà* "already" are frequently used with the *plus-que-parfait*.

Nous sommes arrivés à la gare en retard, et le train était déjà parti.	*We arrived late at the station, and the train had already left.*
Il n'avait pas encore fini son examen quand la cloche a sonné.	*He had not finished his exam yet when the bell rang.*

- The *plus-que-parfait* is used in an "if"-clause with *si* to describe a hypothetical situation that would have led to a different outcome:

si + ***PLUS-QUE-PARFAIT*** **("if"-CLAUSE), CONDITIONAL PERFECT (MAIN CLAUSE)**

Si j'avais su, je ne serais pas venu.	*If I had known, I would not have come.*

See also the unit on the conditional.

Exercise

A *Complete the following sentences with the correct form of the verb in parentheses, choosing between the* passé composé *and pluperfect.*

1. Mme Dupont est restée au bureau tard parce qu'elle ______________ (ne pas finir) son travail.
2. Ce matin Julie ______________ (se réveiller) en retard parce qu'elle ______________ (se coucher) après minuit.
3. Nous avons travaillé jusqu'à 7 heures aujourd'hui parce que nous ______________ (partir) tôt hier.
4. Quand nous ______________ (arriver) au cinéma, le film ______________ (déjà commencer).
5. À la fin de la pièce, Paul m'a demandé si j'______________ (comprendre) l'histoire parce que lui, il ______________ (ne rien comprendre)!

VERBS
the future

Tense Formation

Infinitive + endings

The stem for the future is the infinitive, with exceptions noted below. For *-re* verbs, the *-e* is dropped before the endings are added.

prendre	prendr-	je prendrai
vendre	vendr-	je vendrai

Endings of the Future Tense

je	-ai	nous	-ons
tu	-as	vous	-ez
il/elle/on	-a	ils/elles	-ont

AVOID THE Blunder

Don't forget to drop the *-e* of the *-re* infinitive before adding the future endings.

✗ je prendreai
✗ il vendrea

Irregular Stems

Some verbs have an irregular stem in the future tense.

INFINITIVE	FUTURE STEM	INFINITIVE	FUTURE STEM
aller	ir-	pleuvoir	pleuvr-
asseoir	assiér-	pouvoir	pourr-
avoir	aur-	recevoir	recevr-
courir	courr-	savoir	saur-
devoir	devr-	tenir	tiendr-
envoyer	enverr-	valoir	vaudr-
être	ser-	venir	viendr-
faire	fer-	voir	verr-
falloir	faudr-	vouloir	voudr-
mourir	mourr-		

aller	*to go*	ils iront	*they will go*
devoir	*to have to*	tu devras	*you will have to*
envoyer	*to send*	vous enverrez	*you will send*
faire	*to do*	nous ferons	*we will do*
pleuvoir	*to rain*	il pleuvra	*it will rain*
savoir	*to know*	tu sauras	*you will know*
tenir	*to hold*	ils tiendront	*they will hold*
voir	*to see*	je verrai	*I will see*

Some verbs have compounds with similar irregular forms, such as *faire* "to do" and *refaire* "to redo," or *envoyer* "to send" and *renvoyer* "to send back." Other verbs, however, only appear to be compounds of similar verbs, for example, *voir* "to see" and *recevoir* "to receive." These two verbs each have their own irregular conjugation pattern: *je verrai,* etc. and *je recevrai,* etc.

AVOID THE *Blunder*

✗ Je receverrai.

Spelling Changes in the Future

■ For verbs that end in *-yer,* the *-y* of the stem changes to *-ie* in all forms of the future tense. Common verbs of this type are *déployer* "to deploy," *employer* "to use," *essayer* "to try," *essuyer* "to wipe," *nettoyer* "to clean," *payer* "to pay," and *s'ennuyer* "to be bored."

je m'ennuierai	nous nous ennuierons
tu t'ennuieras	vous vous ennuierez
il s'ennuiera	ils s'ennuieront

AVOID THE *Blunder*

Don't forget to add an *-e* in the ending of the future of *-yer* verbs, even if it is not pronounced.

✗ Il s'ennuira.
✗ Nous essairons.

■ For all verbs ending in *-e-* + a consonant + an infinitive ending, the *-e-* changes to *-è-* in all forms of the future tense. Common verbs of this type are *acheter* "to buy," *achever* "to finish," *amener* "to bring," *élever* "to raise," *emmener* "to take," *enlever* "to remove," *geler* "to freeze," *lever* "to lift," *peser* "to weigh," and *se promener* "to go for a walk."

je promènerai	nous promènerons
tu promèneras	vous promènerez
il/elle/on promènera	ils/elles promèneront

Note that verbs ending in *-é-* + a consonant + an infinitive ending do not change in the future.

je répéterai	nous répéterons
tu répéteras	vous répéterez
il/elle/on répétera	ils/elles répéteront

As in the present tense, *appeler, jeter* and most other verbs ending in *-eler* and *-eter* do not follow this rule. Instead, the final consonant of the stem is doubled in all but the *nous* and *vous* forms. Common verbs with this pattern are *épeler* "to spell out," *étinceler* "to sparkle," *renouveler* "to renew," and *feuilleter* "to turn pages."

jeter

je jetterai	nous jetterons
tu jetteras	vous jetterez
il/elle/on jettera	ils/elles jetteront

AVOID THE *Blunder*

✗ Je jèterai.
✗ Ils appèleront.

Uses of the Future

The future tense is used with certain expressions of time.

demain	*tomorrow*
demain matin/soir	*tomorrow morning/evening*
après-demain	*the day after tomorrow*
lundi/mardi prochain	*next Monday/Tuesday*
la semaine / l'année prochaine	*next week/year*
le mois prochain	*next month*
plus tard	*later*
dans (+ *period of time*)	*in* (+ period of time)
un jour	*one day*

The Future Versus the Immediate Future

As in English, the future tense is used in French to describe future events in a general way.

Il y aura des orages cet été.	*There will be storms in the summer. (Summer is coming, and everyone knows there are usually storms in summer.)*

When the details preceding a future event make it certain to happen, the immediate future is used (*aller* + infinitive).

Il va y avoir un orage.	*There's going to be a storm. (The sky is extremely overcast, and conditions are ripe for a storm.)*

AVOID THE Blunder

When you see evidence that something is about to happen (or certain to happen), use the immediate future rather than the future.

✗ Il y a de gros nuages noirs dans le ciel. Il pleuvra.

The immediate future is also used to show the subject's intention.

Je vais aller en France cet été.	*I am going to go to France next summer.*
Nous allons rentrer tôt ce soir.	*We intend to go home early tonight.*

Quand Clauses

In French, when the main verb of a sentence is in the future or the imperative, the verb that follows *quand* must be in the future (or future perfect). English uses the present tense after "when."

Dès qu'il fera beau, je ferai du jardinage.	*As soon as the weather is nice, I will work in the yard.*
Quand je serai grand, je serai pompier.	*When I grow up, I will be a firefighter.*
Mettez de l'huile dans l'eau, et l'huile flottera.	*Put oil in water, and the oil will float.*

AVOID THE Blunder

✗ Je ferai du jardinage quand il fait beau.
✗ Quand je suis grand, je serai pompier.
✗ Dès que j'arrive, je dinerai.

In a future context, the future (or future perfect) tense is required after the following expressions of time.

quand	*when*
lorsque	*when*
dès que	*as soon as*
aussitôt que	*as soon as*
une fois que	*once*
après que	*after*

Une fois que tu auras acheté un casque, tu pourras faire de la moto.	*Once you buy a helmet, you will be able to go ride a motorcycle.*
Après que nous serons arrivés à l'hôtel, nous irons voir la plage.	*After we arrive at the hotel, we'll go see the beach.*

Si-Clauses

To express a rationale for doing something, French and English both use a construction with *si*/"if."

FRENCH PATTERN

si + subject + present verb + subject + future verb

ENGLISH PATTERN

"if" + subject + present verb + subject + future verb

S'il fait beau demain, nous irons à la plage.	*If the weather is nice tomorrow, we will go to the beach.*
Si tu étudies, tu comprendras.	*If you study, you will understand.*
Si tu ne paies pas tes factures, tu auras des ennuis.	*If you don't pay your bills, you will get in trouble.*

In *si*-clauses, *si* is followed by the present even if the context expresses the future. In *quand* clauses, *quand* must be followed by the future if the main verb is in the future.

AVOID THE Blunder

Don't use the future tense immediately after *si*.

✗ S'il fera beau demain, nous irons à la plage.

When Not to Use Future

After certain expressions, the subjunctive must be used instead of the future. Common expressions of this type are *avoir peur que* "to be afraid" and *souhaiter que* "to hope." See the unit on the subjunctive.

AVOID THE Blunder

✗ Il souhaite que tu viendras le voir l'été prochain.

Exercises

A *Complete the following sentences with the correct future form of the verb in parentheses.*

1. Nous ____________________ (faire) la cuisine.
2. Elle ____________________ (venir) me rendre visite tous les jours.
3. Vous ____________________ (descendre) au sous-sol.
4. Nous ____________________ (envoyer) les messages.
5. Ils ____________________ (étudier) aux États-Unis.
6. Il y ____________________ (avoir) beaucoup de gens.
7. Tu ____________________ (voir) que c'est assez facile.
8. Un jour, vous ____________________ (savoir) la vérité.
9. Où ____________________-vous (aller) pour les vacances?

B *Express the following in French.*

1. *When I grow up, I will be a flight attendant.*

   ____

2. *If the flight is canceled, I will go home.*

   ____

3. *If you* (vous) *look outside, you can see the trees.*

   ____

4. *As soon as I arrive in Paris, I will phone my parents.*

   ____

VERBS
the future perfect

Tense Formation

Future tense of *avoir* or *être* + past participle

The future perfect is formed by using the future forms of the auxiliary verb *avoir* or *être* plus the past participle.

j'aurai parlé	nous aurons parlé
tu auras parlé	vous aurez parlé
il/elle aura parlé	ils/elles auront parlé
je serai allé(e)	nous serons allé(e)s
tu seras allé(e)	vous serez allé(e)(s)
il/elle sera allé(e)	ils/elles seront allé(e)s

See the unit on the *passé composé* for formation of the past participle, determination of which auxiliary to use with a specific verb, and agreement of the past participle with a subject or object.

Uses of the Future Perfect

In French and English, the future perfect expresses actions that will be accomplished by a certain time in the future or before another future action.

The future perfect is used more frequently in French than in English, which tends to use the present perfect or the present tense instead.

Dès que vous aurez fini votre examen, vous pourrez partir.	*As soon as you have finished your exam, you will be able to leave.* (PRESENT PERFECT) *As soon as you finish your exam, you will be able to leave.* (PRESENT)
Dès que je serai rentré, je vous appellerai.	*As soon as I am home, I will call you.* (PRESENT)

Quand tu auras fini ton travail, tu pourras jouer.	*When you are finished with your work, you will be able to play.* (PRESENT)

AVOID THE *Blunder*

Don't use the past tense in a dependent clause in French if the main verb is in the future.

✗ Quand vous avez fini votre examen, vous pourrez partir.
✗ Dès que je suis rentré, je vous appellerai.

■ In English, the expression "by" + a date is common with the future perfect. *Par,* the literal equivalent of "by," is never used in this context.

Nous aurons fini avant demain.	*We will be done by tomorrow.*

AVOID THE *Blunder*

Don't use *par* as an expression of time to translate "by."

✗ Nous aurons fini par demain.

Possible translations of "by" + a date in a future context follow.

d'ici demain	*by tomorrow*
d'ici trois jours	*(by) three days from now / within three days*
d'ici la semaine prochaine	*by next week*
avant	*by, before*
dans	*in*
après que	*after*

D'ici demain, nous aurons fini.	*We will be done by tomorrow.*
Il sera rentré d'ici trois jours.	*He will be back within three days.*

■ After *après que,* when the subject of the two clauses is the same, French prefers to use the perfect infinitive instead of the future perfect.

Après que nous serons arrivés à l'hôtel, nous irons voir la plage. Après être arrivés à l'hôtel, nous irons voir la plage.	*After we arrive at the hotel, we will go see the beach.*

Exercise

A *Complete the following sentences with the correct form of the verb in parentheses, choosing from the present, future, future perfect, and immediate future tenses.*

1. Quand il ______________ (finir) la vaisselle, il pourra sortir.
2. Tu me montreras tes photos quand tu ______________ (rentrer) de vacances.
3. Quand j'aurai fini de manger, je ______________ (partir).
4. Quand vous ______________ (sortir), n'oubliez pas de fermer la porte à clé.
5. Il est tard; nous ______________ (partir) tout de suite.
6. Si tu ______________ (être) sage, nous t'emmènerons au zoo.
7. Quand vous ______________ (arriver) au carrefour, vous tournerez à gauche.
8. Julie est enceinte de huit mois. Elle ______________ (avoir) un bébé dans un mois.

VERBS
the present conditional

Formation

Infinitive + endings

The stem for the conditional is the infinitive, with exceptions noted below. For *-re* verbs, the *-e* is dropped before the endings are added.

prendre	prendr-	je prendrais
vendre	vendr-	je vendrais

Endings of the Conditional

je	-ais	nous	-ions
tu	-ais	vous	-iez
il/elle/on	-ait	ils/elles	-aient

The endings of the conditional are the same as the *imparfait* endings.

AVOID THE Blunder

Don't forget to drop the *-e* of the *-re* infinitive before adding the conditional endings.

✗ je prendreais
✗ il vendreait

Irregular Stems

The stem of the conditional has the same irregular forms and the same spelling changes as the future tense. For a list of the irregular stems of the conditional, see the unit on the future.

Characteristics of the Conditional

Unlike the English conditional, which is a two-word verb form ("would" + verb), the French *conditionnel* is a simple tense (a one-word verb with specific endings).

Je **dormirais**.	***I would sleep***.
Je **parlerais**.	***I would speak***.

There are two exceptions: "could" (from French *pouvoir* "to be able to") and "should" (from French *devoir* "to have to"), whose one-word forms match the French one-word conditional.

Je **pourrais**.	***I could***.
Je **devrais**.	***I should***.

AVOID THE Blunder

✗ Je serais être content d'avoir un bateau.
(when "I would be glad to have a boat" is meant)

✗ Il ferait lire, s'il avait le temps.
(when "He would read if he had time" is meant)

The *-s* of the ending of the first-person singular form in the conditional distinguishes it from the ending of the first-person singular form of the future.

Je ferai mes devoirs ce soir. (FUTURE)	*I will do my homework tonight.*
Je ferais mes devoirs maintenant si j'avais le temps. (CONDITIONAL)	*I would do my homework now, if I had time.*

The *imparfait* and the conditional are very similar in form.

je parlais (*IMPARFAIT*)	*I was talking*
je parlerais (CONDITIONAL)	*I would talk*

AVOID THE Blunder

Don't drop any syllable when forming the conditional, or you may end up with the *imparfait* instead.

Je parlais. (when "I would talk" is meant)

Uses of the Conditional

Expression of a Daydream: The "If"-Clause

The conditional expresses what would happen if current or future conditions were different.

Si j'avais le temps, je lirais le journal tous les matins.	*If I had time, I would read the paper every morning.*

The condition, introduced by *si* "if," is expressed by the imperfect. The result is expressed by the conditional in the main clause.

FRENCH PATTERNS	*si* + *imparfait,* conditional
	conditional, *si* + *imparfait*
ENGLISH PATTERNS	"if" + past, conditional
	conditional, "if" + past

You may reverse the order of the clauses without a change in meaning, but the clauses themselves remain the same.

Si vous aviez beaucoup d'argent, que feriez-vous?	*If you had a lot of money, what would you do?*
Que feriez-vous si vous aviez beaucoup d'argent?	*What would you do if you had a lot of time?*

AVOID THE Blunder

Don't put the conditional in the *si*-clause.

✗ Si vous auriez beaucoup d'argent, que feriez-vous?
✗ Si j'aurais le temps, je lirais le journal tous les matins.

Note that when the main verb is in the conditional, the *imparfait* is used in the *si*-clause even though the context of the hypothesis is the present.

AVOID THE Blunder

✗ Qu'est-ce que tu ferais si tu gagnes à la loterie?
✗ Qu'est-ce que tu ferais si tu as le temps?

The Future in the Past

As in English, the conditional is used in French to express the future in a past context, usually in reported speech.

Hier, il a dit qu'il m'aiderait.	*Yesterday he said that he would help me.*
Hier la météo a dit qu'il ferait beau aujourd'hui.	*Yesterday the Weather Service said that it would be nice today.*

AVOID THE *Blunder*

Don't use the future tense in a dependent clause when the main verb is in the past.

✗ Hier la météo a dit qu'il fera beau aujourd'hui.

Polite Requests and Wishes

- To express a polite request, use the conditional of *pouvoir*—either *pourrais-tu* or *pourriez-vous*—followed by the infinitive. The present tense is acceptable, but the conditional is more polite.

Pouvez-vous passer le sel, s'il vous plait?	*Can you pass the salt, please?*
Pourriez-vous passer le sel, s'il vous plait?	*Could you pass the salt, please?*

AVOID THE *Blunder*

Don't use the conditional of the main verb to express a polite request.

✗ Ouvriez-vous la fenêtre, s'il vous plait?
✗ Me passerais-tu le sel, s'il te plait?
✗ M'indiqueriez la rue Bouchet, s'il vous plait?

Note that in English, "could" is also the past tense of "can." In this context it must be translated by a past tense of *pouvoir* in French—never by the conditional.

AVOID THE *Blunder*

✗ Il ne pourrait pas trouver leur maison.
(when "He could not find their house" is meant)

- To express a wish or desire, use *aimer* or *vouloir* in the conditional. They both mean "would like."

J'aimerais aller à Tahiti.	*I would like to go to Tahiti.*
Ils voudraient faire un voyage.	*They would like to take a trip.*

In a question, *aimer* or *vouloir* expresses an offer.

Qu'est-ce que tu aimerais? *What would you like?*
Voudrais-tu que je t'aides? *Would you like me to help you?*

Don't use *aimeriez-vous* to express a request.

✗ Aimeriez-vous ouvrir la fenêtre, s'il vous plait?

Vouloir—but not *aimer*—can also be used in the present tense to express a wish, although the conditional is more polite.

M. Martin veut parler au directeur. *Mr. Martin wants to talk to the director.*

M. Martin voudrait parler au directeur. *Mr. Martin would like to talk to the director.*

AVOID THE Blunder

Don't use *aimer,* which in the present tense simply means "to like," to express a wish.

✗ J'aime faire un voyage.
(when "I would like to take a trip" is meant)

Advice

The conditional of *devoir,* followed by the infinitive of the main verb, is used to give advice. It is the equivalent of English "should" or "ought to."

Tu as l'air épuisé. Tu devrais te reposer. *You look exhausted. You should rest.*

AVOID THE Blunder

✗ Tu te reposerais. (when "You should rest" is meant)

For further details on "would" and "could," see page 321 in the unit on constructions.

Indignation

As in English, the conditional (present or past, depending on the context) is often used to express indignation in French.

Tu pourrais te laver les mains avant le diner!	*You could wash your hands before dinner!*
Tu aurais pu me demander la permission!	*You could have asked for my permission!*
Ça t'embêterait de te pousser?!	*Would it bother you to move over?!*

Unconfirmed Information

The news often reports events that are too recent to be confirmed. The expressions "apparently," "it appears that," and "it seems that" reflect the uncertainty of these reports. In French, the conditional (present or past, depending on the context) is used in these situations.

Il y a eu une explosion. Dix mineurs seraient toujours dans la mine.	*There has been an explosion. Ten miners are apparently still in the mine.*
L'incendie de ce matin aurait détruit deux maisons.	*This morning's fire has apparently destroyed two homes.*

Exercises

A *Express the following sentences in French.*

1. *If we were not in class today, we would be at home.*

   ____

2. *Could you* (vous) *tell me where the restrooms are, please?*

   ____

3. *They hoped that the movie would be interesting.*

   ____

4. *I would go to Europe if I had enough money.*

   ____

5. *They should go to the library more often.*

   ____

6. *What would you* (tu or vous) *like to do tonight?*

   ____

7. *I could not understand the message. So I did not answer.*

____

8. *Would you* (tu) *like me to help you?*

____

9. *You* (tu) *could at least apologize!*

____

B *Complete the following sentences with the correct conditional or* imparfait *form of the verb in parentheses. Pay attention to whether the missing verb form is in the* si*-clause or the main clause.*

1. Si la maison était sale, vous ______________ (faire) le ménage.
2. Si nous achetions des billets, nous ______________ (pouvoir) voir le spectacle.
3. Nous jouerions, s'il ______________ (ne pas y avoir) de cours.
4. Si vous étiez pressés, vous ______________ (partir) maintenant!
5. Je te ______________ (téléphoner) si j'avais ton numéro!
6. Si tu voulais aller dans un endroit romantique, où ______________-tu (aller)?
7. Vous ne ______________ (être) pas en retard si vous vous dépêchiez!
8. Si vous ______________ (étudier) plus efficacement, vous passeriez moins de temps avec vos livres.
9. Si tu prenais ta voiture, tu ______________ (arriver) à l'heure.

VERBS
the past conditional

Tense Formation

Conditional of *avoir* or *être* + past participle

The past conditional is formed by using the conditional forms of the auxiliary verb *avoir* or *être* plus the past participle.

j'aurais parlé	nous aurions parlé
tu aurais parlé	vous auriez parlé
il/elle aurait parlé	ils/elles auraient parlé
je serais allé(e)	nous serions allé(e)s
tu serais allé(e)	vous seriez allé(e)(s)
il/elle serait allé(e)	ils/elles seraient allé(e)s

See the unit on the *passé composé* for formation of the past participle, determination of which auxiliary to use with a specific verb, and agreement of the past participle with a subject or object.

In English, the past conditional is a three-word verb form, except for "could" (*j'aurais pu* "I could have") and "should" (*j'aurais dû* "I should have"). In French, the *conditionnel passé* is a two-word form.

J'**aurais dansé** toute la nuit.	*I **would have danced** all night.*
J'**aurais aimé** venir avec toi.	*I **would have liked** to go with you.*

AVOID THE Blunder

Don't use the English three-word form to conjugate the French past conditional.

✗ J'aurais eu dansé toute la nuit.
✗ J'aurais eu aimé venir avec toi.

Uses of the Past Conditional

A Hypothesis in a Past Context: The "If"-Clause

The present conditional expresses what would happen if current or future conditions were different. The past conditional, however, expresses what would have happened at some point in the past if conditions had been different.

L'accident aurait pu être plus grave.	*The accident could have been worse.*

The construction of a sentence containing a *si-*/"if"-clause is the same in French and English. The main verb is in the past conditional, and the verb of the *si*-clause is in the pluperfect, as the following chart shows.

FRENCH PATTERNS	*si* + pluperfect, past conditional
	past conditional, *si* + pluperfect
ENGLISH PATTERNS	"if" + pluperfect, past conditional
	past conditional, "if" + pluperfect

S'il avait plu hier, nous n'aurions pas pu aller à la plage.	*If it had rained yesterday, we would not have been able to go to the beach.*
Nous n'aurions pas pu aller à la plage s'il avait plu hier.	*We would not have been able to go to the beach if it had rained yesterday.*

AVOID THE Blunder

When using the past conditional in French, be sure to use the pluperfect in the *si*-clause.

✗ Si j'ai étudié plus, j'aurais probablement réussi.
✗ Si je savais, je ne serais pas venu.

Often, a hypothesis in a past context expresses a regret.

Si j'avais étudié plus, j'aurais probablement réussi à mon examen.	*If I had studied more, I would probably have passed my exam.*
Si j'avais su, je ne serais pas venu.	*If I had known, I would not have come.*

The Future Perfect in the Past

Just as the conditional is used to express the future in a past context, the past conditional expresses the future perfect in a past context.

Je pensais que nous aurions fini avant la nuit.	*I thought we would have been done before dark.*

Exercises

A *Express the following in French, using the past conditional in the main clause.*

1. *What would we have done without you* (vous)*?*

 ____

2. *If I had known your number, I would have called you* (tu).

 ____

3. *If you* (tu) *had not come to help me, I would never have finished this work.*

 ____

4. *She would have met the wolf if she had gone into the forest.*

 ____

B *Complete the following sentences with the correct present or past conditional form of the verb in parentheses. Pay attention to whether the missing verb form is in the si-clause or the main clause.*

1. Si nous nous étions dépêchés, nous ______________ (ne pas rater) le train.
2. Si elle avait su, elle ______________ (ne pas sortir) avec ce garçon.
3. S'il n'y avait pas de cours, nous ______________ (aller) au ciné.
4. Si vous étiez pressés, vous ______________ (partir) maintenant!
5. S'il n'y avait pas d'examen, les étudiants ______________ (pouvoir) rentrer chez eux.
6. Il ______________ (arriver) en retard s'il n'avait pas pris un taxi.

VERBS
the subjunctive mood

The subjunctive expresses actions in a more "subjective" way than other verb forms do. Since it may prove too subtle to determine subjectivity, it is easier to learn to recognize the situations and expressions that trigger the subjunctive.

The subjunctive (present or past) is used in a dependent clause introduced by *que* when the subject of the main verb

- is trying to persuade someone to do something
- expresses emotion about something that has happened, is happening, or is going to happen
- expresses doubt about something that has happened, is happening, or is going to happen
- is searching for desirable qualities of someone or something that may not exist

Expressions That Trigger the Subjunctive

A trigger expression can be an impersonal verb form, like *il faut* "it is necessary," or it can be a verb conjugated with any subject. A number of nonverbal expressions (mostly conjunctions) can also trigger the subjunctive.

■ The verb of the trigger expression can be conjugated in any tense, including the conditional.

Ça me plairait que tu fasses ça rien que pour moi.	*I would like it if you did this just for me.*
Ils ont aimé que les enfants servent le repas.	*They liked it that the kids served dinner.*

When the verb of the trigger expression is in a past tense, the verb of the dependent clause can be in either the present or past subjunctive, and the difference affects the meaning of the sentence.

□ If the dependent verb is in the present subjunctive, it indicates that the actions of the main and dependent verbs took place at the same time.

J'étais désolé qu'ils se battent.	*I was sorry that they were fighting.*

☐ If the dependent verb is in past subjunctive, it indicates that the action of the dependent clause took place before the main verb's action. (See the unit on the past subjunctive.)

J'étais désolé qu'ils se soient battus.	*I was sorry that they had had a fight.*

AVOID THE Blunder

✗ Je suis désolé qu'ils se battent.
(when "I am sorry that they fought" is meant)

Keep in mind that the *que* following each trigger expression introduces a new subject and a verb in the subjunctive.

PATTERN trigger expression + *que* + subject 2 + verb 2 in the subjunctive

If a second subject is not expressed after a trigger expression, *que* cannot be used and the verb of the dependent clause is an infinitive.

TWO SUBJECTS

Je veux que tu finisses aujourd'hui.	*I want you to finish today.*

ONE SUBJECT

Il ne veut pas finir aujourd'hui.	*He does not want to finish today.*
Je suis content de partir.	*I am glad I'm leaving.*

AVOID THE Blunder

✗ Je suis content que je parte en vacances.
✗ Vous êtes déçus que vous perdiez le match.

Note that the *que* that introduces the subjunctive clause is not the same *que* as the relative pronoun.

AVOID THE Blunder

✗ Le livre que je lise est intéressant.
✗ Le travail que tu fasses est difficile.

AVOID THE *Blunder*

Don't omit *que* after a trigger expression.

✗ J'ai peur il soit malade.

Uses of the Subjunctive

To Persuade or Give Advice

If the subject of the main verb directly or indirectly wants, forbids, allows, wishes, etc. someone else to do or not do something, now or in the future, the dependent verb is in the present subjunctive.

il est essentiel que	*it is essential*
il est important/utile/bon que	*it is important/useful/good*
il faut que	*it is necessary*
il vaut mieux que	*it is better to*
accepter / vouloir bien que	*to accept*
aimer mieux que	*to prefer*
attendre que	*to wait for*
avoir besoin que	*to need*
avoir envie que	*to want*
demander que	*to ask*
empêcher que	*to prevent (from)*
être d'accord pour que	*to agree*
éviter que	*to avoid*
exiger que	*to demand*
insister que	*to insist*
interdire que	*to forbid*
ordonner que	*to command*
permettre que	*to allow*
préférer que	*to prefer*
proposer que	*to propose*
refuser que	*to refuse*
souhaiter / désirer / avoir envie que	*to wish, want*
supporter que	*to bear*
vouloir que	*to want*

Mes parents veulent que je devienne avocat.	*My parents want me to become a lawyer.*
Il faut que les avocats soient honnêtes.	*Lawyers must be honest.*

Maman veut bien que je sorte ce soir.	*Mom agrees to let me go out tonight.*

To Express Emotion or Judgment

If the subject of the main verb expresses love, hate, regret, surprise, fear, joy, sadness, pride, etc. about something that is happening or will happen, the verb in the dependent clause is in the present subjunctive. If the emotion is about something that has happened, the verb in the dependent clause is in the past subjunctive.

étonner	*to surprise*
ça m'/t'/l'/nous/vous/les étonne que	*it surprises me/you/him/her/us/you/them that*

Some of the other verbs expressing emotion are the following.

amuser	*to entertain*
déranger	*to bother, disturb*
intéresser	*to interest*

Ça me surprend qu'il soit si méchant.	*I am surprised he is so mean.*
Ça me dérange que tu fasses du bruit.	*It bothers me that you are making noise.*

If the main clause has an impersonal subject + an adjective expressing emotion or judgment + *que*, the verb in the dependent clause is in the subjunctive. Some of the adjectives that express emotion or judgment in this pattern include the following.

il est + *adjective* + que	*it is* + adjective + *that*
amusant	*funny*
bizarre	*strange*
dommage	*a pity*
étonnant	*surprising*
fou	*crazy*
honteux	*shameful*
regrettable	*regrettable*

Il est bizarre qu'elle ne sorte jamais.	*It is strange that she never goes out.*
Il est dommage que les enfants ne puissent pas venir pour les fêtes.	*It is a pity the kids can't come for the holidays.*

If the main clause has a personal subject + *être* + an adjective expressing emotion or judgment + *que,* the verb in the dependent clause is in the subjunctive. Some of the adjectives that express emotion or judgment in this pattern include the following.

être + *adjective* + que	*to be* + adjective + *that*
content	*glad*
désolé	*sorry*
fier	*proud*
flatté	*flattered*
inquiet	*worried*
surpris	*surprised*
triste	*sad*

Sa mère est inquiète qu'il soit en retard.	*His mother is worried that he is late.*

Some of the verbs expressing emotion or judgment that trigger the subjunctive include the following.

admirer que	*to admire*
aimer que	*to like*
avoir honte que	*to be ashamed*
avoir peur que / craindre que	*to be afraid, fear*
détester que	*to dislike*
regretter que	*to regret*
s'inquiéter que	*to worry*

Ses parents n'aiment pas qu'elle sorte seule.	*Her parents don't like for her to go out alone.*
J'admire que tu puisses faire ça.	*I admire that you can do this.*
J'ai peur qu'il pleuve samedi prochain.	*I am afraid it might rain next Saturday.*

Other expressions and constructions that trigger the use of the subjunctive in the dependent clause include the following.

Comment se fait-il que...?	*How come . . . ?*
avoir de la chance que	*to be lucky that*
je comprends que	*I understand that*
Que...!	*That . . . !*

Comment se fait-il que vous soyez toujours en retard?	*How come you're always late?*
Tu as de la chance que je sois de bonne humeur, sinon...	*You are lucky I am in a good mood, otherwise . . .*
Que je lui fasse des excuses? Jamais!	*That I apologize to him? Never!*

Il est + an adjective and *c'est* + an adjective mean the same thing, although *c'est* + an adjective is more informal.

To Express Doubt

If the subject of the main verb expresses doubt about something that is happening or will happen, the verb in the dependent clause is in the present subjunctive. If the doubt is about something that has happened, the verb in the dependent clause is in the past subjunctive.

douter que	*to doubt*
nier que	*to deny*

Le prof doute qu'il ait une bonne excuse.	*The teacher doubts that he has a good excuse.*
Elle nie qu'il veuille partir.	*She denies that he wants to leave.*

AVOID THE Blunder

Don't confuse *douter* "to doubt" with *se douter* "to suspect," which is not followed by the subjunctive.

✗ Je doute qu'il n'a pas d'excuse.
(when "I suspect that he does not have an excuse" is meant)

If the main clause has an impersonal subject + an adjective expressing doubt + *que,* the verb in the dependent clause is in the subjunctive. Some of the adjectives that express doubt in this pattern include the following.

il est + *adjective* + que	*it is* + adjective + *that*
douteux	*doubtful*
faux	*false*
impensable	*unthinkable*
impossible	*impossible*
incroyable	*incredible*

Il est impossible que vous réussissiez seul.	*It is impossible that you succeed by yourself.*

Some impersonal expressions of doubt that trigger the subjunctive are the following.

il n'y a aucune chance que	*there's not a chance that*
ce n'est pas la peine que	*it is not worth the trouble that*
il n'est pas question que	*there is no way that*

Il n'y a aucune chance qu'il arrive à l'heure.	*There's not a chance of him arriving on time.*

Verbs of Opinion in Interrogative (Inversion Only) and Negative Constructions

ne pas croire que	*to not believe*
ne pas penser que	*to not think*
ne pas trouver que	*to not find*
ne pas être certain/sûr que	*to not be sure*

Je ne pense pas qu'il ait le temps de finir.	*I don't think he has time to finish.*
Pensez-vous qu'elle puisse réussir?	*Do you think she can succeed?*
Je ne crois pas que cet ouvrier soit très travailleur.	*I don't believe that this worker is very industrious.*
—Penses-tu que la planète soit carrée?	*"Do you think the planet is square?"*
—Non, je ne pense pas qu'elle soit carrée.	*"No, I do not think it is square."*

AVOID THE *Blunder*

✗ Penses-tu que la planète est carrée?
✗ Je ne crois pas qu'il est sérieux.

If the subject of the main verb expresses an opinion in an affirmative statement, the dependent verb is in the indicative. See the section on when not to use the subjunctive on page 232.

Searching for Someone/Something

If the subject of the main verb is searching for or inquiring about someone or something with specific characteristics, those characteristics are expressed in a relative clause with a subjunctive verb.

INDICATIVE

Nous avons une maison qui a un jardin.	*We have a house that has a backyard.*

SUBJUNCTIVE

Nous voulons une maison qui ait un jardin.	*We want a house that would have a backyard.*

INDICATIVE

Kurt est une personne qui sait parler allemand.	*Kurt is someone who can speak German.*

SUBJUNCTIVE

Y a-t-il quelqu'un qui sache parler allemand ici?	*Is there someone who can speak German here?*

AVOID THE Blunder

Don't forget to use the subjunctive after *vouloir, chercher,* etc. + a relative pronoun.

✗ Nous voulons une maison qui a un jardin.

The trigger verbs that express such inquiry include the following.

avoir besoin	*to need*
avoir envie	*to want*
chercher	*to look for*
vouloir	*to want*
connaitre (*in negative and interrogative constructions only*)	*to know*
exister (*in negative and interrogative constructions only*)	*to exist*
il y a (*in negative and interrogative constructions only*)	*there is*

Using the subjunctive after these verbs indicates that the object of the search may not exist.

Conjunctions

The following nonverbal expressions must introduce a clause whose verb is in the subjunctive. If a noun or infinitive follows one of these expressions, use the corresponding preposition if there is one. The chart shows the conjunctions and their corresponding prepositions.

CONJUNCTION		PREPOSITION
à condition que / pourvu que	*provided that*	à condition de
à moins que	*unless*	à moins de
avant que	*before*	avant de
bien que	*although*	—
de peur que	*for fear that / for fear of*	de peur de
en attendant que	*while waiting*	en attendant de
il est temps que	*it is time that / it is time to*	il est temps de
jusqu'à ce que	*until*	jusqu'à
pour que	*in order to/for*	pour
sans que	*without*	sans

Il est temps que vous fassiez des excuses. — *It is time for you to apologize.*

Ils iront à la piscine pourvu qu'il fasse beau. — *They will go to the pool provided that the weather is nice.*

Like any trigger expression, conjunctions introduce a second subject. In the absence of one, the infinitive is used and the conjunction is replaced by the equivalent preposition.

TWO SUBJECTS

J'ai acheté ce livre pour que tu le lises. — *I bought this book so that you can read it.*

ONE SUBJECT

J'ai acheté ce livre pour le lire. — *I bought this book to read it.*

AVOID THE *Blunder*

Don't use a conjunction before an infinitive or a noun.

✗ Il doit rentrer avant que minuit.
✗ Il est temps que partir.

However, the conjunctions *à moins que, bien que, jusqu'à ce que,* and *pourvu que* must be followed by the subjunctive even if both verbs have the same subject.

Il sortira avec nous à moins qu'il ait trop de travail.	*He will go out with us unless he has too much work to do.*
Je t'attendrai bien que je sois pressée.	*I will wait for you, even though I am in a hurry.*

AVOID THE Blunder

Don't use an infinitive after *à moins que, bien que, jusqu'à ce que,* or *pourvu que.*

✗ Je t'attendrai bien qu'être pressée.

Differences Between French and English

Use of the subjunctive is not common in English. By contrast, it is used often in everyday French. Even though the construction may seem unfamiliar to English speakers, the subjunctive is not a rare or fancy form in French.

The following examples illustrate some very common uses of the subjunctive.

Le prof veut que ses étudiants réussissent.	*The teacher wants his students to succeed.*
Je voudrais que tu fasses la vaisselle, s'il te plait.	*I would like you to do the dishes, please.*
Je n'aime pas que tu rentres après minuit.	*I do not like it that you come home past midnight.*
Nous ne pensons pas qu'il ait fait ça seul.	*We don't think he did that all alone.*

AVOID THE Blunder

✗ Le prof veut ses étudiants réussir.
✗ Je te veux faire la vaisselle.
✗ Elle veut il partir.

The English translation of a sentence with the subjunctive often has an object pronoun used as the subject of an infinitive.

He wants ***them*** *to succeed.*
I'd like ***you*** *to come here.*

In French, using a pronoun before an infinitive usually indicates that it is the object of the verb's action, not its subject.

Qu'est-ce que tu veux que je fasse?	*What do you want me to do?*
Qu'est-ce que tu veux me faire?	*What do you want to do to me?*

AVOID THE *Blunder*

✗ Qu'est-ce que tu veux me faire?
(when "What do you want me to do?" is meant)

No Future in the Subjunctive Mood

In a future context, if the main verb is a trigger expression, the verb in the dependent clause is in the subjunctive instead of the future or immediate future.

Les organisateurs de la fête ont peur qu'il pleuve le jour de la fête.	*The organizers of the party fear that it might rain on the day of the party.*
Nous souhaitons que vous veniez nous voir l'année prochaine.	*We wish that you would come see us next year.*

AVOID THE *Blunder*

Don't use the future after a trigger expression.

✗ Les organisateurs de la fête ont peur qu'il pleuvra le jour de la fête.
✗ Il est important que vous serez à l'heure demain.

AVOID THE *Blunder*

✗ Il est étonnant qu'il aille pleuvoir demain.
(when "It is surprising that it is going to rain tomorrow" is meant)
✗ Ils sont furieux que le prof aille donner un examen la veille des vacances. (when "They are furious that the teacher is going to give an exam the day before the break begins" is meant)

If the sentence is ambiguous without the future, an expression of time may need to be used to give a more precise context.

Il faut que vous soyez à l'heure.	*You must be on time (in general).* *You must be on time (for a particular appointment to come).*
Il faut que vous soyez à l'heure demain matin.	*You must be on time tomorrow morning.*

When Not to Use the Subjunctive

In some circumstances, even though a sentence has a trigger expression, the subjunctive is not used.

Single Subject

In the absence of a second subject, the verb of the dependent clause must be the infinitive, even if the main verb is a "trigger" verb.

TWO SUBJECTS

Je voudrais que mes enfants partent en vacances.	*I would like for my children to go on vacation.*

ONE SUBJECT

Je voudrais partir en vacances.	*I would like to go on vacation.*

AVOID THE Blunder

✗ Je veux que je rentre chez moi.
✗ Paul est content qu'il parte en vacances.

If the trigger expression is *être* + an adjective or an expression with *avoir* (for example, *avoir besoin/envie/honte/peur*), use *de* before the infinitive.

Je suis content de partir en vacances.	*I am glad to be going on vacation.*
Avez-vous peur de prendre l'avion?	*Are you afraid of flying?*

"Phony" Trigger Expressions

Sometimes what appears to be a trigger expression is not, and the dependent verb is in the indicative. A verb can look like a trigger for the subjunctive when it is followed by *que* + a second subject.

- Several very common verbs are never followed by the subjunctive.

entendre dire	*to hear that*
espérer	*to hope*
il parait	*rumor has it*
savoir	*to know*
se souvenir que	*to remember*

J'espère que vous vous reposerez.	*I hope that you will rest.*
Il parait que Pierre a eu un accident.	*I hear that Pierre had an accident.*
Je sais que tu dis la vérité.	*I know you are telling the truth.*

□ *Entendre dire* is always conjugated in the *passé composé* and introduces a verb that is usually in the pluperfect.

J'ai entendu dire que Pierre avait eu un accident.	*I heard that Pierre had an accident.*

AVOID THE Blunder

✗ J'entends dire que tu as gagné le loto.

□ The verb *espérer* is not a trigger verb, and it is often followed by the future or the *passé composé,* but rarely by the present.

Nous espérons que vous vous remettrez vite.	*We hope you recover fast.*
J'espère que tu as passé de bonnes vacances.	*I hope you had a nice holiday.*

AVOID THE Blunder

✗ J'espère qu'il fait beau demain.

AVOID THE Blunder

Don't confuse *espérer que* "to hope," which is followed by the indicative, with *souhaiter que* "to wish," which is followed by the subjunctive.

✗ J'espère que votre voyage soit agréable.
✗ Nous souhaitons que vous viendrez nous voir l'année prochaine.

- Verbs introducing reported speech, such as *affirmer* "to affirm," *comprendre* "to understand," *dire* "to say," *écrire* "to write," *expliquer* "to explain," *promettre* "to promise," *raconter* "to tell," and *répondre* "to answer," do not introduce a verb in the subjunctive unless they are reporting a command. (See the unit on reported speech.)

Le professeur dit que ses étudiants sont intéressants.	*The professor says that his students are interesting.*
Il a expliqué qu'il s'était trompé.	*He explained that he had made a mistake.*

AVOID THE Blunder

Don't confuse the verbs that introduce reported speech with trigger expressions that introduce the subjunctive.

✗ Je dis que vous soyez têtu!
✗ Il a expliqué qu'il se soit trompé.

- After verbs of perception, such as *écouter* "to listen to," *entendre* "to hear," *regarder* "to watch," and *voir* "to see," the infinitive is used in French. The English and French sentences have similar constructions.

Elle a regardé les bateaux partir.	*She watched the boats leave.*
Elle l'a entendu entrer.	*She heard him come in.*
J'ai vu l'avion décoller.	*I saw the plane take off.*

AVOID THE Blunder

✗ J'ai vu que l'avion décolle.

Verbs of Opinion

When the main clause of a sentence expresses an opinion, the verb in the dependent clause may be either indicative or subjunctive, depending on the construction of the sentence. If the subject of the main verb expresses an opinion or certainty in an affirmative statement, the verb in the dependent clause is in the indicative (any tense). If the main clause is a question using inversion or is negative, the verb in the dependent clause is in the subjunctive.

AFFIRMATIVE

Je pense qu'il fera beau demain.	*I think it will be nice tomorrow.*
Le professeur trouve que ses étudiants ont bien travaillé.	*The professor thinks (finds) that his students have done well.*

NEGATIVE

Je ne pense pas qu'il fasse beau demain.	*I don't think it will be nice tomorrow.*

QUESTION USING INVERSION

Trouvez-vous que vos étudiants aient bien travaillé?	*Do you think that your students have done well?*

AVOID THE *Blunder*

✗ Mes parents pensent que je sois un étudiant sérieux.
✗ Elle ne croit pas que tu mens.

The following chart shows how some common verbs of opinion are used with both the indicative and the subjunctive.

AFFIRMATIVE	NEGATIVE/QUESTION USING INVERSION
je pense que + *indicative*	je ne pense pas que + *subjunctive* penses-tu que + *subjunctive*
je crois que + *indicative*	je ne crois pas que + *subjunctive* crois-tu que + *subjunctive*
je suppose que + *indicative*	je ne suppose pas que + *subjunctive* supposes-tu que + *subjunctive*
il semble que + *indicative*	il ne semble pas que + *subjunctive* (te) semble-t-il que + *subjunctive*
il est évident que + *indicative*	il n'est pas évident que + *subjunctive* est-il évident que + *subjunctive*

AFFIRMATIVE	NEGATIVE/QUESTION USING INVERSION
il est vrai que + *indicative*	il n'est pas vrai que + *subjunctive* est-il vrai que + *subjunctive*
il est certain/sûr que + *indicative*	il n'est pas certain que + *subjunctive* est-il certain que + *subjunctive*

If *il semble que* is in a question, it is usually accompanied by an object pronoun.

Te semble-t-il qu'ils aient raison? *Does it seem (to you) that they are right?*

Exercises

A *Complete the following sentences with either the indicative or present subjunctive of the verb in parentheses. Be aware of the distinction between true trigger expressions and "phony" ones.*

1. Je suis sûre que vous me ________________ (comprendre).
2. J'espère que vous ________________ (conjuguer) le subjonctif correctement.
3. Nous sommes contents qu'il ________________ (faire) beau aujourd'hui.
4. Je doute qu'il ________________ (être) à l'heure.
5. Nous savons que cette affaire ________________ (être) sérieuse.
6. Les profs préfèrent que nous ________________ (avoir) de bons résultats.
7. Maman ne veut pas que nous ________________ (boire) du vin.

B *Express the following in French.*

1. *I am surprised that you are going to Europe next summer.*

____

2. *It is a pity that they are leaving early.*

____

3. *What do you* (vous) *want us to do?*

____

4. *I am sad that I am leaving tomorrow.*

____

5. *I would like for my children to be happy in life.*

____

6. *He is afraid he will lose his hat.*

____

7. *She does not think he is telling the truth.*

____

VERBS
the present subjunctive

Tense Formation

ils form of the present indicative − *-ent* ending + endings

parler	ils parlent	parl-
finir	ils finissent	finiss-
vendre	ils vendent	vend-

Endings of the Present Subjunctive

je	-e	nous	-ions
tu	-es	vous	-iez
il/elle/on	-e	ils/elles	-ent

For regular verbs, the *nous* and *vous* forms of the present subjunctive are often identical to the *nous* and *vous* forms of the *imparfait.*

SUBJUNCTIVE	*IMPARFAIT*
que nous parlions	nous parlions
que nous finissions	nous finissions

For *-er* verbs, the present subjunctive looks like the present indicative, except for the *nous* and *vous* forms.

SUBJUNCTIVE	INDICATIVE
que je parle	je parle
que tu parles	tu parles
qu'il parle	il parle
qu'ils parlent	ils parlent

In learning the subjunctive conjugations, it is useful to memorize each form with *que* in front: *que je dorme, que tu dormes,* etc.

Two-Stem Verbs

Verbs that alternate between two stems in the present indicative maintain that alternation in the subjunctive. For *je, tu, il/elle,* and *ils/elles,* the subjunctive is formed regularly, on the stem of the *ils* form, but the stem of the *nous* and *vous* forms is the stem of the *nous* form of the present indicative.

Common verbs of this type are *appeler* "to call," *boire* "to drink," *devoir* "to have to," *payer* "to pay," *prendre* "to take," *se promener* "to go for a walk," *tenir* "to hold," and *venir* "to come."

PRESENT	SUBJUNCTIVE
je bois (STEM 1)	que je boives
nous buvons (STEM 2)	que nous buvions
je paie (STEM 1)	que je paie
nous payons (STEM 2)	que nous payions
je promène (STEM 1)	que je promène
vous promenez (STEM 2)	que vous promeniez
je viens (STEM 1)	que je vienne
vous venez (STEM 2)	que vous veniez

AVOID THE Blunder

Don't forget the *i* in the *nous* and *vous* forms of verbs whose stem ends in *-y*.

✗ que nous payons
✗ que vous employez

Nine Verbs with Irregular Subjunctive Forms

Verbs of all three groups follow the conjugation patterns above, with nine exceptions: *aller* "to go," *avoir* "to have," *être* "to be," *faire* "to do," *falloir* "must," *pleuvoir* "to rain," *pouvoir* "can," *savoir* "to know," and *vouloir* "to want" are not formed according to the same pattern as the other verbs.

aller	avoir	être
que j'aille	que j'aie	que je sois
que tu ailles	que tu aies	que tu sois
qu'il aille	qu'il ait	qu'il soit
que nous allions	que nous ayons	que nous soyons
que vous alliez	que vous ayez	que vous soyez
qu'ils aillent	qu'ils aient	qu'ils soient

faire	falloir	pleuvoir
que je fasse		
que tu fasses		
qu'il fasse	qu'il faille	qu'il pleuve
que nous fassions		
que vous fassiez		
qu'ils fassent		

pouvoir	**savoir**	**vouloir**
que je puisse	que je sache	que je veuille
que tu puisses	que tu saches	que tu veuilles
qu'il puisse	qu'il sache	qu'il veuille
que nous puissions	que nous sachions	que nous voulions
que vous puissiez	que vous sachiez	que vous vouliez
qu'ils puissent	qu'ils sachent	qu'ils veuillent

AVOID THE Blunder

Don't put an *i* in the ending of the *nous* and *vous* forms of *avoir* and *être*.

✗ que nous ayions
✗ que vous soyiez

Uses of the Present Subjunctive

For uses of the present subjunctive, see the unit on the subjunctive mood.

Exercise

A *Complete the following sentences with the correct present subjunctive form of the verb in parentheses.*

1. Il est normal que les étudiants ______________ (avoir) besoin de vacances.
2. Il est bon que vous ______________ (étudier) avec vos amis.
3. Il est dommage que tu ______________ (ne pas pouvoir) rester ici plus longtemps.
4. Il est important que vous ______________ (faire) de l'exercice pour rester en forme.
5. Mon père ne veut pas que je ______________ (sortir) le soir pendant la semaine.
6. Il est nécessaire que tu ______________ (promener) ton chien deux fois par jour.
7. Il est plus prudent qu'il ______________ (revenir) avant minuit.
8. Il faut que vous ______________ (aller) voir ce film. Il est formidable!
9. Il est sage que nous ______________ (boire) beaucoup d'eau quand il fait chaud.
10. Il est important que les enfants ______________ (dormir) beaucoup.
11. Il ne faut pas que tu ______________ (boire) autant de Coca.
12. Il est bon que nous ______________ (payer) nos factures à temps.

VERBS
the past subjunctive

Tense Formation

Subjunctive of *avoir* or *être* + past participle

The past subjunctive is formed by using the subjunctive of the auxiliary verb *avoir* or *être* plus the past participle.

que j'aie parlé	que nous ayons parlé
que tu aies parlé	que vous ayez parlé
qu'il/elle ait parlé	qu'ils/elles aient parlé
que je sois allé(e)	que nous soyons allé(e)s
que tu sois allé(e)	que vous soyez allé(e)(s)
qu'il/elle soit allé(e)	qu'ils/elles soient allé(e)s

See the unit on the *passé composé* for formation of the past participle, determination of which auxiliary to use with a specific verb, and agreement of the past participle with a subject or object.

Uses of the Past Subjunctive

The past subjunctive is triggered by the same expressions as the present subjunctive. See the unit on the subjunctive mood.

The past subjunctive is used *relative to the action of the trigger expression*. It expresses an event that occurred before the action of the trigger expression in the main clause.

Il est triste que nous n'ayons pas pu vous voir.	*It is sad we could not see you.*
Il est impossible que tu aies échoué.	*It is not possible that you failed.*
Je suis déçu que tu ne sois pas venu hier soir.	*I am disappointed that you did not come last night.*

AVOID THE Blunder

Don't use the past subjunctive simply to introduce a past action.

✗ Je suis désolé qu'ils se soient battus.
(when "I was sorry that they were fighting" is meant)

In the absence of a second subject, the perfect infinitive is used instead of the past subjunctive. The rules are the same as for the present infinitive replacing the present subjunctive.

SUBJUNCTIVE CONSTRUCTION

Le prof est content que nous ayons réussi à l'examen.	*The teacher is glad that we did well on the exam.*

INFINITIVE CONSTRUCTION

Je suis content d'avoir réussi à mon examen.	*I am glad I did well on my exam.*

Past Subjunctive or Present Subjunctive

Compare the following examples.

Je suis désolé qu'ils se battent.	*I am sorry that they are fighting.*
Je suis désolé qu'ils se soient battus.	*I am sorry that they had a fight.*
J'étais désolé qu'ils se battent.	*I was sorry that they were fighting.*
J'étais désolé qu'ils se soient battus.	*I was sorry that they had had a fight.*

■ If the action of the verb in the dependent clause occurs after or at the same time as the action of the trigger expression, the present subjunctive is used for the verb in the dependent clause.

J'aimerais que nous sortions ensemble samedi prochain. (AFTER)	*I'd like to go out together next Saturday.*
Le pâtissier est content que les clients aiment ses gâteaux. (CONCURRENT)	*The baker is glad that the customers like his pastries.*

■ If the action of the verb in the dependent clause happened before the action of the trigger expression, the past subjunctive is used for the verb in the dependent clause.

Les organisateurs ont peur que les gens ne se soient pas amusés. (BEFORE)	*The organizers are afraid that people did not have fun.*
Nous sommes fiers que l'équipe nationale ait gagné la coupe. (BEFORE)	*We are proud that the national team won the cup.*

AVOID THE Blunder

Don't forget to use the past subjunctive if the action of the verb in the dependent clause took place before the action of the trigger expression.

✗ Nous sommes fiers que l'équipe nationale gagne la coupe. (when "We are proud that the national team won the cup" is meant)
✗ Je suis contente que tu sortes avec moi samedi dernier. (when "I am glad that you went out with me last Saturday" is meant)

ACTION OF THE DEPENDENT VERB	TENSE OF THE DEPENDENT VERB
Same time as that of the main verb	Present subjunctive
After that of the main verb	Present subjunctive
Before that of the main verb	Past subjunctive

Exercise

A *Complete the following sentences with the correct present or past subjunctive form of the verb in parentheses.*

1. Nous regrettons que nos enfants ____________________ (ne pas venir) en France avec nous l'été dernier.
2. Ce prof d'histoire ne croit pas que Christophe Colomb ____________________ (découvrir) notre continent.
3. Mme Martin est très en retard ce soir et M. Martin a peur qu'elle ____________________ (rater) le dernier bus.
4. Nous sommes contents que vous ____________________ (pouvoir) venir chez nous samedi prochain. La fête sera très sympa.
5. Les parents de Julie voudraient qu'elle ____________________ (aller) chez le docteur parce qu'ils ont peur qu'elle ____________________ (attraper) un mauvais virus quand elle était en vacances.

REPORTED SPEECH

When you relate someone's words without directly quoting the person, you are using reported speech. As in English, the words being reported can be a statement, a question, or a command.

DIRECT QUOTE

—C'est une surprise pour Papa, m'a dit Maman.	*"It is a surprise for Dad," Mom said to me.*

REPORTED SPEECH

Maman m'a dit que c'était une surprise pour Papa.	*Mom told me it was a surprise for Dad.*

DIRECT QUOTE

—Est-ce que le train est à l'heure? a-t-il demandé.	*"Is the train on time?" he asked.*

REPORTED SPEECH

Il a demandé si le train était à l'heure.	*He asked if the train was on time.*

In reported speech, changes must be made to the original quote; these may include changing the subject and objects (and words that refer to them), the verb, word order, and punctuation, as the following examples show.

—Veux-tu ma veste? Il a demandé si je voulais sa veste.	*"Do you want my jacket?"* *He asked if I wanted his jacket.*
—Vous ne nous avez pas écrit! Ils se sont exclamés que nous ne leur avions pas écrit.	*"You did not write to us!"* *They exclaimed that we did not write to them.*
—Ça va mieux? Il m'a demandé si j'allais mieux.	*"Are you feeling better?"* *He asked if I felt better.*

AVOID THE *Blunder*

✗ Ils ont dit que nous ne vous avions pas écrit.
(from "—Vous ne nous avez pas écrit!")
✗ Elle a dit qu'elle était rentrée chez moi à 2 heures.
(from "—Je suis rentrée chez moi à 2 heures.")

Reporting a Statement

In French, as in English, when reporting what someone says (present tense), the verb tense of the original quote is kept. When reporting what someone said (past tense), the verb tense used in the dependent clause varies. See the chart on page 248 in this unit.

- Reported speech is very similar in construction to the subjunctive, but declarative verbs used in reported speech (such as *demander* "to ask," *dire* "to say," and *s'exclamer* "to exclaim") are not followed by the subjunctive. The subjunctive is used in reported speech only to replace a direct command that was in the imperative. See the unit on the subjunctive mood.

REPORTED SPEECH	declarative verb + *que* + subject 2 + verb 2 in the indicative
SUBJUNCTIVE	trigger expression + *que* + subject 2 + verb 2 in the subjunctive

AVOID THE *Blunder*

Learn to distinguish verbs that introduce reported speech from trigger expressions for the subjunctive.

✗ Le professeur dit que ses étudiants soient intéressants.
✗ Je déclare que vous ayez tort, madame!

Common introductory verbs for reporting statements follow.

affirmer	*to state*
ajouter	*to add*
annoncer	*to announce*
comprendre	*to understand*
déclarer	*to declare*
dire	*to say, tell*
écrire	*to write*
expliquer	*to explain*
indiquer	*to show*
lancer	*to call out*
promettre	*to promise*
raconter	*to tell*
remarquer	*to note*
répondre	*to answer*
s'écrier	*to exclaim*

AVOID THE Blunder

Don't use *parler* to introduce reported speech.

✗ Je t'ai parlé qu'il serait en retard!

☐ In English, you can omit the word "that" following a declarative verb. In French, you cannot omit *que*.

Il a dit qu'il allait partir.	*He said (that) he was going to leave.*
Ils ont expliqué qu'ils ne pouvaient pas venir.	*They explained (that) they could not come.*

AVOID THE Blunder

✗ Il a dit il allait partir.
✗ Il a répondu nous avions tort.
✗ Elle a annoncé le repas était servi.

Tense Agreement for Reported Speech

When the introductory verb is in past tense, the tenses of the dependent clause will vary.

TENSE/MOOD IN THE ORIGINAL QUOTE	TENSE/MOOD IN REPORTED SPEECH
PRESENT	***IMPARFAIT***
Il a dit, —Je le veux. *He said, "I want it."*	Il a dit qu'il le voulait. *He said that he wanted it.*
IMPARFAIT	***IMPARFAIT***
Il a dit, —Elle pleurait souvent. *He said, "She cried often."*	Il a dit qu'elle pleurait souvent. *He said that she cried often.*
PASSÉ COMPOSÉ	**PLUPERFECT**
Il a dit, —Tu n'as pas fini. *He said, "You have not finished."*	Il a dit que tu n'avais pas fini. *He said that you had not finished.*
PLUPERFECT	**PLUPERFECT**
Il a dit, —Tu ne l'avais pas dit. *He said, "You had not said it."*	Il a dit que tu ne l'avais pas dit. *He said that you had not said it.*
FUTURE	**CONDITIONAL**
Il a dit, —Tu auras un zéro. *He said, "You will get a zero."*	Il a dit que tu aurais un zéro. *He said that you would get a zero.*
CONDITIONAL	**CONDITIONAL**
Il a dit, —Ça pourrait être difficile. *He said, "It could be difficult."*	Il a dit que ça pourrait être difficile. *He said that it could be difficult.*
IMPERATIVE	**SUBJUNCTIVE OR INFINITIVE**
Il a dit, —Fais tes devoirs. *He said, "Do your homework."*	{ Il a dit que tu fasses tes devoirs. Il t'a dit de faire tes devoirs. } *He told you to do your homework.*

AVOID THE Blunder

When reporting what someone said (past tense), don't forget to change the verb tense in the dependent clause.

✗ Il a dit que tu auras un zéro.
✗ Il a déclaré qu'il le veut.

Reporting a Command

To report a command, either the subjunctive or the infinitive can be used, although the infinitive introduced by *de* is usually preferred.

Il a dit que tu fasses tes devoirs. Il t'a dit de faire tes devoirs.	*He told you to do your homework.*
Il m'a dit que j'attende. Il m'a dit d'attendre.	*He told me to wait.*

With the infinitive, it is common to add an indirect object pronoun before the introductory verb to indicate the subject of the infinitive.

Elle leur a dit de se dépêcher. *She told them to hurry.*
Nous lui avons demandé de partir. *We asked her to leave.*

AVOID THE Blunder

Don't use the direct object pronoun as the subject of an infinitive.

✗ Sa mère l'a dit de se dépêcher.
✗ Je les ai dit de partir.

Reporting a Question

Common introductory verbs include *ne pas comprendre* "not to understand," *demander* "to ask," *se demander* "to wonder," *s'inquiéter* "to worry," *ne pas savoir* "not to know," and *vouloir savoir* "to want to know." These verbs cannot be followed by *que* when they introduce a question.

Inversion cannot be used to report a question.

—Êtes-vous malades? *"Are you sick?"*
Il a demandé si nous étions malades. *He asked if we were sick.*

AVOID THE Blunder

✗ Il a demandé si étions-nous malades.

Reporting Yes/No Questions

For yes/no questions that use *est-ce que* or inversion, *si* "if" introduces the reported question.

DIRECT QUESTION	REPORTED QUESTION
—Est-ce que tu as compris? —As-tu compris?	Il a demandé si j'avais compris.
—Est-ce que vous vous êtes amusés?	Il a demandé si nous nous étions amusés.

AVOID THE *Blunder*

Don't keep *est-ce que* when reporting a question.

✗ Il a demandé est-ce que j'avais compris.

The indirect object pronoun is often added to a reported question.

Il m'a demandé si j'avais compris. *He asked me if I had understood.*

Reporting Information Questions

Questions seeking information are expressed as follows in direct and reported speech.

DIRECT QUESTION	REPORTED QUESTION
qu'est-ce que...?	demander ce que...
que...?	demander ce que...
qu'est-ce qui...?	demander ce qui...
qui est-ce qui...?	demander qui...

Il m'a demandé ce que je voulais. *He asked (me) what I wanted.*
Il a demandé ce qui s'était passé. *He asked what had happened.*

Note that question words asking "what" change to *ce qui* and *ce que* in reported speech.

AVOID THE *Blunder*

✗ Il m'a demandé qu'est-ce que je voulais.
✗ Il a voulu savoir qu'est-ce qui s'était passé.

Other interrogative words remain the same as in direct questions.

comment...?	demander comment...
où...?	demander où...
pourquoi...?	demander pourquoi...
qui...?	demander qui...
Elle voulait savoir où j'allais.	*She wanted to know where I was going.*
Il lui a demandé pourquoi elle partait.	*He asked her why she was leaving.*
Il a demandé qui avait gagné.	*He asked who had won.*

Exercise

A *Complete the reported-speech sentences. All introductory verbs are in the past. There may be more than one way to express the sentence in French.*

1. Julie a dit, —Je n'ai pas faim.

   Julie a dit ______________________.

2. Sa mère lui a répondu, —Finis ta soupe!

   Sa mère lui a répondu ______________________.

3. Le passager a demandé, —Le train est-il à l'heure?

   Le passager a demandé ______________________.

4. Le policier a demandé, —Qu'est-ce qui s'est passé?

   Le policier a demandé ______________________.

5. Le professeur a demandé, —Vous comprenez?

   Le professeur voulait savoir ______________________.

6. Sa mère a dit, —Va au lit!

   Sa mère ______________________.

7. Il m'a demandé, —Qu'est-ce que tu ferais si tu voyais un martien?

   Il m'a demandé ______________________.

8. Paul m'a demandé, —Vas-tu m'inviter?

   Paul m'a demandé ______________________.

QUESTIONS AND ANSWERS

In French, as in English, there are two question types: the yes/no question and the information question. Each type can be formed in several ways: using intonation only, using inversion, and using *est-ce que*. A question mark always ends a question.

A question can be thought of in terms of building blocks. The first block is the yes/no question (core block). With a question word (block 2) added to the core block, the question expands to become an information question. Finally, a preposition (block 3) can be added to the information question.

STATEMENT	Elle danse.
CORE BLOCK	Danse-t-elle? OR Est-ce qu'elle danse?
+ BLOCK 2	**Comment** danse-t-elle? OR **Comment** est-ce qu'elle danse?
+ BLOCK 3	**Avec qui** danse-t-elle? OR **Avec qui** est-ce qu'elle danse?

Yes/No Questions

In English, a yes/no question is introduced by "do you," "are you," etc. In French, no auxiliary verb is added to the conjugated verb to form a question.

Est-ce qu'il parle anglais? Parle-t-il anglais?	*Does he speak English?*
Écris-tu? Est-ce que tu écris?	*Are you writing?*

AVOID THE *Blunder*

Don't introduce an auxiliary verb when forming a yes/no question.

✗ Êtes-vous déjeuner au restaurant?
✗ Que fait-il faire?

Forming a Question Using Inversion

In this form of question, the order of the subject pronoun and verb is reversed and a hyphen is inserted between them. This is the more formal way of asking a question, and it is usually reserved for written expression.

Déjeunez-vous au restaurant à midi?	*Do you eat out for lunch?*
Parle-t-il anglais?	*Does he speak English?*
As-tu fini ton travail?	*Did you finish your work?*
Allez-vous partir?	*Are you going to leave?*
Viendras-tu avec moi?	*Will you come with me?*
Est-il malade?	*Is he sick?*

AVOID THE *Blunder*

Don't forget the hyphen between the verb and subject when they are inverted.

✗ As tu fini? ✗ Où es tu?

- Inversion with *je* is extremely rare and is reserved for literary style.

Où suis-je? (LITERARY)
Où est-ce que je suis? (PREFERRED) } *Where am I?*

AVOID THE *Blunder*

Don't confuse question inversion (adding *-t-* before a pronoun) with adding *s-* to a *tu* imperative form before a pronoun.

✗ Va-t-y? ✗ Y vas-il?

- If the subject of a verb that ends in a vowel is *il, elle,* or *on*, *-t-* must be added between the verb and the pronoun.

Parle-t-il chinois?	*Does he speak Chinese?*
Finira-t-elle son travail à temps?	*Will she finish her work on time?*
Mange-t-on bien ici?	*Is this a good place to eat?*

AVOID THE *Blunder*

✗ Parle-elle chinois?
✗ Finira-il son travail?

■ If a noun is the subject of a verb, it cannot be moved around in the sentence, except in some information questions (see the section on information questions in this unit). Only a subject pronoun (*tu, vous, elle,* etc.) can follow the verb in inversion. As a result, the verb in this form of question is surrounded by two subjects: The noun subject precedes it and the corresponding subject pronoun follows it.

Alain aime-t-il danser?	*Does Alain like to dance?*
Julie et Pierre travaillent-ils bien?	*Do Julie and Pierre work hard?*
La maison est-elle agréable?	*Is the house pleasant?*

AVOID THE *Blunder*

In a yes/no question, don't invert a noun subject and the verb.

✗ Est la maison agréable?
✗ Aime Alain danser?

■ In the *passé composé* (or any compound tense), the subject and the auxiliary *être* or *avoir* are inverted. The past participle remains where it is.

Es-tu sorti?	*Did you go out?*
As-tu fini?	*Have you finished?*
Sont-ils revenus?	*Have they returned?*

AVOID THE *Blunder*

In the *passé composé,* don't invert the subject and past participle.

✗ Êtes arrivés-vous?
✗ Avez fait-vous vos devoirs?

■ If the sentence has an object pronoun, the rules of placement of the pronoun are the same as for a statement, and the pronoun must precede the infinitive (if there is one) or the conjugated verb. (See the unit on subjects, objects, and their pronouns.)

Le regardez-vous?	*Are you looking at it?*
T'ennuies-tu?	*Are you bored?*
Se sont-ils parlé?	*Did they talk to each other?*
Irez-vous leur parler?	*Will you go talk to them?*

AVOID THE *Blunder*

Even if you think it looks "wrong," do start a question with an object pronoun when necessary.

✗ Regardez-vous le?
✗ Ennuies-toi tu?

Using *est-ce que* to Form a Question

est-ce que + sentence

Est-ce que is simply a "tag" that indicates a sentence is interrogative; it is never translated in English. After *est-ce que*, no changes are made to the sentence and the order of words is the same as for a statement. This is the simplest and easiest way to ask a question.

Est-ce que vous déjeunez au restaurant à midi?	*Do you eat out for lunch?*
Est-ce qu'il parle anglais?	*Does he speak English?*
Est-ce que vous avez visité Paris?	*Did you visit Paris?*
Est-ce que Julie et Marc sont contents?	*Are Julie and Marc satisfied?*

AVOID THE *Blunder*

Don't combine *est-ce que* with inversion.

✗ Est-ce que sont-ils déjà partis?
✗ Est-ce que t'ennuies-tu ici?

Answering a Yes/No Question

To answer a yes/no question, English often uses only the auxiliary verb from the question.

"Do you like it?" "I do."
"Are you there?" "I am."

In French, *oui* or *non* can be used to give a short answer, or an adverb can be used, but a French equivalent for an English auxiliary verb cannot be used.

—Tu l'aimes? —Non.
—Tu es là? —Oui.

AVOID THE Blunder

✗ —Est-ce que tu as fini? —Oui, j'ai.
(when "Have you finished?" "I have." is meant)
✗ —Est-ce qu'elle aime le chocolat? —Oui, elle fait.
(when "Does she like chocolate?" "She does." is meant)
✗ —Est-ce que tu lis? —Je suis.
(when "Are you reading?" "I am." is meant)

An adverb or adverbial expression can replace *oui* or *non*.

bien sûr	*sure / of course*
certainement	*certainly*
Avec plaisir.	*I'd love to.*
Pourquoi pas?	*Why not?*

—Veux-tu sortir ce soir?	*"Do you want to go out tonight?"*
—Avec plaisir.	*"I'd love to."*

If the answer is negative, the adverb is preceded by *pas*.

Pas maintenant.	*Not now.*
Pas encore.	*Not yet.*
Pas question!	*No way!*
Pas du tout.	*Not at all.*

—Partons!	*"Let's go!"*
—Pas encore.	*"Not yet."*
—Veux-tu diner?	*"Do you want to eat?"*
—Pas maintenant.	*"Not now."*

Information Questions

A question word such as *quand* "when," *pourquoi* "why," or *où* "where" must introduce an information question (block 2). The core block can be *est-ce que* or inversion. The following examples show information questions asked in both ways. For lists of question words, see the charts on pages 259–271 in the section on the question words in this unit.

Quand sont-ils arrivés? Quand est-ce qu'ils sont arrivés?	*When did they arrive?*
Pourquoi as-tu dit un mensonge? Pourquoi est-ce que tu as dit un mensonge?	*Why did you tell a lie?*

If the question word is combined with a preposition (block 3), the preposition comes first, before the question word.

D'où êtes-vous?	*Where are you from?*
Avec qui est-ce qu'ils sont sortis?	*Whom did they go out with?*
Pour qui est-ce que vous travaillez?	*Whom do you work for?*
Avec quoi est-ce que tu as écrit?	*What did you write with?*

AVOID THE Blunder

Don't place the preposition at the end of the question, as is often done in English.

✗ Qui travaillez-vous pour?
✗ Qui est-il sorti avec?
✗ Qu'est-ce que tu as écrit avec?

Forming an Information Question with *est-ce que*

question word + *est-ce que* + sentence

Où est-ce que vous déjeunez?	*Where do you have lunch?*
Pourquoi est-ce que Pierre est parti?	*Why did Pierre leave?*

Forming an Information Question Using Inversion

question word + sentence with the subject pronoun and verb inverted

Où déjeunez-vous?	*Where do you have lunch?*
Pourquoi pleures-tu?	*Why are you crying?*

If the subject is a noun instead of a pronoun, however, there are two inversion methods.

□ As in a yes/no question, a double subject can be introduced, but this form is usually reserved for written expression.

Quand Pierre est-il parti?	*When did Pierre leave?*

□ Unlike in a yes/no question, the order of the noun subject and verb can be reversed in most questions.

If the verb does not have a direct object, the order of noun subject and verb can and should be reversed. Information questions with *pourquoi* are the only exception. Note that information questions with *qui* can be tricky (see page 267 in this unit).

INVERSION WITHOUT A DIRECT OBJECT

Quand part Pierre?	*When does Pierre leave?*
Où déjeune Alice?	*Where does Alice have lunch?*
Combien coutent ces fleurs?	*How much are these flowers?*

Unlike the rather formal inversion of yes/no questions (*Aimez-vous le thé?*), this type of inversion is preferred to the *est-ce que* form in everyday language.

AVOID THE Blunder

Don't insert a hyphen or *-t-* between the verb and noun subject.

✗ Comment danse-t-Alain?
✗ Où va-t-Alice?
✗ Quand part-Pierre?

In fact, inversion is the preferred form for asking an information question that has a noun as its subject. The following chart contrasts noun subject–verb inversion and double subject (written style) inversion.

PREFERRED FORM	NORMAL INVERSION FORM
Où vont les enfants cet été? *Where are the children going this summer?*	Où les enfants vont-ils cet été?
À qui parle le facteur? *Whom is the mailman talking to?*	À qui le facteur parle-t-il?
Combien coutent ces fleurs? *How much are these flowers?*	Combien ces fleurs coutent-elles?
Comment va ta grand-mère? *How is your grandmother doing?*	Comment ta grand-mère va-t-elle?
Quand reviennent vos voisins? *When are your neighbors coming back?*	Quand vos voisins reviennent-ils?

AVOID THE Blunder

Don't reverse the order of the noun subject and verb if the verb has a direct object.

✗ Quand a écrit votre mari un poème? (un poème = direct object)
✗ Où met le livreur les fleurs? (les fleurs = direct object)

If the verb has a direct object, the *est-ce que* form is used.

INVERSION WITH A DIRECT OBJECT

Quand est-ce que votre mari a écrit un poème?	*When did your husband write a poem?*
Où est-ce que le livreur met les fleurs?	*Where does the delivery man put the flowers?*

■ The preferred form of inversion (noun subject–verb inversion) is almost always used after *que* (as object), but not after *qu'est-ce que.*

Que fait votre mari? (SIMPLE) Qu'est-ce que fait votre mari? (AWKWARD)	*What does your husband do?*
Que veut cette personne? (SIMPLE) Qu'est-ce que veut cette personne? (AWKWARD)	*What does this person want?*

The Question Words

Asking "When?"

quand	*when*
yes/no question + souvent	*how often*
à quelle heure	*at what time*
combien de temps y a-t-il que y a-t-il longtemps que	*how long ago*
depuis quand + *present tense*	*since when*

Quand pars-tu?	*When do you leave?*
Est-ce que tu vas souvent à la gym?	*How often do you work out?*
À quelle heure finis-tu?	*At what time are you done?*
Combien de temps y a-t-il que tu as écrit ça?	*How long ago did you write that?*

AVOID THE Blunder

Don't translate "how often" word for word into French.

✗ Combien souvent vas-tu au cinéma?

AVOID THE Blunder

Don't use liaison after *quand,* except in *quand est-ce que,* where the liaison is a /t/ sound.

Answering *Quand?*

- General

à (+ *time*)	*at* (+ time)
vers (+ *time*)	*around* (+ time)
le matin	*in the morning*
dans la journée	*during the day*
le soir	*in the evening, at night*

- Frequency

toujours	*always*
tout le temps	*all the time*
souvent	*often*
parfois, de temps en temps	*sometimes, from time to time*
presque toujours/jamais	*almost always/never*
jamais	*never*
le lundi/le mardi	*on Mondays/Tuesdays*
tous les lundis/mardis	*every Monday/Tuesday*
tous les jours/mois	*every day/month*
une fois par jour/mois	*once a day / a month*
deux fois par jour/mois	*twice a day / a month*

- Present

maintenant	*now*
tout de suite	*right now*
en ce moment	*now, at this time*
aujourd'hui	*today*
ces jours-ci	*these days*

- Past

récemment	*recently*
autrefois	*formerly, in the old days*
il y a + *amount of time*	amount of time + *ago*
avant-hier	*the day before yesterday*
hier	*yesterday*
hier matin	*yesterday morning*
hier soir	*last night*
la semaine dernière	*last week*
le mois / l'an dernier	*last month/year*
lundi dernier	*last Monday*

AVOID THE Blunder

Don't use *nuit* to express "at night" or "last night."

✗ hier nuit ✗ la nuit je me couche à dix heures

AVOID THE Blunder

Don't use *hier* to mean "last" (in the sense of "the previous") with *semaine* "week," *mois* "month," or *an* "year."

✗ hier semaine
✗ hier mois
✗ hier an

- Future

à l'avenir	*in the future*
dans + *amount of time*	*in* + amount of time
bientôt	*soon*
dès que + *future tense*	*as soon as* + present tense
après	*after*
ce soir	*tonight*
demain	*tomorrow*
demain matin	*tomorrow morning*
demain soir	*tomorrow night*
après-demain	*the day after tomorrow*
la semaine prochaine	*next week*
le mois / l'an prochain	*next month/year*
lundi prochain	*next Monday*

Dernier and *prochain* must agree in gender with the noun they describe. They are placed after the noun.

l'année dernière	*last year*
les jours prochains	*the coming days*

AVOID THE Blunder

Don't place *dernier* or *prochain* before the noun in an expression of time.

✗ le dernier mois
✗ le prochain an

Asking "Where?"

où	*where*
d'où	*where from*
où	*where to*
à quel endroit	*in what location*

Où habites-tu?	*Where do you live?*
Où veux-tu aller?	*Where do you want to go?*
D'où es-tu?	*Where are you from?*
À quel endroit as-tu mis mes clés?	*Where did you put my keys?*

Answering *Où?*

ici	*here*
là	*here/there*
là-bas	*over there*
partout	*everywhere*
nulle part	*nowhere*

Questions with *où* can also be answered by prepositional phrases. The most common prepositions used in this way follow.

à	*at*
chez	*at (someone's) house*
dans	*in*
derrière	*behind*
devant	*in front of*
en	*at*
vers	*toward, around*

See the unit on prepositions.

Asking "How?": Manner and Degree

comment	*how*

comment + *verb*	*how* + verb
Comment voyagez-vous?	*How do you travel?*
yes/no question + adjective	*how* + adjective + verb
Est-ce que c'est difficile?	*How difficult is it?*
yes/no question + adverb	*how* + adverb + verb
Est-ce qu'elle chante bien?	*How well does she sing?*
Est-ce que vous avez vraiment besoin de ça?	*How badly do you need this?*

AVOID THE *Blunder*

Don't pronounce the *t* of *comment* in a question, except in the fixed question *Comment allez-vous?*

✗ Comment a-t-il fait? (with "Comment" /t/ pronounced)
✗ Comment es-tu tombé? (with "Comment" /t/ pronounced)

Answering *Comment?*

bien	*well*
mieux	*better*
mal	*badly*
moins bien	*less well*
an adverb of manner or degree	
en + *gerund*	*by/while + ______ing*
Je suis tombé en courant.	*I fell running.*

Asking "How Many?" and "How Much?"

combien de + *noun without article*	*how much*
combien de + *noun without article*	*how many*
yes/no question + adverb	*how much* + verb
combien de temps	*how long*
combien + *verb*	*how much* (in a money context)
Combien de temps as-tu mis?	*How long did it take you?*
Combien de voitures ont-ils?	*How many cars do they have?*
Tu l'aimes vraiment?	*How much do you love him/her?*
Combien as-tu dépensé?	*How much did you spend?*
C'est combien?	*How much is it?*
Combien ça coute?	*How much does it cost?*
Combien gagnez-vous par jour?	*How much do you make per day?*

Liaison never occurs after *combien.*

AVOID THE Blunder

Don't use *combien* for abstract things that cannot be counted.

✗ Combien intéressant est ce livre?
✗ Combien l'aimes-tu?

Answering *Combien?*

An expression of quantity replaces an article before a noun.

Il a beaucoup de chance.	*He is lucky.*
Tu as bu trop de coca.	*You drank too much Coke.*

AVOID THE Blunder

✗ trop du coca ✗ beaucoup de la chance

beaucoup (de)	*a lot*
un peu (de)	*a little*
peu (de)	*little*
assez (de)	*enough*
pas assez (de)	*not enough*
aucun(e)	*none, not any*
pas du tout	*not at all*
plus (de)	*more*
moins (de)	*less*
autant (de)	*as much, as many*

For more expressions of quantity, see the unit on determiners.

Asking "Why?"

pourquoi	*why*
pourquoi / pour quoi faire	*what for*
pour quelle raison / pour quelles raisons	*what is the reason / what are the reasons*
dans quel but	*to what end*

comment se fait-il que + *subjunctive*	*how come* + ______
Comment ça se fait?	*How come?*

Pourquoi pleurez-vous?	*Why are you crying?*
Pourquoi as-tu dit ça?	*What did you say that for?*
Pour quelles raisons voulez-vous ce poste?	*For what reasons do you want this position?*
Dans quel but a-t-il écrit cette lettre?	*To what end did he write this letter?*
Comment se fait-il que tu n'aies pas encore fini?	*How come you're not done yet?*

Answering *Pourquoi?*

parce que + *verb*	*because* + verb
à cause de + *noun*	*because of* + noun
pour + *infinitive*	*in order to* + verb
pour + *noun*	*for* + noun
la raison pour laquelle	*the reason why*

Il a quitté la ville à cause du climat.	*He left town because of the weather.*
C'est la raison pour laquelle il est parti.	*That's the reason why he left.*

AVOID THE Blunder

Don't use a noun after *parce que;* use *à cause de* instead.

✗ Il est parti parce que le climat.

Asking "What?"

The question word "what" has several equivalents in French: *que, qu'est-ce que,* and *qu'est-ce qui*. To choose the right form, it is necessary to determine the function of "what" in the question. It can be the verb's subject (as in "What caused that accident?") or object (as in "What do you want?").

AVOID THE Blunder

Don't answer a question that begins with *que* using a noun that refers to a person.

✗ —Qu'est-ce qui a causé l'accident? —C'est Paul.
✗ —Qu'est-ce qui se passe? —Julie.

- *Que* can be used in a question with inversion (the short form) or with *est-ce qu-* (the long form). In the long form, the first *que* indicates that the unknown is a thing, and the second *qu-* word indicates its function in the sentence: subject (*qui*) or object (*que*).

SUBJECT: qu'est-ce qui

Qu'est-ce qui se passe?	*What is happening?*

OBJECT: qu'est-ce que

Qu'est-ce que tu fais? Que fais-tu?	*What are you doing?*

The chart below shows the functions of *que* in questions.

que + est-ce qu- AS SUBJECT: Qu'est-ce qui...

Qu'est-ce qui a causé l'accident?	*What caused the accident?*
Qu'est-ce qui est arrivé?	*What happened?*

que + est-ce qu- AS OBJECT: Qu'est-ce que...

Qu'est-ce que tu veux?	*What do you want?*
Qu'est-ce qu'il va faire?	*What is he going to do?*

que (SHORT FORM) AS OBJECT: Que + INVERSION

Que dis-tu?	*What do you say?*

Note that there is no short form for *que* as a subject. In the short form, *que* only functions as an object.

AVOID THE Blunder

✗ Qu'a causé l'accident?

Note that in the question *qu'est-ce qui*, the second *qu-* word indicates the function of the question word; *qui* does not denote a person.

AVOID THE Blunder

✗ Qu'est-ce qui est arrivé? (when "Who arrived?" is meant)

■ In everyday language, asking "what?" instead of saying "excuse me" is common. It can either express surprise or indicate that you did not hear something. In this context, *quoi* can be used, although *comment* is more formal.

—Sa voiture a été volée. —Quoi? *"His car was stolen." "What?"*

AVOID THE Blunder

Don't use *que* to express "what" in an exclamation.

✗ "Que!"

Preposition + "What"

To ask "with what," "at what," "for what," etc. in French, *que* and *qu'est-ce que* change to *quoi* and *quoi est-ce que* after the preposition.

Avec quoi as-tu écrit?	*What did you write with?*
À quelle heure arriveront-ils?	*At what time will they arrive?*
De quoi parles-tu?	*What are you talking about?*

AVOID THE Blunder

Don't use *que* and *qu'est-ce que* after a preposition.

✗ Avec qu'est-ce que tu as écrit?
✗ Pour qu'est-ce que tu as fait ça?
✗ À que jouez-vous?

Don't start a question with *quoi* or *quoi est-ce que.*

✗ Quoi est-ce que tu veux?
✗ Quoi faites-vous?

Asking "Who?" or "Whom?"

The question word "who" has several equivalents in French: *qui, qui est-ce que,* and *qui est-ce qui.* To choose the right form, it is necessary to determine its function in the question. It can be the verb's subject (as in "Who did this?") or object (as in "Whom do you prefer?").

- In a question, *qui* can be used in a short form (without inversion) if it is the subject of a verb. The long form (with *est-ce qu-*) can be used whether *qui* functions as the verb's subject or object.

Qui est-ce qui travaille le dimanche?
Qui travaille le dimanche? } *Who works on Sundays?*

Qui est-ce qui a commencé?
Qui a commencé? } *Who started?*

- In the long form, the first *qui* indicates that the unknown is a person, and the second *qu-* word indicates its function in the sentence: subject (*qui*) or object (*que*).

SUBJECT: qui est-ce qui

Qui est-ce qui a ouvert la porte? — *Who opened the door?*

OBJECT: qui est-ce que

Qui est-ce que vous préférez? — *Whom do you prefer?*

AVOID THE Blunder

Don't start a question with any word but *qui* when asking about a person.

✗ Qu'est-ce qui est arrivé? (when "Who arrived?" is meant)

The chart below shows the functions of *qui* in questions.

qui + est-ce qu- AS SUBJECT: Qui est-ce qui...

Qui est-ce qui a commencé? — *Who started?*
Qui est-ce qui veut un bonbon? — *Who wants a piece of candy?*

qui (SHORT FORM) AS SUBJECT: Qui + VERB

Qui a commencé? — *Who started?*

qui + est-ce qu- AS OBJECT: Qui est-ce que...

Qui est-ce que tu as invité? — *Whom did you invite?*

qui (SHORT FORM) AS OBJECT: Qui + INVERSION

Qui as-tu invité? — *Whom did you invite?*

- Note that *qui* (the short form) can be used as the verb's subject or object. If it is an object, the subject and verb that follow must be inverted.

- In the short form with *qui* as object, if the subject of the verb is a noun, the subject must be doubled or the meaning of the question will change.

Qui Bernard aime-t-il?	*Whom does Bernard love?*
Qui Marie invite-t-elle?	*Whom does Marie invite?*

If the subject is not doubled and the noun subject and verb are inverted anyway (as in most information questions), the meaning of the question changes completely.

Qui aime Bernard?	*Who loves Bernard?*
Qui invite Marie?	*Who invites Marie?*

AVOID THE Blunder

Don't invert a noun subject and verb in a question with *qui* as object.

✗ Qui aime Bernard? (when "Whom does Bernard love?" is meant)

With *qui* as subject, all adjectives (both descriptive and possessive) must be masculine singular and the verb must be third-person singular.

Qui a bien fait ses devoirs aujourd'hui?	*Who did their homework today?*

AVOID THE Blunder

✗ Qui ont fait leurs devoirs?

Preposition + "Whom"

To ask "with whom," "for whom," etc. in French, *qui* and *qui est-ce que* are used after the preposition.

À qui as-tu écrit? À qui est-ce que tu as écrit?	*Whom did you write to?*
Pour qui travaillez-vous? Pour qui est-ce que vous travaillez?	*For whom do you work?*

AVOID THE Blunder

Don't use *qui* or *qui est-ce qui* after a preposition in a question.

✗ Qui est-ce que tu as écrit à?

"Who?" and "What?": A Summary

If it is a person being asked about, the question begins with *qui.*

If it is a thing being asked about, the question begins with *que.*

- ☐ If a preposition precedes *qui,* either *qui* or *qui est-ce que* is used.

AVOID THE Blunder

Don't insert *est-ce* ***qui*** after a preposition.

✗ À qui est-ce qui tu parles?

- ☐ If a preposition precedes *que,* either *quoi* or *quoi est-ce que* is used.

Avec quoi est-ce que tu joues?	*What are you playing with?*

AVOID THE Blunder

Don't put a preposition at the end of a question in French, even though this is common practice in English.

✗ Qui sont-ils sortis avec?

Questions of Choice: *quel*

The interrogative adjective *quel* asks "what" or "which" about a noun.

Quel est le livre que tu préfères?	*What is the book you prefer?*
Quels cours prends-tu ce semestre?	*Which classes are you taking this semester?*

As an adjective, *quel* must agree in gender and number with the noun it is asking about.

	MASCULINE	FEMININE
SINGULAR	quel	quelle
PLURAL	quels	quelles

Quelle est la couleur que tu préfères?	*What color do you prefer?*
Quels sont tes chanteurs préférés?	*Who are your favorite singers?*

- *Quel* may be used in two different constructions:

- *quel est* + noun (+ relative clause)

Quelle est ton adresse?	*What is your address?*
Quels sont les meilleurs restaurants ici?	*Which are the best restaurants here?*
Quel est ce bruit?	*What is that noise?*
Quel est le livre que tu préfères?	*Which book do you prefer?*
Quelle est la couleur que tu aimes le moins?	*What color do you like the least?*
Quelle est la chose dont tu as le plus envie?	*What thing do you want the most?*

AVOID THE Blunder

Don't omit a definite determiner (*le, ce, mon,* etc.) in the construction *quel est* + noun.

✗ Quel est chanteur favori?
✗ Quelle est couleur que tu préfères?

- *quel* + noun + *est-ce que* or inversion

In this construction, *quel* replaces the article before the noun.

Quelle couleur est-ce que tu préfères? Quelle couleur préfères-tu?	*Which color do you prefer?*
Quel livre est-ce que tu as lu? Quel livre as-tu lu?	*Which book have you read?*

AVOID THE Blunder

Don't keep the article that *quel* replaces.

✗ Quelle la couleur préfères-tu?

- If a preposition precedes *quel*, the construction *quel* + noun is used.
  preposition + *quel* + noun + *est-ce que* or inversion

De quel instrument est-ce que vous jouez? De quel instrument jouez-vous?	*What instrument do you play?*

AVOID THE Blunder

✗ À quelle est l'heure du rendez-vous?

Quel or *qu'est-ce que*?

Both of these question words translate "what," but their usage is different.

- *Quel* introduces a noun or *être* + a noun.

Quel âge a-t-il?	*How old is he? (What age does he have?)*
Quelle est ton adresse?	*What is your address?*

- *Qu'est-ce que* introduces a clause.

Qu'est-ce que tu vas faire?	*What are you going to do?*

To ask for the definition of a noun, however, *qu'est-ce que* is used with the noun.

Qu'est-ce qu'un masque?	*What is a mask?*

AVOID THE Blunder

Don't use *qu'est-ce que* + noun to translate "what" unless you are asking for a definition.

✗ Qu'est-ce que ta couleur préférée?

Exercises

A *Express the following questions in French, using the* est-ce que *form first, then using inversion. Both forms may not be possible for some items.*

1. *Whom would you* (tu) *like to dance with?*

___

___

2. *Do your* (tu) *brothers play tennis every day?*

___

___

3. *Who runs the fastest?*

___

___

4. *What is her profession?*

___

___

5. *Which instrument do you* (vous) *play?*

___

___

6. *Are you* (tu) *going to succeed?*

___

___

7. *Did they* (elles) *have fun?*

___

___

B *Write questions to ask for the information provided in the phrases and clauses in bold type, using the* est-ce que *form first, then using inversion. Both forms may not be possible for some items.*

1. Luc écoute **de la musique classique**.

___

___

2. Luc s'intéresse **aux voitures.**

3. Je préfère **le vert.**

4. Julie arrivera à la maison **à 7 heures.**

5. Les Français aiment **le vin rouge**.

6. Virginie aime **Paul**.

7. **Je suis fatiguée** aujourd'hui.

8. Il a passé les vacances **avec ses parents.**

9. Elle rentre à la maison **à pied.**

10. Ils sont allés **en France.**

11. Il dit cela **parce que c'est vrai.**

C *Complete the following sentences with a form of* quel *or* qu'est-ce que.

1. ____________________ tour est la plus haute? La tour Eiffel ou la tour Montparnasse?
2. ____________________ on peut faire d'intéressant ici?
3. ____________________ candidat a été élu?
4. ____________________ sont les directives pour cet exercice?
5. ____________________ est votre opinion?
6. ____________________ vous allez faire ce soir?
7. ____________________ sont les cours les plus intéressants?
8. ____________________ veux-tu?
9. ____________________ vous voulez boire?

VOCABULARY

WORDS

Cognates

Cognates are words that look alike and share a common meaning in French and English. Following are some common cognates.

acteur	*actor*
animal	*animal*
banane	*banana*
capital	*capital*
contrôle	*control*
directeur	*director*
faveur	*favor*
moteur	*motor*
patient	*patient*
professeur	*professor*
référence	*reference*
satisfaction	*satisfaction*

False Cognates

Les faux amis "false friends" are words that look alike in French and English, but don't have the same meaning at all. They are referred to as "false friends" because they are so misleading. Following are some common "false friends."

ENGLISH WORD	FRENCH WORD	MEANING OF FRENCH WORD
NOUNS		
advertisement	avertissement	*warning*
apology	apologie	*eulogy*
angina	angine	*sore throat*
bachelor	bachelier	*student who passed the* baccalauréat
car	car	*bus*
carpet	carpette	*small rug*
college	collège	*junior high school*
commode	commode	*chest of drawers*
conductor	conducteur	*driver*
deception	déception	*disappointment*

ENGLISH WORD	FRENCH WORD	MEANING OF FRENCH WORD
fabric	fabrique	*factory*
figure	figure	*face*
glass	glace	*ice*
injury	injure	*insult*
journey	journée	*day*
lecture	lecture	*reading*
library	librairie	*bookstore*
location	location	*rental*
mode	mode	*fashion*
pain	peine	*sorrow*
patron	patron	*boss*
place	place	*town square, seat*
pub	pub	*advertisement*
sentence	sentence	*verdict*
trouble	trouble	*confusion*
VERBS		
to achieve	achever	*to finish*
to attend	attendre	*to wait for*
to bless	blesser	*to hurt, injure*
to date	dater	*to put a date on (something)*
to deliver	délivrer	*to free*
to demand	demander	*to ask*
to edit	éditer	*to publish*
to engage	engager	*to hire*
to file	filer	*to spin*
to hurt	heurter	*to hit, collide with*
to pretend	prétendre	*to claim*
to quit	quitter	*to leave (a place)*
to rest	rester	*to stay*
to support	supporter	*to bear*
to travel	travailler	*to work*
ADJECTIVES/ADVERBS		
actual	actuel	*current*
engaged	engagé	*hired*
gross	gros/grosse	*fat*
large	large	*wide*
eventually	éventuellement	*possibly*

Translating from English to French

A single word in a language can denote several different things or concepts, but may need to be translated by several different words in another language. For instance, English "country" can mean both "countryside" and "homeland." The French word for "countryside" is *la campagne*, whereas the word for "homeland" is *le pays*.

AVOID THE Blunder

✗ Nous avons passé les vacances au pays.
(when "We spent our vacation in the countryside" is meant)

When looking up a word in the dictionary, it is important to pay attention to the various subentries that indicate the different meanings that the word can have. It is often not a good idea to select the very first word of the very first subentry.

It usually helps to think of two words in English to express what you want to say. If the first word seems difficult to put into French, perhaps the second one will be easier. Less frequently used English words can be a great help to your French vocabulary.

Il a continué à marcher.	*He kept on walking.* *He continued to walk.*
Elle est partie vite.	*She took off quickly.* *She departed quickly.*

The Noun "Time"

- *heure*

Quelle heure est-il?	*What time is it?*
C'est l'heure de partir.	*It's time to go.*
Il est à l'heure.	*He is on time.*
C'est l'heure du diner.	*It's dinnertime.*

AVOID THE Blunder

✗ Quel temps est-il? (when "What time is it?" is meant)

- *fois*

la première fois	*the first time*
deux fois	*two times*

AVOID THE Blunder

✗ Il est tombé trois temps.

- *temps*

Le temps passe vite.	*Time flies.*
Nous n'avons pas le temps.	*We don't have time.*
à la mi-temps	*at half-time*

- *époque*

à l'époque des Romains	*in Roman times*
à l'époque de Louis XIV	*in the time of Louis XIV*

- *moment*

au moment de leur mariage	*at the time of their wedding*
C'est le moment!	*Now is a good time!*

- *mesure* (music)

Il a gardé la mesure.	*He kept time.*

- The expression "to have a good time" is not translated with the word *temps*. Instead, the reflexive verb *s'amuser* is used.

Nous nous sommes bien amusés en vacances.	*We had a good time on vacation.*

AVOID THE Blunder

✗ Nous avons eu un bon temps en vacances.

The Noun "People"

In French, *gens* is a noncount noun that is always masculine plural. If a specific number describes "people" in English, *personnes* is used instead of *gens* in French.

AVOID THE Blunder

Don't use a verb in the singular after the noun *gens*.

✗ Les gens est fou.

Les gens sont fous dans cette ville!	*People are crazy in this town!*
Il y a des gens qui n'aiment pas le chocolat.	*Some people don't like chocolate.*
Ces gens ont été très aimables.	*Those people were very pleasant.*
tous les gens	*everyone*

BUT

Quatre personnes ont été blessées.	*Four people were injured.*
—Combien de personnes sont venues? —Je ne sais pas, beaucoup de gens.	*"How many people came?"* *"I don't know, a lot of people."*

AVOID THE Blunder

Don't use the word *personne* to express "people," if possible.

✗ Toutes les personnes étaient élégantes.
(when "Everyone looked smart" is meant)
✗ Il y avait des personnes intéressantes.
(when "There were some interesting people" is meant)

- The following expressions of quantity can be used with *gens.*

des gens	*some people*
peu de gens	*few people*
beaucoup de gens	*a lot of people*
trop de gens	*too many people*
tous les gens	*everyone*
(pas) assez de gens	*(not) enough people*
plus de gens	*more people*
moins de gens	*fewer people*
autant de gens	*as many people*

AVOID THE Blunder

Don't use counting expressions of quantity with *gens.*

✗ Deux gens se marient. ✗ Combien de gens sont venus?

The Verb "To Leave"

Partir, s'en aller, sortir, quitter, and *laisser* can all mean "to leave," but each has a different nuance and is used in a different situation.

AVOID THE Blunder

The verb *aller* is never translated "to go" in the sense of "to leave."

✗ Il est temps d'aller. (when "It is time to go" is meant)
✗ Nous voulions aller. (when "We wanted to go" is meant)

■ *Partir* is an intransitive verb. Since it cannot have an object, the place that is being left cannot be directly named.

C'est l'heure de partir.	*It is time to leave.*
Partez discrètement.	*Leave discreetly.*
Les coureurs sont partis!	*The runners are off!*

If the place is named, the preposition *de* is used before the place being left.

Je pars toujours de la maison à 8 heures.	*I always leave the house at eight.*

AVOID THE Blunder

✗ Je pars la maison à huit heures.

In a compound tense, *partir* takes *être* as its auxiliary.

Quand êtes-vous partis?	*When did you leave?*

AVOID THE Blunder

Don't forget to make the past participle agree with the subject.

✗ Ils sont arrivé. ✗ Elle est sorti.

■ *S'en aller* indicates a more immediate departure than *partir*; if the verb "to leave" is in the "-ing" form, it is best to translate it by *s'en aller.*

Le train part à 19h45.	*The train leaves at 7:45* P.M.
Vite! Le train s'en va!	*Quick! The train is leaving!*
C'est l'heure, je m'en vais.	*It's time. I'm going/leaving.*

In the imperative, *s'en aller* is preferred to *partir.*

Va-t'en!	*Leave!*
Ne t'en va pas!	*Don't leave!*
Allons-nous en!	*Let's leave!*
Allez-vous en tout de suite!	*Leave immediately!*

S'en aller is very rarely used in the past tense; *partir* is used instead.

AVOID THE Blunder

✗ Je m'en suis allé à 5 heures.

■ *Sortir* is an intransitive verb. Since it cannot have an object, the place that is being left cannot be directly named. If the place is named, the preposition *de* is used. Unlike *partir*, *sortir* emphasizes physical movement out of a place, for instance, out of a container.

Le poussin sort de l'œuf.	*The chick comes out of the egg.*

Used alone, *sortir* can mean "to go out," as a social event.

Nous sortons toujours le samedi soir.	*We always go out on Saturday night.*
Pierre et Julie sortent ensemble.	*Pierre et Julie are dating.*

□ In a compound tense, *sortir* takes *être* as its auxiliary, and the past participle agrees with the subject.

Elles sont sorties.	*They went out.*

Sortir can be used as a transitive verb (with a direct object) to express "to get (something) out" of a place.

Il sort un lapin de son chapeau.	*He is pulling a rabbit out of his hat.*
Il sort la poubelle.	*He takes the trash can out.*

In its transitive usage, *sortir* takes *avoir* as its auxiliary in compound tenses.

AVOID THE Blunder

✗ Il est sorti la poubelle.

■ *Quitter* is a transitive verb and must have an expressed object. It means to leave a person or a place.

Ne me quitte pas.	*Don't leave me.*
Nous quittons la maison vers midi.	*We leave the house around noon.*

In a compound tense, *partir* and *sortir* take *être,* and the past participle agrees with the subject. *Quitter* takes *avoir,* and its past participle agrees with the object, if one precedes *avoir*. (See the unit on the *passé composé* for agreement of the past participle.)

Elle est partie.	*She left.*
Ils sont sortis.	*They went out.*
Vous avez quitté la maison.	*You left the house.*

■ Like *quitter, laisser* is a transitive verb and must have an expressed object. *Laisser* means to leave something behind, on purpose or accidentally.

Elle laisse son bébé à la crèche tous les matins. — *She leaves her baby at the day care center every morning.*
J'ai laissé mes gants dans la voiture. — *I left my gloves in the car.*

AVOID THE Blunder

✗ J'ai quitté mon parapluie dans le bus.

The Verb "To Live"

Two French verbs can translate "to live": *habiter* and *vivre*. Both verbs are intransitive, but each one has a specific meaning.

- As a general rule, when a location is named, *habiter* is used.

Paul habite chez ses parents.	*Paul lives at his parents'.*
Louis XIV habitait à Versailles.	*Louis XIV lived in Versailles.*
Nous habitons dans une maison.	*We live in a house.*

- When the verb "to live" is used in a more abstract sense or with a date, as opposed to a place, *vivre* is used.

Louis XIV a vécu au dix-septième siècle.	*Louis XIV lived in the 17th century.*
Ils vécurent heureux jusqu'à la fin.	*They lived happily ever after.*

AVOID THE Blunder

✗ Ils sont morts ou ils habitent?
✗ Louis XIV a habité au 17ème siècle.

The Verb "To Know"

Both *savoir* and *connaitre* mean "to know," but they are used in different contexts.

- *Savoir* is used when one has a thorough knowledge of something, knows a fact, or knows how to do something. It is always followed by a direct object, which can be a noun, a verb in the infinitive, or a clause.

Nous savons notre leçon.	*We know our lesson.*
Savez-vous danser le tango?	*Can you dance the tango?*
Est-ce que tu sais nager?	*Can you swim?*
Il sait que tu as dit la vérité.	*He knows that you told the truth.*
Je sais que Mme Joulet travaille à l'hôpital.	*I know that Mrs. Joulet works at the hospital.*

AVOID THE Blunder

Don't use *connaitre* + an infinitive or clause.

✗ Je connais nager.
✗ Il connait qu'elle habite à Austin.

■ *Connaitre* expresses acquaintance or familiarity with a person, concept, or place—to know of the existence of something.

Connaissez-vous les Joulet?	*Do you know the Joulets?*
Connais-tu la philosophie de Kant?	*Are you familiar with Kant's philosophy?*
Je ne connais pas cette chanson.	*I am not familiar with this song.*

If "to know" can be replaced by "to be familiar with," *connaitre* is used.

Je ne sais pas cette chanson.	*I do not know (the words to) that song.*
Je ne connais pas cette chanson.	*I am not familiar with that song.*

□ As a pronominal verb, *connaitre* usually has the reciprocal meaning "to know one another."

Nous nous connaissons depuis longtemps.	*We have known each other for a long time.*

■ In the *passé composé, savoir* and *connaitre* change meaning.

□ *Savoir* in the *passé composé* means "to find out."

Quand elle l'a su, elle s'est mise à rire.	*When she found out, she started to laugh.*

□ *Connaitre* and *se connaitre* in the *passé composé* mean "to meet for the first time" and must have a direct object.

—Où avez-vous connu votre mari?	"*Where did you meet your husband?*"
—Nous nous sommes connus au Mexique.	"*We met (each other) in Mexico.*"

AVOID THE Blunder

Don't forget to use *être* instead of *avoir* when using *connaitre* as a reciprocal verb.

✗ Nous nous avons connus.

Verbs of Transportation and Movement

The verbs "to fly," "to drive," "to walk," "to swim," "to ride," etc. can name a skill or a way of traveling.

- To express a way of traveling, French uses the construction *aller* + *en/à* + means of travel.

  - *aller* + *en* + means of travel

Je suis allé à Dallas en voiture.	*I drove to Dallas.*
Nous irons à Paris en avion.	*We will fly to Paris.*
Ils vont en voiture partout.	*They drive everywhere.*
Elle va au travail en bus.	*She rides the bus to work.*

  - *aller* + *à* + means of travel

Ils vont à l'école à pied.	*They walk to school.*
Ils y vont à cheval.	*They go there on horseback.*
Il y va à la nage.	*He swims there.*

AVOID THE Blunder

✗ Nous avons conduit à Dallas.
✗ J'ai volé de Houston à Paris.
✗ Nous détestons voler.

- The French literal equivalents of "to fly" (*voler*), "to drive" (*conduire*), "to walk" (*marcher*), "to swim" (*nager*), "to ride" (*monter*), etc. are only used to name the skills of "flying," driving," etc.

Les aigles volent très haut.	*Eagles fly very high.*
Il conduit bien pour un débutant.	*He drives well for a beginner.*
J'ai mal au genou et je ne peux pas marcher.	*My knee hurts, and I can't walk.*
Elle nage bien.	*She swims well.*
Il court vite.	*He runs fast.*
Vous montez bien (à cheval).	*You ride horses well.*

- Many English verbs of motion are followed by a preposition. For the equivalent French verbs, the movement indicated by the English preposition is included in the meaning of the verb itself.

Il a traversé la rivière à la nage.	*He swam across the river.*
Je suis monté en courant.	*I ran upstairs.*
Elle a traversé la rue à pied.	*She walked across the street.*

AVOID THE Blunder

✗ Il a nagé à travers la rivière.
✗ Il a couru en haut.

"To Have To"

In English, "to have to" expresses obligation, and it replaces "must" when "must" cannot be used. The French verb *devoir* is equivalent to "must" and "to have to."

Je dois travailler ce soir.	*I have to work tonight.*
Est-ce que tu dois partir si tôt?	*Do you have to leave so soon?*

AVOID THE Blunder

Don't automatically translate "to have to" by the verb *avoir.* If you can replace "have to" with "must," use *devoir.*

✗ J'ai travailler.
✗ J'ai eu partir tôt.
✗ Il aura avoir se lever tôt.

The Preposition "On"

The French equivalent of "on" is *sur*, but many expressions with "on" are not translated by expressions with *sur. Sur* indicates "on" in a physical way only.

sur la télé	*on top of the television set*
sur le piano	*on top of the piano*
sur le train	*on (the roof of) the train*

Following is a list of common expressions in which "on" cannot be translated by *sur*.

à la télé	*on television*
dans l'avion / en avion	*on the plane*
dans le métro	*on the subway*
dans le bus	*on the bus*
dans le train	*on the train*
au mur	*on the wall*
au travail	*on the job*
de service	*on duty*

en vacances	*on vacation*
lundi	*on Monday*
le lundi	*on Mondays*
le jour de Noël	*on Christmas Day*
au piano	*on the piano*
à droite	*on the right*
à gauche	*on the left*
prendre des médicaments	*to be on medication*
se droguer	*to be on drugs*

AVOID THE Blunder

✗ sur le métro (when "on the subway" is meant)
✗ sur l'avion (when "on the plane" is meant)
✗ sur la radio (when "on the radio" is meant)

The Adjective "Nice"

The adjective "nice" can be used to describe a wide variety of nouns in English. In French, each variety has its own equivalent for "nice."

- To describe a person's character or manners as "nice," *agréable, gentil*, or *sympathique* can be used.

Marie est une personne très agréable.	*Marie is very nice.*
Sois gentil avec ta petite sœur!	*Be nice to your little sister!*

AVOID THE Blunder

Don't use *gentil* to describe a thing.

✗ Vous avez une gentille maison.

- To describe the weather as "nice," *beau* is used.

Il fait beau aujourd'hui.	*The weather is nice today.*
Quand il fait beau, nous sortons.	*When it is nice out, we go out.*

AVOID THE Blunder

✗ Il est beau. (when "It is nice" is meant (it = the weather))

- To describe an object as "nice," *joli* or *beau* can be used.

Elle porte une jolie robe.	*She is wearing a nice dress.*
Ils vivent dans une jolie petite maison.	*They live in a nice little house.*
C'est une jolie bague.	*It is a nice ring.*
Cet arbre est joli.	*This tree looks nice.*

- To describe time as "nice," *bon* or *agréable* can be used.

As-tu passé de bonnes vacances?	*Did you have a nice vacation?*
Passe un bon moment!	*Have a nice time!*
Nous avons passé un moment agréable.	*We had a very nice time.*

- "Nice" is sometimes used instead of "very" to indicate a higher degree. The adverb *bien* is used to translate this usage in French.

Ce café est bien fort.	*This coffee is nice and strong.*
Il aime son thé bien sucré.	*He likes his tea nice and sweet.*

- To describe an event or object as "nice," French uses *être* + *bien.*

C'était bien?	*Was it nice?*
Ton diner était vraiment bien.	*Your dinner was very nice.*
C'est très bien.	*It's very nice.*
Très bien.	*Nice job.*

AVOID THE Blunder

✗ La soirée était bonne.

Expressions with "nice" are very common in English, but can be tricky to translate into French.

Il a un joli nom.	*His name has a nice ring to it.*
Ça sent bon ici.	*It smells nice here.*
Ça fait du bien.	*It feels nice.*
C'est joli.	*It looks nice.*

□ When translating the adverb "nicely," the same guidelines are followed.

Il m'a aidé gentiment.	*He helped me nicely.*

Translating from French to English

The Verb *devoir*

- *devoir* + noun = "to owe"

As a transitive verb, *devoir* indicates that one owes something (a direct object) to someone (an indirect object), with the direct object immediately following the verb, before the indirect object.

Je dois de l'argent à mon garagiste.	*I owe my mechanic some money.*
Nous devons le respect à nos parents.	*We owe respect to our parents.*

AVOID THE *Blunder*

Don't place the indirect object before the direct object.

✗ Je dois mon garagiste de l'argent.

- *devoir* + infinitive

If *devoir* is followed by an infinitive, it may have several different meanings.

□ *Devoir* can express a strong obligation, like "must" in English.

Il doit finir son travail avant de sortir.	*He must finish his work before going out.*

□ *Devoir* can express a logical conclusion, like "must" in English.

Le prof n'est pas en classe, il doit être malade.	*The teacher is not in class. He must be sick.*

□ *Devoir* can express a prediction, something that is or was scheduled to happen.

Son livre doit sortir bientôt.	*His book is due to come out soon.*
Son train devait arriver à 20h, mais il a eu du retard.	*His train was supposed to arrive at 8 P.M., but it got delayed.*

AVOID THE *Blunder*

Don't automatically translate *devoir* by "must."

- In the present conditional, *devoir* is used to give advice, like "should" or "ought to" in English. See the unit on the conditional.

Tu devrais faire plus de sport.	*You should exercise more.*
Tu ne devrais pas fumer autant.	*You should not smoke so much.*

- In the past conditional, *devoir* expresses regret about something that has been done, like "should (not) have" in English.

Je n'aurais pas dû dire un mensonge.	*I should not have told a lie.*
Tu n'aurais pas dû faire ça.	*You should not have done that.*
Tu aurais dû mieux te préparer.	*You should have prepared better.*

AVOID THE *Blunder*

Don't forget the circumflex accent on the *u* of *dû* to distinguish it from the partitive *du*.

Depuis

Depuis can be the equivalent of "since," as well as of "for."

- *depuis* + period of time = "for"

Depuis followed by an expression that represents a duration (as opposed to a date) can be translated by "for" in a past or present context. This construction considers how long the action lasted, from the moment it started *up to the present*. The French verb must be in the present tense, while its English counterpart is in the present perfect.

Nous nous connaissons depuis 10 ans.	*We've known each other for 10 years.*
Nous habitons ici depuis des années.	*We have lived here for years.*
Nous sommes mariés depuis 5 ans.	*We have been married for 5 years.*
Elle fait du yoga depuis 6 mois.	*She's been doing yoga for 6 months.*

AVOID THE *Blunder*

✗ Nous nous sommes connus depuis 10 ans.
✗ Nous avons été mariés depuis 5 ans.

Depuis can be replaced by two other expressions.

- *Il y a* + period of time + *que*

Il y a 5 ans que nous sommes mariés.	*We have been married for 5 years.*
Il y a 2 jours que nous sommes en vacances.	*We've been on vacation for 2 days.*

- *Ça fait* + period of time + *que*

Ça fait 10 ans que nous nous connaissons.	*We've known each other for 10 years.*

AVOID THE Blunder

Don't confuse *il y a* + period of time + *que* with *il y a* "ago."

✗ Nous nous sommes connus il y a 10 ans.
(when "We have known each other for 10 years" is meant)

In a past context, the main verb is in the *imparfait* and *depuis* indicates that the action was going on up to the moment when it was interrupted. In English, the pluperfect is used.

depuis + period of time
ça faisait + period of time + *que*
il y avait + period of time + *que*

Je lisais depuis une heure quand tu es arrivé. Ça faisait une heure que je lisais quand tu es arrivé.	*I had been reading for an hour when you arrived.*
J'enseignais le français depuis 3 ans quand je suis enfin allé à Paris. Il y avait 3 ans que j'enseignais le français quand je suis enfin allé à Paris.	*I had been teaching French for 3 years when I finally went to Paris.*

- *depuis* + date = "since"

If *depuis* is followed by a date or another specific point in time, the time expression indicates the starting point of an action that extends up to the present moment.

Elle fait du yoga depuis mai.	*She has been doing yoga since May.*
Elle a 21 ans depuis le 30 septembre.	*She's been 21 since September 30.*
Elles se connaissent depuis qu'elles ont suivi le même cours.	*They've known each other since they took the same class.*

AVOID THE Blunder

✗ Nous nous sommes connus depuis 1990.
(when "We have known each other since 1990" is meant)
✗ J'ai roulé depuis midi.
(when "I have been driving since noon" is meant)

- *depuis* in a sentence with the *passé composé*

To indicate that an action has *not* been going on for a while, or to indicate how long it has been since that action *last* happened, English uses "for" or "in" with the verb in the present perfect.

In French, these concepts are expressed using *depuis* + period of time or *il y a longtemps que* or *ça fait longtemps que* + period of time, with the *passé composé* in the negative form. Although the English sentence may be affirmative or negative, its French equivalent must be negative.

Je n'ai pas vu Anna depuis des mois.	*I have not seen Anna in/for months.*
Ils ne sont pas rentrés en France depuis 2 ans.	*They have not been back to France in two years.*
Ça fait des siècles que je ne les ai pas vus.	*It's been ages since I last saw them.*

AVOID THE Blunder

✗ Ça fait des siècles que je les ai vus.
(when "It's been ages since I last saw them" is meant)
✗ Il y a longtemps que j'ai mangé du chocolat.
(when "It's been a long time since I ate some chocolate" is meant)

In a past context, the main verb is in the pluperfect. With the expression using *il y a* or *ça fait,* the main verb must be in the *imparfait.*

Je n'avais pas vu Anna depuis des mois.	*I had not seen Anna in/for months.*
Ça faisait des siècles que je ne les avais pas vus.	*It had been ages since I had seen them.*

Il y a

Il y a is the French equivalent of "ago." Like its English counterpart, *il y a* is used in a sentence with a past tense because it indicates the moment in time when an action began or took place.

Nous nous sommes connus il y a 10 ans.	*We met 10 years ago.*
Elle a commencé ses études il y a 20 ans!	*She started college 20 years ago!*

AVOID THE Blunder

Don't confuse *il y a* "ago" with *il y a* + period of time + *que,* which can replace *depuis.*

✗ Il y a 10 ans qu'elle commence ses études!
(when "She started college 10 years ago!" is meant)

The Noun *temps*

The French noun *temps* can mean "time" (see also the section on the noun "time," above), as well as "weather."

- *Temps* itself is rarely used in the context of weather, except in the following question.

Quel temps fait-il?	*What is the weather like?*
Il fait beau.	*The weather is nice.*
Il fait mauvais.	*The weather is bad.*

AVOID THE Blunder

✗ Le temps fait beau.

- Although it ends in *s, temps* is almost always singular. In some uncommon expressions, it can be plural.

Ce marin sort par tous les temps.	*This sailor goes out in any weather.*
Les temps sont durs.	*Times are hard.*

AVOID THE Blunder

✗ tous les temps (when "all the time" is meant)

Common expressions with *temps* follow.

(juste) à temps	*in the nick of time*
Il était temps!	*In the nick of time! / What kept you?*

en même temps	*at the same time*
perdre son temps	*to waste one's time*
ces derniers temps	*lately*
de temps en temps	*from time to time*
c'était le bon temps	*those were the good old days*
en temps voulu	*in due time*
en temps normal	*under normal circumstances*

AVOID THE Blunder

✗ au même temps

Expressions with *faire*

- Sports expressions

In French, two expressions are used to name the practice of sports: *jouer à,* which is reserved for team sports, and *faire de,* which includes individual sports as well as team sports.

Mon fils joue au foot.	*My son plays soccer.*
Pierre fait du judo et de la natation.	*Pierre practices judo and swims.*

Common sports names that can only be expressed with *faire de* follow.

l'alpinisme	*mountain climbing*
l'aviron	*rowing*
la boxe	*boxing*
la course	*running*
le cyclisme	*cycling*
l'équitation	*horseback riding*
le judo	*judo*
la natation	*swimming*
le ski	*ski*
la voile	*sailing*

Since *faire de* can be used with both types of sports, use *faire de* rather than the more restrictive *jouer à.*

AVOID THE Blunder

✗ Paul et Alain jouent au ski.
✗ Julie joue à la natation.

Faire peur and *faire mal*

In the expressions *faire peur* and *faire mal, faire* indicates that the subject imposes *peur* "fear" or *mal* "pain" on another person or animal. The preposition *à* that follows *faire peur* and *faire mal* introduces an indirect object.

Ne faites pas peur aux animaux du zoo.	*Don't scare the animals in the zoo.*
Ne leur faites pas peur.	*Don't scare them.*
Le dentiste a fait mal à Paul.	*The dentist hurt Paul.*
Le dentiste lui a fait mal.	*The dentist hurt him.*

In *avoir peur* and *avoir mal,* the subject himself or herself feels *peur* or *mal,* without the intervention of another person.

Julie a mal aux dents.	*Julie has a toothache.*
J'ai très peur des serpents.	*I am very afraid of snakes.*

AVOID THE Blunder

✗ Il a peur aux enfants. (when "He scares the children" is meant)
✗ Elle fait mal aux dents. (when "She has a toothache" is meant)

Faire faire

Faire + verb means "to have something done" by someone else. The tenses of *faire* and of English "to have" must be equivalent.

J'ai fait agrandir cette photo. (PAST)	*I had this picture blown up.*
Elle se fait faire un tatouage. (PRESENT)	*She is getting a tattoo.*
Il va faire réparer sa voiture. (FUTURE)	*He is going to have his car fixed.*

With *faire* + verb, the placement of an object pronoun does not follow the usual rules. The guidelines are as follows, in order of precedence.

- If *faire* is an infinitive, the object pronoun precedes it.

Il va la faire réparer.	*He is going to have it fixed.*

AVOID THE Blunder

✗ Il va faire la réparer.

☐ If *faire* is conjugated, the object pronoun precedes it.

Il la fait réparer.	*He has it fixed.*

AVOID THE Blunder

✗ Il fait la réparer.

☐ If *faire* is a past participle, the object pronoun precedes the conjugated auxiliary and *fait* does not agree with it.

Il l'a fait réparer.	*He had it fixed.*

AVOID THE Blunder

Don't make the past participle *fait* agree with the object pronoun; it is invariable.

✗ Je les ai faites réparer.

The Verb *manquer*

The verb *manquer* "to miss" is always transitive: It must have a direct or indirect object expressed in the sentence. Its meaning depends on the type of object.

■ *Manquer* + direct object = "to miss" (as, for instance, to fail to make it to an appointment). The verb *rater,* which also means "to miss," can replace *manquer* in this usage.

Je suis en retard; je vais manquer mon train.	*I'm late; I am going to miss my train.*
Je suis désolé de vous avoir manqué.	*I am sorry I missed you.*

Manquer cannot be used to translate "to miss" (meaning "to fail") as an intransitive verb; *rater* is used instead.

Il a essayé deux fois et il a raté deux fois.	*He tried twice and he missed twice.*

■ *Manquer à* = "to be missed by (someone)." The French construction *manquer à* is the reverse of "to miss (someone)": The English subject becomes the object in French.

Le soldat manque à sa mère.	*The mother of the soldier misses him.*
Tu me manques.	*I miss you.*

Note that the object of *manquer à* is indirect.

Vous manquez à vos parents.	*Your parents miss you.*
Vous leur manquez.	*They miss you.*
Il manque à sa mère.	*His mother misses him.*
Il lui manque.	*She misses him.*

AVOID THE Blunder

✗ Je te manque. (when "I miss you" is meant)

Aussi

- *Aussi* = "too, also, as well." When *aussi* means "too," its position in the sentence can vary in French and English.

Je voudrais y aller aussi.	*I would like to go too.*
Ils sont aussi arrivés à 6 heures.	*They too arrived at 6 o'clock.*
Achète du pain et aussi des croissants.	*Buy some bread, and also some croissants.*

- *Aussi* = "as," an indicator of equality in comparisons. If *aussi* can be replaced by *plus* or *moins*, it is an expression of comparison.

Il chante aussi mal que moi.	*He sings as badly as I.*
Il chante moins mal que moi.	*He sings better than I.*
Il chante plus mal que moi.	*He sings worse than I.*

Like "as" in English, *aussi* must immediately precede the word it describes, which can be an adjective or adverb.

Tu es aussi grand que ton père.	*You are as tall as your father.*
Le gâteau est aussi bon que la brioche.	*Cake is as good as brioche.*

AVOID THE Blunder

✗ Le gâteau est bon que la brioche aussi.

Comme

- *Comme* = "as" (in the function of). No article follows *comme* in this usage.

Comme interprète, elle est excellente. — *As an interpreter, she is excellent.*

However, *comme* is not the equivalent of "as" in an expression of comparison; *aussi* is used instead.

Il est aussi grand que son père. — *He is as tall as his father.*
Les maisons sont aussi belles ici. — *The houses are as beautiful here.*

AVOID THE Blunder

✗ Il est comme grand que son père.
✗ Les maisons sont comme belles.

- *Comme* = "like" in a comparison. *Comme* is often used in informal and rather generic comparisons, after a noun, adjective, or verb. In this simplified comparison, which mirrors the English construction, *comme* can introduce a stress pronoun, a person's name, or a noun preceded by an article.

une femme comme les autres — *a woman like any other*
Je suis comme toi. — *I am like you.*
Il s'habille comme un clown. — *He dresses like a clown.*
Il chante comme Pavarotti. — *He sings like Pavarotti.*
Elle est comme une mère pour moi. — *She is like a mother to me.*

AVOID THE Blunder

Don't forget to use an article when *comme* means "like."

✗ Il s'habille comme clown.
(when "He dresses like a clown" is meant)

Heureusement

The adverb *heureusement* is based on the adjective *heureux,* which means "happy." However, *heureusement* is not the equivalent of "happily."

- In literary style, *heureusement* means "in a clever way."

Il a écrit une lettre heureusement tournée. — *He wrote a cleverly phrased letter.*

■ In everyday usage, *heureusement* is the equivalent of "fortunately, luckily." In this sense, it is often followed by *que* or it can appear alone as a sentence adverb.

Heureusement, personne n'a été blessé. Heureusement que personne n'a été blessé.	*Luckily, no one was hurt.*
Heureusement, j'avais prévu ça. Heureusement que j'avais prévu ça.	*Fortunately, I had planned for that.*

■ The adjective *heureux* is used to translate the expression "happily" in the expression "happily ever after."

Ils vécurent heureux jusqu'à la fin de leur vie.	*They lived happily ever after.*

AVOID THE Blunder

Don't translate "happily" as *heureusement.*

✗ Ils vécurent heureusement jusqu'à la fin de leur vie.
(when "They lived happily ever after" is meant)

Expressing Temperature

■ To describe the temperature outdoors, the impersonal expression *il fait* is used, followed by an invariable adjective.

Il fait chaud.	*It is hot.*
Il fait très froid.	*It is very cold.*
Il faisait frais hier.	*It was cool yesterday.*

AVOID THE Blunder

Don't use *être* to describe the weather, even though English uses "to be."

✗ Il était frais hier.
✗ Il sera chaud demain.
✗ Il est chaud en été.

■ To describe the temperature of an object, *être* is used, followed by an adjective that can vary in gender and number.

Mon café est froid.	*My coffee is cold.*
Ces petits pains sont chauds.	*These buns are hot.*

■ To express the temperature of a person, *avoir* is used, followed by an invariable adjective.

J'ai chaud. Je vais mettre la climatisation.	*I feel hot. I am going to turn on the air conditioning.*
Vous tremblez. Avez-vous froid?	*You are shivering. Are you cold?*

AVOID THE Blunder

Don't use *être* + adjective to express how hot or cold a person feels.

✗ Es-tu chaud? (when "Are you cold?" is meant)
✗ Elle est froide. (when "She is cold." is meant)

To express that a person feels fine, *être bien* is used instead of *avoir* + adjective.

—Tu as chaud?	*"Are you hot?"*
—Non, je suis bien.	*"No, I am fine."*

Exercises

A *Express the following in French.*

1. *He tried four times.*

 ___

2. *All the people wore hats.*

 ___

3. *Can you* (tu) *speak Italian?*

 ___

4. *I know this poem by heart.*

 ___

5. *We flew to Houston.*

 ___

6. *He has to work tonight.*

 ___

7. *The weather is nice.*

 ___

8. *Did you* (tu) *miss me?*

 ___

9. *I know they met in Switzerland.*

 ___

10. *Is it too hot?* (weather)

 ___

11. *He lived in the 20th century.*

 ___

12. *I left my book on the subway.*

 ___

13. *She missed her train three times this week.*

 ___

B *Express the following in English.*

1. Elle fait l'apologie de son ancien professeur.

    ____

2. Elle se lave la figure.

    ____

3. Va à la librairie.

    ____

4. Ils se sont connus en vacances.

    ____

5. Tu me manques.

    ____

6. Son article doit être publié le mois prochain.

    ____

7. Heureusement qu'ils étaient déjà partis!

    ____

8. Il a froid.

    ____

9. Je vous manque.

    ____

PREPOSITIONS

The Rules

A preposition is an invariable word that links the noun or pronoun that follows to other elements of a sentence. It often follows a verb to introduce a phrase that expresses location, time, manner, etc.

A French preposition usually keeps its meaning, regardless of the verb it follows. By contrast, an English preposition is often absorbed into the meaning of the verb it follows. When an English preposition is clearly part of the meaning of a verb ("to look for" and "to look after," for example), it is helpful to consult a dictionary before translating the verb and preposition separately into French.

AVOID THE *Blunder*

✗ Il a marché dehors. (when "He walked out" is meant)
✗ Je regarde pour mes clés.
(when "I am looking for my keys" is meant)
✗ Regarde après les enfants.
(when "Look after the children" is meant)
✗ Il a cassé vers le haut avec sa copine.
(when "He broke up with his girlfriend" is meant)

- If a pronoun is needed after a preposition, a stress pronoun is used.

Viens avec moi.	*Come with me.*
Il a chanté pour elle.	*He sang for her.*
Nous sommes partis sans eux.	*We left without them.*
Tu fais comme moi.	*You do like me.* (*You do as I do.*)

AVOID THE *Blunder*

✗ Elle est sortie avec il.
✗ Fais-le pour me.
✗ J'ai besoin d'ils.

The preposition *à* is rarely followed by a pronoun, except to express ownership.

Ce livre est à moi.	*This book is mine.*
C'est à vous.	*It is yours.*

■ In French, a sentence never ends with a preposition, although this is very common in English.

Avec qui as-tu joué?	*Whom did you play with?*
Pour qui ont-ils voté?	*Whom did they vote for?*

AVOID THE *Blunder*

✗ Qui joues-tu avec?
✗ Qui allez-vous chez?

■ The only verbal form that can follow a preposition is an infinitive, except with the preposition *en*.

Elle a envie de danser.	*She feels like dancing.*
Il s'amuse à se cacher.	*He is having fun hiding.*
Elle fait le régime pour maigrir.	*She is on a diet to lose weight.*

AVOID THE *Blunder*

✗ Elle fait le régime pour elle maigrit.
✗ J'ai acheté ça pour te fais plaisir.

■ In general, French prepositions carry less meaning than English prepositions. As a result, they often have to be developed to render the full English meaning.

un cadeau **de la part de** maman	*a gift **from** Mom*
Il l'a aidée **à sortir de** la voiture.	*He helped her **out of** the car.*
Elle prend le bus **pour aller au** travail.	*She rides the bus **to** work.*
Il est marié **et il a des** enfants.	*He is married **with** children.*

Beyond a list of meanings, bilingual dictionaries give examples of the usage of a word. These are particularly helpful to choose the word or expression that best fits the context. They should be carefully reviewed before translating a verb + preposition construction from English to French.

For example, *hors de* means "outside." The meaning of the sentence *Il l'a aidée hors de la voiture* is "He helped her outside the car," not "He helped her out of the car." Similarly, *à* usually means "at" when it does not follow a verb of motion, and the sentence *Elle prend le bus au travail* indicates that she gets on the bus at her workplace (*prendre* is not a verb of motion).

AVOID THE Blunder

✗ Il l'a aidée hors de la voiture.
✗ Elle prend le bus au travail.

à

The preposition *à* is spelled with an accent, to distinguish it from the third-person singular form of the present tense of *avoir.*

Il a une maison.	*He has a house.*
Il est à la maison.	*He is at home.*

à + Infinitive

Before an infinitive, the preposition *à* is not translated in English (see the unit on the infinitive).

Je vais t'aider à faire ton travail.	*I will help you to do your work.*
Nous nous préparons à partir.	*We are getting ready to leave.*
Ne continue pas à pleurer.	*Don't continue to cry.*

à + Noun

After a verb, *à* can introduce an indirect object or a prepositional phrase that expresses location or manner.

INDIRECT OBJECT

Il parle à Julie.	*He talks to Julie.*
Demande à ta mère.	*Ask your mother.*

PREPOSITIONAL PHRASE

Il va à l'école.	*He goes to school.*
Je l'ai fait à la main.	*I did it by hand.*

See also the unit on subjects, objects, and their pronouns.

■ If the definite article *le* or *les* follows *à*, the following contracted forms are used.

à + le = au
à + les = aux

Nous sommes au jardin.	*We are in the backyard.*
Ne parlez pas aux étrangers dans la rue.	*Do not talk to strangers on the street.*

AVOID THE Blunder

✗ Il parle à le professeur.
✗ Il répond à les messages.

■ Before the name of a city, *à* expresses "in" or "to," with or without motion.

Il habite à Dallas.	*He lives in Dallas.*
Nous allons à Dijon.	*We are going to Dijon.*

Before the name of a masculine country, *à* + definite article expresses "in" or "to," with or without motion.

The name of a country is masculine if it ends in any letter other than *e,* for example, *le Nicaragua, le Pérou, le Canada,* and *le Danemark.* Exceptions are *le Mexique, le Zaïre,* and *le Cambodge.*

Il part au Brésil.	*He is leaving for Brazil.*
Paul habite aux États-Unis.	*Paul lives in the United States.*

■ *À* is used before specific expressions of time.

Je pars à midi.	*I leave at noon.*
Le train arrive à 18h30.	*The train arrives at 6:30 P.M.*

À is used before an ordinal number that describes a century.

au vingtième siècle	*in the twentieth century*

À is not used before years; *en* is used instead.

en 2006	*in 2006*
en l'an 2000	*in the year 2000*

AVOID THE Blunder

✗ Il est né à 1974.
✗ Le film a été fait à 2001.

■ À + a definite article is used before certain nouns to express how something is done.

C'est écrit à la main.	*It is handwritten.*
une peinture à l'huile	*an oil painting*

AVOID THE Blunder

✗ C'est fait par main.

de

de + Infinitive

Before certain infinitives, the preposition *de* is not translated in English. For a list of such verbs, see page 154 of the unit on the infinitive.

Il a choisi d'apprendre le français.	*He chose to learn French.*
Il a oublié de prendre ses clés.	*He forgot to take his keys.*
Il est content de travailler ici.	*He is happy to work here.*
Évite de manger trop.	*Avoid eating too much.*

If *de* does not express "of" or "from," it is not translated in English.

■ After verbs like *défendre* "to forbid," *demander* "to ask," *dire* "to tell," and *ordonner* "to order," *de* introduces a reported command (see the unit on reported speech). The object of the main verb and the subject of the infinitive must refer to the same person(s).

Il nous a dit de faire attention.	*He told us to be careful.*
Nous vous demandons de vous taire.	*We are asking you to be quiet.*

AVOID THE Blunder

✗ Nous avons demandé de Julie faire attention.
(when "We asked Julie to be careful" is meant)

■ *venir de*

When the verb *venir* is followed by *de* + an infinitive, it expresses the recent past. The English equivalent is "to have just done something."

Le cours vient de commencer.	*Class has just begun.*

de + Noun

■ If the definite article *le* or *les* follows *de*, the following contracted forms are used.

de + le = du
de + les = des

C'est le jour du cours de français.	*It is the day of the French class.*
Il revient des États-Unis.	*He is back from the United States.*

■ In an expression of quantity, *de* replaces the article before a noun.

Nous avons des amis.	*We have friends.*
Nous avons peu d'amis.	*We have few friends.*
Vous avez de la chance.	*You are lucky.*
Vous avez beaucoup de chance.	*You are very lucky.*

AVOID THE Blunder

✗ Vous avez assez de l'argent.
✗ Il y a beaucoup des livres.
✗ Nous avons peu des amis.

After a negative verb other than a verb of preference and *être, de* replaces the indefinite and partitive articles (see also the unit on determiners).

Il n'a pas d'argent.	*He has no money.*
Nous ne voulons pas de chat.	*We don't want a cat / cats.*

■ *de* = "from." *De* indicates place of origin, with or without motion. Common expressions using *de* follow.

venir de + *noun*	*to come from*
être de	*to be from*
sortir de	*to get out of*
arriver de	*to arrive from*
Il sort du bain.	*He gets out of the bath.*
Nous arrivons du travail.	*We arrive from work.*

To express origin from cities and countries, the following guidelines apply.

■ "from" + city = *de* + no article

Il est de Marseille.	*He is from Marseille.*
Nous arrivons de Paris.	*We are arriving from Paris.*

- "from" + country with feminine name = *de* + no article

Elle est d'Italie.	*She is from Italy.*
Ils sont de République Dominicaine.	*They are from the Dominican Republic.*

- "from" + country with masculine name = *de* + definite article

Ils sont des États-Unis.	*They are from the United States.*
Elle vient du Brésil.	*She comes from Brazil.*

AVOID THE Blunder

✗ Elle est de la France.
✗ Ils viennent de Mexique.

- *de* = "about" after verbs like *parler* "to talk" and *penser* "to think"

Parlez-moi de vos enfants.	*Tell me about your children.*
Que penses-tu de mon nouveau chapeau?	*What do you think about my new hat?*

De cannot be used to express "about" after a noun; *sur* or *au sujet de* is used instead. (*De* after a noun expresses possession.)

C'est un film de Rodin.	*It is a film by Rodin.*
C'est un film sur Rodin.	*It is a film about Rodin.*
une histoire de la guerre	*a history of the war*
une histoire sur la guerre	*a story about the war*

AVOID THE Blunder

✗ C'est un film de Rodin. (when "It is a film about Rodin" is meant)

Note that "about" has a broader range of meanings than *de*.

- "about" = "approximately" (expressed by *environ* + location/number/period of time or by *vers* + date/time)

C'est à environ 100 km.	*It's about 100 kilometers away.*
Ça nous prendra environ 4 heures.	*It will take us about four hours.*
Nous dinerons vers 20h.	*We will have dinner around 8 P.M.*

- "about" + infinitive = "be on the verge of" (expressed by *être sur le point de* + infinitive)

Le train est sur le point de partir.	*The train is about to leave.*

- *de* = "in" in a superlative construction

la maison la plus jolie du quartier	*the prettiest house in the neighborhood*
l'étudiant le plus travailleur de la classe	*the most hard-working student in the class*

AVOID THE Blunder

✗ la maison la plus jolie dans le quartier
✗ C'est l'étudiant le plus drôle dans la classe.

- *de* = "in" in some expressions of time

huit heures du matin	*eight in the morning (8 A.M.)*
quatre heures de l'après-midi	*four in the afternoon (4 P.M.)*

AVOID THE Blunder

✗ quatre heures dans le matin

en

en + Present Participle

En + a present participle is a very common construction in French. It is the equivalent of "while ______ing," "by ______ing," "in ______ing," or "upon ______ing."

- *En* + a present participle indicates cause. It answers the question *Comment est-ce arrivé?* ("How did it happen?"). The verb in the result clause is in the *passé composé* or the pluperfect.

Je me suis blessé en coupant du pain.	*I got hurt (while) cutting bread.*

- *En* + a present participle describes how something is done. It answers the question *Comment* + main verb*?*

Comment gagne-t-il sa vie?	*How does he earn his living?*
Il gagne sa vie en vendant des crêpes.	*He earns his living (by) selling crêpes.*
Comment allume-t-on la télé?	*How do you turn on the TV?*
On allume la télé en appuyant sur le bouton.	*The TV is turned on by pushing on the button.*

- *En* + a present participle denotes simultaneity between two actions performed by the same subject.

Il déjeune en lisant le journal.	*He has lunch while reading the paper.*
Il prend sa douche en chantant.	*He sings while in the shower.*

- As an expression of time, *en* + a present participle indicates what happened or will happen at a precise moment.

J'ai trouvé le paquet en ouvrant la porte.	*I found the package upon opening the door.*
Je vous appellerai en arrivant.	*I will call you upon arriving.*

Other Uses of *en*

- Before all countries with a feminine name and before countries with a masculine name that begins with a vowel (like *Iran, Irak,* and *Israël*), *en* expresses "to" or "in," with or without motion.

Nous voyagerons en Europe cet été.	*We will travel in Europe this summer.*
Ils habitent en Allemagne.	*They live in Germany.*
la guerre en Irak	*the war in Iraq*

AVOID THE Blunder

✗ Nous allons à l'Europe.
✗ Ils vivent à France.

- *En* indicates the material something is made of.

C'est une bague en or.	*It is a gold ring.*
une planche en bois	*a wooden board*

- *En* means "in" before years (but not centuries) and seasons (except *printemps*).

Il est né en 1980.	*He was born in 1980.*
Nous skions en hiver.	*We ski in winter.*

AVOID THE Blunder

✗ en printemps

- *En* means "in" before the name of a language.

C'est écrit en italien.	*It is written in Italian.*
Céline Dion chante en anglais et en français.	*Céline Dion sings in English and in French.*

- *En* indicates how long it takes, took, or will take to do something.

Il a fini en une heure.	*He was done in one hour.*

en or *dans*?

Both of these prepositions can be translated by "in" in English.

- Expressing time

□ In an expression of time, *dans* denotes a projection into the future, with a verb in the future, future perfect, or imperative.

Nous aurons fini le cours dans une heure.	*The class will be over in an hour.*
Dans 15 ans, il pourra prendre sa retraite.	*In 15 years, he will be able to retire.*
Revenez dans cinq minutes.	*Come back in five minutes.*

AVOID THE Blunder

Don't use *dans* in a past context.

✗ Il a fini son travail dans deux minutes.
(when "He finished his work in two minutes" is meant)

□ *En* introduces a duration expressed as a period of time, and the verb of the sentence can be in a present, past, or future tense.

Nous avons fini en cinq minutes.	*We finished in five minutes.*
Tu fais toujours tes devoirs en deux minutes!	*You always do your homework in two minutes!*
Je peux réparer ça en une heure.	*I can repair this in one hour.*

If an English verb is in the future tense, only context can determine which translation of "in" should be used in French.

Il finira en cinq minutes. (MEANING *It will take him five minutes.*) Il finira dans cinq minutes. (MEANING *He will be done five minutes from now.*)	*He will finish in five minutes.*

■ Expressing place or state of being

□ *En* is used with abstract nouns to express "in a state of." There is no determiner after *en*.

La France était en guerre.	*France was at war.*
Ne te mets pas en colère.	*Don't get angry.*
Les travailleurs sont en grève.	*The workers are on strike.*
en général	*in general*
en italiques	*in italics*

AVOID THE Blunder

Don't use *en* before a determiner + noun combination.

✗ Il va en sa chambre.
✗ Entrez en la maison.

□ *Dans* means "in" before a noun that is preceded by a determiner.

dans une boite en carton	*in a cardboard box*
dans la forêt de Sherwood	*in Sherwood Forest*
Il habite dans la maison de sa mère.	*He lives in his mother's house.*

If a prepositional phrase with *en* is modified (by an adjective, for instance), *en* changes to *dans*.

Il voyage en bateau.	*He travels by boat.*
Il voyage dans un bateau luxueux.	*He travels in a luxury boat.*
Nous arrivons en France.	*We arrive in France.*
Nous arrivons dans une France méconnaissable.	*We arrive in an unrecognizable France.*

sans

sans + Noun

The noun that follows *sans* "without" cannot be preceded by a partitive or indefinite article.

Ce matin il est parti sans argent.	*This morning, he left without any money.*
C'est un homme sans foi ni loi.	*He is a lawless man.*

AVOID THE Blunder

✗ Il est parti sans de l'argent.

Other determiners can follow *sans.*

Elle est partie sans ses gants.	*She left without her gloves.*
Sans ce papier, j'aurai des ennuis.	*Without this paper, I will get in trouble.*
Sans la pluie, les plantes mourraient.	*Without rain, plants would die.*

sans + Verb

Sans + verb is expressed in English as "without ______ing." If the verb after *sans* has the same subject as the main verb, *sans* + an infinitive is used.

Il est sorti sans faire de bruit.	*He left without making a sound.*

If the subjects are different, *sans* + a clause with the subjunctive is used. (See also the unit on the subjunctive.)

Il est sorti sans que les autres l'entendent.	*He left without the others hearing.*

AVOID THE Blunder

✗ Nous sommes sortis sans l'entendre.
(when "We left without her hearing (us)" is meant)

jusqu'à

Jusqu'à expresses "until" in expressions of space and time.

- When it indicates location, *jusqu'à* means "as far as."

Allez jusqu'au carrefour.	*Go as far as the intersection.*
Il va à pied jusqu'au centre-ville.	*He walks all the way to downtown.*

- In expressions of time, *jusqu'à* means "until a certain moment."

Nous resterons jusqu'à dimanche.	*We'll stay until Sunday.*
Nous avons regardé la télé jusqu'à minuit.	*We watched TV until midnight.*

If a conjugated verb follows *jusqu'à*, the construction *jusqu'à ce que* + subjunctive is used.

Nous attendrons jusqu'à ce que tu sois là.	*We will wait until you are here.*
Il boira jusqu'à ce que le verre soit vide.	*He will drink until the glass is empty.*

AVOID THE Blunder

Don't forget to use *jusqu'à ce que* in place of *jusqu'à* when a verb follows this French expression for "until."

✗ Ils attendront jusqu'à tu sois là.

chez

Chez means "at/to (someone)'s place," with or without motion.

J'habite chez mes parents.	*I live at my parents'.*
Venez chez moi.	*Come to my place.*
Il est de chez nous.	*He is from around here.*
Tu habites à coté de chez nous.	*You live near our house.*
Je dois aller chez le docteur.	*I must go to the doctor's.*

AVOID THE Blunder

Don't use *chez,* a preposition, as equivalent to the noun *maison.*

✗ Il habite dans chez.
✗ Ils ont acheté une chez.

Don't use *dans* or *à* with *chez.*

✗ Je rentre à chez moi.
✗ J'ai laissé mes gants à chez Pierre.

chez + Name of Business

When a business or store is referred to by the profession or occupation of the person who runs it, *chez* is used (not *à*).

Tu vas à la boulangerie.	*You go to the bakery.*
Tu vas chez le boulanger.	*You go to the baker's.*

A business can be referred to by the name of the place (with *à*) or by the name of the person who runs it (with *chez*). For some businesses, both the store and the person can be named, for others only one or the other is possible.

chez un antiquaire	*at an antique store*
chez le dentiste	*at the dentist's*
chez le docteur	*at the doctor's*

chez l'esthéticienne	*at the beauty parlor*
chez le fleuriste	*at the flower shop*
chez le juge	*in the judge's office*
chez le photographe	*at the camera store*
à la boucherie	*at the butcher shop*
chez le boucher	*at the butcher's*
à la boulangerie	*at the bakery*
chez le boulanger	*at the baker's*
à l'épicerie	*at the (corner) grocery store*
chez l'épicier	*at the grocer's*
à la librairie	*at the bookstore*
chez le libraire	*at the bookstore*
à la pharmacie	*at the pharmacy*
chez le pharmacien	*at the pharmacist's*
à la poissonnerie	*at the fish market*
chez le poissonnier	*at the fish vendor's*
au salon de coiffure	*at the hair salon*
chez le coiffeur	*at the hairdresser's*

Exercise

A *Complete the following sentences with the correct preposition. If no preposition is needed, write an* X.

1. Les enfants obéissent __________ leurs parents.
2. Est-ce que tu cherches __________ quelque chose?
3. Venez __________ nous samedi.
4. Il a appris __________ skier à 6 ans.
5. J'attends __________ le bus.
6. Je resterai ici __________ tu me dises de partir.
7. Je dois aller __________ le coiffeur.
8. Irez-vous __________ Mexique ou __________ Europe cet été?
9. J'ai oublié __________ éteindre la lumière.
10. Tu habites __________ un appartement ou __________ une maison?
11. Il n'acceptera jamais __________ faire ce travail.
12. Je viens __________ arriver. Je suis fatigué.
13. Vous avez le plus beau chat __________ quartier.
14. Revenez __________ une heure, je n'ai pas fini.
15. Elle portait une robe __________ satin et des chaussures __________ cuir.
16. Qu'est-ce qu'il y a __________ cette boite?
17. Pour maigrir, il faut éviter __________ le sucre.
18. Elle est née __________ 1936.
19. Va __________ le pharmacien, s'il te plait.
20. Regardez __________ ces petits chiens adorables!
21. __________ qui vas-tu demander?
22. Pourriez-vous m'aider __________ ouvrir cette fenêtre, s'il vous plait?
23. Sortez __________ mon bureau.

CONSTRUCTIONS

Certain common English constructions seem to translate easily into French, because the words appear to have direct equivalents in French. Following are English constructions that are trickier to translate than they might seem.

Translating the "-ing" Form

The *-ant* form of a French verb (its present participle) is the literal counterpart of the English "-ing" form, but they are not equivalent in usage.

- "to be + ______ing" = conjugated verb in French

There is no exact French equivalent for "to be + ______ing." The corresponding conjugated form of the French verb must be used.

Je parle.	*I am talking.*
Tu partais.	*You were leaving.*
Je pleurerai.	*I will be crying.*
À quoi pensais-tu?	*What were you thinking about?*

AVOID THE Blunder

Don't use *être* + ______*ant* to express "to be + ______ing."

✗ Je suis parlant.
✗ Nous sommes partant.
✗ Ils sont apprenant.

The French equivalent of "was/were + ______ing" is the *imparfait,* never the *passé composé.*

Elle lisait quand le téléphone a sonné.	*She was reading when the phone rang.*
Tu faisais quelque chose? Je t'ai interrompu?	*Were you doing something? I interrupted you?*

AVOID THE *Blunder*

✗ Qu'est-ce que tu as fait? (when "What were you doing?" is meant)
✗ Il a plu. (when "It was raining" is meant)

- "to be + ______ing" = French infinitive

This construction can be used only if both verbs have the same subject.

Je n'aime pas conduire.	*I don't like driving.*
Elle a peur de perdre ses clés.	*She is afraid of losing her keys.*

If the subjects are different, *que* + a clause in the subjunctive is used.

Elle n'aime pas que son fils conduise vite.	*She doesn't like her son driving fast.*

- "while + ______ing" = *en* + *-ant* verb form

This construction can be used only if both verbs have the same subject. The present participle is invariable.

Elle écoute en souriant.	*She listens, smiling.*
Ils apprennent en s'amusant.	*They learn while having fun.*
Elle a fait la vaisselle en regardant la télé.	*She did the dishes while watching TV.*
Elle s'est blessée en courant.	*She got hurt while running.*

Nouns Used as Adjectives

English often uses a noun to describe another noun. In French, only an adjective can describe a noun directly.

le restaurant universitaire	*the university cafeteria*
une guerre mondiale	*a world war*

AVOID THE *Blunder*

✗ des enfance souvenirs
✗ une couleur photo

If no adjective exists, French uses a noun preceded by a preposition (often *de*). The noun that follows the French preposition corresponds to the noun that comes first in the English expression.

fourrure d'animal	*animal fur*
le calendrier des manifestations	*events calendar*
une bague en or	*a gold ring*
souvenirs d'enfance	*childhood memories*
les catégories du concours	*contest categories*
une photo en couleur	*a color photo*

AVOID THE *Blunder*

✗ l'animal de la fourrure (when "animal fur" is meant)

Problematic Conditional Forms

"Would"

"Would" has several meanings in English, and context is crucial in translating it correctly into French.

- "Would" is the auxiliary for the conditional in English. In French, the present conditional is a simple tense (no auxiliary needed), with endings that mark it as conditional. "Would" is not translated as a word by itself.

J'irais si j'avais le temps.	*I would go if I had time.*
Laverais-tu ta voiture s'il pleuvait?	*Would you wash your car if it were raining?*

AVOID THE *Blunder*

✗ Je ferais aller. (when "I would go." is meant)
✗ Ferais-tu laver ta voiture?
(when "Would you wash your car?" is meant)

- "would" = "used to"

When "would" means "used to," it describes a habitual past action. In French, the *imparfait* is used to express this usage.

Quand j'étais petite, je rendais visite à ma grand-mère tous les jeudis.	*When I was little, I would visit my grandmother every Thursday.*
Quand il faisait beau, nous allions au lac.	*When it was nice, we would go to the lake.*

AVOID THE Blunder

Don't automatically translate "would" by the conditional in French.

✗ Quand j'étais petite, j'irais chez ma grand-mère.
✗ Quand il faisait beau, nous irions au lac.

■ "wouldn't" = "did not want to"

When "wouldn't" means "was/were not willing to," the *imparfait* or *passé composé* of *vouloir* is used in French.

Cet enfant n'a pas voulu obéir à son professeur et il a été puni.	*That child would not obey his teacher, and he was punished.*
Je lui ai demandé, mais il n'a pas voulu le faire.	*I asked him, but he wouldn't do it.*

■ The following guide may be used to determine the appropriate French equivalent of "would."

□ If "would" can be replaced by "wanted to" in the English sentence, use *vouloir* in the past tense in French.

□ If "would" can be replaced by "used to" in the English sentence, use *vouloir* in the *imparfait* in French.

□ If "would" cannot be replaced by another word or phrase, use the conditional in French.

AVOID THE Blunder

✗ J'aimais visiter Paris. (when "I would like to visit Paris" is meant)
✗ Je rendrais visite à ma grand-mère tous les jeudis.
(when "I would visit my grandmother every Thursday" is meant)

"Could"

"Could" has several meanings in English, and context is crucial in translating it correctly into French.

■ When "could" is the conditional of "can" in English, the conditional of *pouvoir* is used in French. (See the unit on the conditional.)

Pourriez-vous m'aider, s'il vous plait?	*Could you help me, please?*
Il pourrait le faire, s'il voulait.	*He could do that if he wanted to.*

Note that "could" is a one-word conditional form in English; it is equivalent to the one-word form in French.

- "could" = "was/were able to"

When "could" is the past tense of "can," the *imparfait* or *passé composé* of *pouvoir* is used in French.

Je n'ai pas pu vous rappeler hier soir parce que je suis rentré trop tard.	*I could not call you back last night, because I got home too late.*
Quand j'étais petite, je ne pouvais pas me coucher après 9 heures.	*When I was little, I could not go to bed past 9 P.M.*

AVOID THE Blunder

✗ Je ne pourrais pas t'appeler hier soir.
(when "I could not call you last night" is meant)

The English Infinitive

Consider the uses of the English infinitive in the following examples.

I would like you to come here.
She wanted him to do his work.
I waited for them to return.
It is necessary for you to finish this.

In these sentences, the second verb is an infinitive, and the object pronoun "you," "him," or "them" is the subject of the infinitive. In French, when the subject of the second verb is different from the subject of the first verb, the infinitive cannot be used.

AVOID THE Blunder

✗ Je te voudrais venir ici.
✗ Elle le voulait faire son travail.

The subjunctive is used instead, except after a verb of perception.

Je voudrais que tu viennes ici.	*I would like you to come here.*
Elle voulait qu'il fasse son travail.	*She wanted him to do his work.*
J'ai attendu qu'ils reviennent.	*I waited for them to return.*
Il faut que tu finisses ça.	*It is necessary for you to finish this.*

- After verbs like *écouter* "to listen to," *entendre* "to hear," *regarder* "to watch," and *voir* "to see," the infinitive is used in French, and the English and French sentences have a similar construction.

Elle a regardé les bateaux partir.	*She watched the boats leave.*
Elle l'a entendu entrer.	*She heard him come in.*
J'ai vu l'avion décoller.	*I saw the plane take off.*

AVOID THE Blunder

✗ Elle a regardé que les bateaux partent.
(when "She watched the boats leave" is meant)

Expressing Possession

French and English express possession and ownership in very different constructions. In French, there are three ways to express possession.

Using *de*

Ownership can be expressed using the preposition *de,* followed by the word that names the owner (a noun, but not a pronoun).

le chat de la voisine	*the neighbor's cat*
l'ami de son père	*his father's friend*
le livre d'un collègue	*a colleague's book*
le chien de Paul	*Paul's dog*

AVOID THE Blunder

Don't use a stress pronoun with *de* to show possession.

✗ C'est le chien d'elle.
✗ le livre de lui

Remember that *de* + *le* and *de* + *les* must be contracted to *du* and *des.*

le cartable du professeur	*the teacher's satchel*
la voiture des Martin	*the Martins' car*

Using *être à*

Ownership can be expressed by *être à* + the owner. The word that names the owner can be a noun or a pronoun. This construction is often used in response to the question *C'est à qui?* ("Whose is it?").

Ce livre est à moi. N'y touche pas!	*This book is mine. Don't touch it!*
Quelle belle voiture! Elle est à vous?	*What a beautiful car! Is it yours?*
C'est à toi? Ou c'est à Paul?	*Is it yours? Or is it Paul's?*
Cette maison est à des amis.	*This house belongs to friends.*

Note that in this construction, *être à* introduces the owner.

Ce livre est à Paul.	*This is Paul's book.*

However, when *être* and *de* are used to express ownership, *être* introduces the object owned, then *de* introduces the owner.

C'est le livre de Paul.	*This is Paul's book.*

AVOID THE *Blunder*

Don't mix *être à* + the owner and *être* + the object + *de* + the owner.

✗ Ce livre est de Paul.
✗ C'est le livre à Paul.
✗ la voiture aux Martin

Using the Possessive Adjective

French possessive adjectives agree in gender and number with the noun that represents the object owned. English possessive adjectives agree in gender and number with the noun that represents the owner.

sa maison (*f.*)	*his/her house*
son sac (*m.*)	*his/her bag*

In the plural, the distinction between masculine and feminine disappears in French. English maintains the distinction between masculine and feminine owners.

ses lunettes (*f. pl.*)	*his/her glasses*
ses amis (*m. pl.*)	*his/her friends*

AVOID THE *Blunder*

Don't mark the gender (masculine or feminine) of the owner in French.

✗ sa livre (when "her book" is meant)
✗ son maison (when "his house" is meant)

	BEFORE A MASCULINE SINGULAR NOUN	BEFORE A FEMININE SINGULAR NOUN	BEFORE A PLURAL NOUN
my	mon	ma	mes
your (sing.)	ton	ta	tes
his/her/one's	son	sa	ses
our	notre	notre	nos
your (pl. OR formal)	votre	votre	vos
their	leur	leur	leurs

AVOID THE Blunder

Don't forget to change *ma* to *mon* before a feminine noun that begins with a vowel.

✗ ma amie Cathy
✗ m'amie Cathy

Don't make the verb agree with the person and number of the possessive adjective.

✗ Notre chambre sommes petite.
✗ Votre chambre n'avez pas la climatisation.
✗ Leur hôtel n'ont pas l'ascenseur.

The English Possessive ('s)

This construction, which is very common in English, does not exist in French. The closest equivalent is a construction with *de* (see page 324).

le sac de Julie	*Julie's bag*
l'ami de mon père	*my father's friend*
le chat de la voisine	*the neighbor's cat*

Note that in French, the order of the nouns is reversed and the word that names the owner comes second.

AVOID THE Blunder

✗ Julie sac
✗ mon père ami
✗ la voisine chat

Summary of Common Errors in Translating from English to French

■ The English infinitive is often translated by the subjunctive in French.

Elle veut qu'ils soient heureux.	*She wants them to be happy.*

AVOID THE Blunder

✗ Elle les veut être heureux.

■ In an English sentence, "that" is often omitted. In French, *que* is never omitted, regardless of its function.

C'est quelqu'un **que** je connais bien.	*She is someone (that) I know well.*
Je pense **que** c'est une bonne idée.	*I think (that) it is a good idea.*

AVOID THE Blunder

✗ C'est quelqu'un je connais bien.

■ English often uses a progressive form "to be + ______ing." There is no equivalent in French.

Il danse.	*He is dancing.*
Je lisais.	*I was reading.*

AVOID THE Blunder

✗ Il est dansant.
✗ J'étais lisant.

■ In English, some conditional forms are identical to past tense forms.

J'ai essayé d'ouvrir la porte, mais je n'ai pas pu.	*I tried to open the door, but I could not.*
Ma grand-mère allait à l'église le dimanche.	*My grandmother would go to church on Sundays.*

AVOID THE Blunder

✗ Je ne pourrais pas ouvrir la porte.
(when "I could not open the door" is meant)

■ The preterit, which is the most widely used past tense in English, is a one-word past tense. Even though the French *imparfait* is also a one-word past tense, it is not equivalent to the preterit in usage.

Il est sorti hier soir.	*He went out last night.*
Que faisiez vous le dimanche?	*What did you do on Sunday?*

AVOID THE Blunder

✗ Il sortait hier soir. (when "He went out last night" is meant)

■ The English object pronoun "him" replaces an indirect object as well as a direct object. In French, the corresponding indirect object pronoun is *lui* and the direct object pronoun is *le*. In order to know whether to use *lui* or *le* for "him," first determine if a specific verb takes a direct or an indirect object.

Est-ce que tu l'as vu?	*Did you see him/her?*
Je lui parle souvent.	*I speak to him/her often.*

AVOID THE Blunder

Don't assume that *lui* is the only equivalent of "him."

✗ Est-ce que tu lui as vu?

■ Many English verbs have a preposition as part of their meaning. Most of the time, that preposition cannot be translated directly into French.

Occupe-toi des enfants.	*Look after the children.*
Je cherche mes clés.	*I am looking for my keys.*
Paul et Julie se sont séparés.	*Paul and Julie broke up.*
Ma voiture est tombée en panne.	*My car broke down.*

AVOID THE *Blunder*

Don't translate an English verb + preposition as two separate entities.

✗ Regarde après les enfants.
✗ Paul et Julie ont cassé vers le haut.
✗ Ma voiture a cassé vers le bas.

Exercises

A *Express the following in French. All "you" verb forms are singular.*

1. *Are you crying?*

    ______

2. *"Is this book yours?" "No, it is Julie's."*

    ______

3. *They would not tell me the truth.*

    ______

4. *She wants them to come home.*

    ______

5. *I hurt myself while working.*

    ______

6. *He has childhood memories he does not want to share.*

    ______

7. *Is it someone you know?*

    ______

8. *Would you go?*

    ______

B *Fill in the blanks with the correct form of the possessive adjective in parentheses.*

1. ______ sœurs (*his*)
2. ______ amie (*her*)
3. ______ chien (*our*)
4. ______ frères (*your*, formal)
5. ______ grands-parents (*my*)
6. ______ mère (*our*)
7. ______ tante (*their*)
8. ______ voiture (*his*)
9. ______ jardin (*her*)
10. ______ fille (*his*)

REVIEW

CATCH THE BLUNDERS 1

In the following paragraphs, each word or phrase printed in blue contains at least one blunder. Correct all the blunders, referring to the English version when necessary, and fill in all the blanks. Then check your answers on pages 348–350.

A Le dernier mardi, Julie est allé au dentiste. Elle ne fait pas aimer cet dentiste. Il est brutal et chaque temps qu'elle va chez il, elle fait mal aux dents après. Elle cherche pour un dentiste autre. Elle espère qu'elle puisse bientôt changer. Pour le moment, elle souffrit. Elle connait que ________ dents qu'on ne soigne pas peuvent devenir le problème grand. Pour exemple, Julie l'oncle a eu beaucoup des problèmes une année il y a. En général, il faut va chez le dentiste un temps un an. Il n'est pas agréable, mais il est nécessaire ________ avoir les dents sains.

Last Tuesday, Julie went to the dentist's. She does not like that dentist. He is brutal, and each time she goes there, her teeth hurt afterwards. She is looking for another dentist. She hopes that she will soon be able to change. For now, she is suffering. She knows that teeth left untreated can become a big problem. For instance, Julie's uncle had a lot of problems a year ago. In general, it is necessary to go to the dentist once a year. It is not pleasant, but it is necessary to have healthy teeth.

B Julie est la fille que Marc a fait la connaissance le dernier Samedi. Elle est américainne, mais elle vient de la Jamaïque. Elle habite à Kingston pendant 6 ans. Sa père a acheté une plantation du café en la montagne il y a 6 ans. Ils ont beaucoup de l'argent et elle travaille dans les tous pays de le monde. Quand elle a arrivé à France, elle est allé en Paris et elle achetait l'appartement petit qu'est agréable. L'immeuble que son appartement est dans est vieil mais il est en bonne état. Elle a tout le confort qu'elle a besoin.

Julie is the girl that Marc met last Saturday. She's an American, but she comes from Jamaica. She has lived in Kingston for 6 years. Her father bought a coffee plantation in the mountains 6 years ago. They have a lot of money, and she travels in all the countries of the world. When she arrived in France, she went to Paris, and she bought a small apartment that's comfortable. The building her apartment is in is old, but it is in good shape. She has all the comfort that she needs.

C Marie ne peux pas prendre de douche cet semaine parce que elle s'est cassée son bras. Sa mère aide la et sa frère faire les courses pour elle pouvoir se reposer. Elle serait aimer écrire une lettre à sa amie Patricia pour la parler qu'elle ne va pas bien. Les deux filles jeunes ne se sont pas écrites pour longtemps. Elle s'ont parlées le dernier mois mais ce mois, Patricia a dit qu'elle n'a plus des minutes sur son portable et qu'elle ne peut pas la téléphoner. Alors Marie est triste et elle est ennuyeuse. Elle ne sait pas qu'est-ce qu'elle pourrait faire pour l'amuser. Elle n'aime pas lisant et sa mère ne veut pas elle regarder la télé tous les temps. Elle pense: "Je voudrais ________ quelqu'un aider moi!"

Marie cannot take showers this week, because she broke her arm. Her mother helps her, and her brother runs her errands so she can rest. She would like to write to her friend Patricia to tell her that she is not doing well. The two young girls have not written for a long time. They talked last month, but this month Patricia said she did not have any more minutes on her cell phone and that she could not call. So Marie is sad and bored. She does not know what she could do to entertain herself. She does not like reading, and her mother does not want her to watch TV all the time. She thinks, "I would like someone to help me!"

D Si je serais un athlète, ma vie serait difficile aussi que gratifiante. Je devrais se lever très tôt tout les matins ________ aller s'entrainer. Je déteste me levant tôt. Avant de partir la maison, je devais prendre mon petit-déjeuner: il faut qu'un athlète a les forces. Qu'est-ce qu'est bon pour le petit-déjeuner de un athlète? Je pense que des œufs et ________ céréale soient bons pour ma santé. Si je gagnerais la médaille à les Olympiques Jeus un jour, je pouvais prendre ma retraite et vivre heureusement jusqu'au fin de mon vie.

If I were an athlete, my life would be as hard as it would be rewarding. I would have to get up very early every morning to go train. I hate getting up early. Before leaving the house, I would have to have breakfast: it is necessary for an athlete to have strength. What is good for an athlete's breakfast? I think that eggs and cereal are good for my health. If I won a medal at the Olympic Games one day, I could retire and live happily ever after (literally, until the end of my life).

E L'été dernier, notre favori restaurant a brulé. On ne sait pas qu'est-ce qui s'est passé. Tout a été calme et tout a coup l'incendie est commencé. Nous avons vus les dégâts sur la télé, et nous avons eu tristes parce que nous aimions cet restaurant. Quel horreur! Il y a eu toujours beaucoup des gens et de l'ambiance était agréable. Un jour un danse professeur donnait un cours de la salsa et nous avons eu un bon temps. Je voudrais de savoir qu'est-ce que les propriétaires veuillent faire maintenant. J'espère qu'ils reconstruisent bientôt.

Last summer, our favorite restaurant burned down. We don't know what happened. Everything was quiet, and all of a sudden the fire started. We saw the rubble on TV and we were sad, because we liked that restaurant. What a horrible thing! There were always a lot of people, and the atmosphere was nice. One day, a dance teacher taught a salsa lesson, and we had a good time. I would like to know what the owners want to do now. I hope they rebuild soon.

F Demain dès que j'arrive au travail, je commençerai ________ ranger mon bureau. Quand j'ai quitté hier nuit, je n'ai rangé rien parce que je n'ai eu pas le temps. Ma mari a téléphoné à moi parce qu'il a oublié son clés ce matin. Il attendait pour moi avant la maison! Alors j'ai devu partir vite pour aller aider lui. Mais je n'aime pas quitter mes affaires en désordre. J'aime les choses être bien organisé.

Tomorrow, as soon as I arrive at work, I will clean up my desk. When I left last night, I did not put anything away, because I did not have time. My husband called me because he had forgotten his keys this morning. He was waiting for me in front of the house! So I had to leave quickly to go help him. But I don't like to leave my stuff lying around. I like things to be well organized.

G Je suis en la premier année au collège. Je pense que ce soit assez difficile mais si je fais les efforts je ferai réussir. Les étudiants autres que j'ai fait la connaissance ont dit à moi ________ je ne dois pas m'inquiéter. Ces étudiants ils ont proposé de s'étudier à l'université bibliothèque. Ce sont très gentils, et je suis content de savoir eux. J'ai un appartement gentil ________ je partage avec un étudiant autre. Il est aussi sympa et nous jouons au judo ensemble. Il n'aime pas des études. Il préfère jouer au sport tous les temps. Moi, je veux que je réussisse. Je travaille beaucoup de. Le cours qu'est difficile pour moi c'est le cours de l'italien. Cet cours est sur mardis et jeudis à 8:30 dans le matin. J'aimerais à apprendre l'Italien, mais je serais préférer un cours que n'est pas dans le matin.

I am in my first year of college. I think that it is fairly difficult but if I make the effort, I will succeed. The other students that I have met told me I should not worry. These students proposed to study together at the university library. They are very nice, and I am glad to know them. I have a nice apartment that I share with another student. He is very nice, and we practice judo together. He does not like his studies. He prefers to play sports all the time. I want to succeed. I work a lot. The class that is hard for me is the Italian class. That class is on Tuesdays and Thursdays at 8:30 A.M. I would like to learn Italian, but I would prefer a class that is not in the morning.

H Samedi le dernier nous avons volé à Dallas ________ voir une exposition de la peinture. Je n'avais pas été en un musée pour deux ans. Il n'y a pas des musée dans la ville ________ nous habitons dans. Au musée du Dallas il y a eu beaucoup de personnes et nous avons attendu pour longtemps avant nous entrions. En le musée, il était très froid parce que les américains aiment ________ climatisation. Nous avons aimé l'exposition, mais quand nous avons sorti, il a fait très chaud dehors, et parce que la différence avec la température intérieuse, j'ai attrapé un rhume. Quand nous rentrions chez nous, je me couchais tout de suite et je dormais pour dix heures. Quel un voyage!

Last Saturday, we flew to Dallas to see a painting exhibit. I had not been in a museum in two years. There are no museums in the city we live in. At the Dallas museum, there were a lot of people and we waited for a long time before we got in. In the museum, it was very cold, because Americans like air conditioning. We liked the exhibit, but when we got out, it was very hot and, because of the difference with the inside temperature, I caught a cold. When we came home, I went to bed right away and I slept for ten hours. What a trip!

I Ma grand-mère Jeanne était la femme extraordinaire. Elle était née dans 1920, en Nice, une ville du sud de ________ France. Sa père était un médecin et sa mère s'occupait de les pauvres et des sans-abris de la ville. Elle les donnaient à manger quand ils étaient faim, et dans l' hiver quand ils étaient malades, elle avait les médicaments pour leurs. Les jours quand elle n'avait pas école, Jeanne allait avec sa mère. Quand elle a devenue grande et qu'elle a fini ses études secondaires, elle décidait d'aller en Paris. Là, elle est allée à l'universitaire parce qu'elle a voulu devenir un docteur comme sa père. Il n'était pas beaucoup des femmes à la université à cet époque. C'était une chose assez extraordinaire quand la femme faisait des études supérieuses. Mais aussitôt qu'elle a commencé ses études, la guerre avec l'Allemagne a commençé. Ses parents voulaient la rentrer à Nice parce qu'ils pensaient que Paris sera trop de dangereux. Mais elle y voulait rester ________ aider les personnes qui étaient misérable parce que la guerre. Comme sa mère elle voulait aider les gens qui souffrissent. Elle est devenu infirmière à l'hopital. C'est là qu'elle a su mon grand-père. À le début elle n'éprouvait ni amitié, ni affection pour lui, mais petit a petit, elle a commencé à lui aimer... et après la guerre ils s'ont mariés. Malheureusement mon grand-père avait un accident et il morté assez jeun. Jeanne ne s'est remarié jamais.

My grandmother Jeanne was an extraordinary woman. She was born in 1920 in Nice, a town in the south of France. Her father was a doctor, and her mother was taking care of the poor and the homeless of the town. She would give them food when they were hungry, and in the winter, when they were sick, she had medications for them. The days when she did not have school, Jeanne would go with her mother. When she grew up and finished high school, she decided to go to Paris. There, she went to college, because she wanted to become a doctor like her father. There weren't many women in college at that time. It was quite an extraordinary thing when a woman went to college. But as soon as she started, the war with Germany began. Her parents wanted her to come home to Nice, because they thought that Paris would be too dangerous. But she wanted to stay there to help the people who were miserable because of the war. Like her mother, she wanted to help those who suffer. She became a nurse at the hospital. That is where she met my grandfather. At the beginning, she felt neither friendship nor affection for him, but little by little, she started to love him . . . and after the war they got married. Unfortunately, my grandfather had an accident and died rather young. Jeanne never remarried.

CATCH THE BLUNDERS 2

This exercise spans the whole book and is intended as a review. A page number in the answer key will send you back to the particular chapter if you need more detailed explanations. Each sentence has one, two, or three errors (the number is indicated in parentheses). Underline the word that has the error, and rewrite the sentence correctly.

1. Leur fille cadete est parisiene. (2)
   Their youngest daughter is from Paris.
2. Elle est très sportife et elle a gagnée beaucoup de trophées intéressantes. (3)
   She is very athletic, and she won many interesting trophies.
3. Ils aiment beaucoup de les films français. (1)
   They like French movies a lot.
4. Vous préférez du chocolat ou du flan? (2)
   You prefer chocolate or flan?
5. Cet maison a l'air inhabité. (2)
   That house looks uninhabited.
6. Paul est un gens qui je vois souvent. (2)
   Paul is someone I see often.
7. Julie l'a donnée les fleurs. (3)
   Julie gave her flowers.
8. Si vous auriez beaucoup de l'argent, qu'est-ce que feriez-vous? (3)
   If you had a lot of money, what would you do?
9. Quand ils étaient petit, ils ont fait ses devoirs à la cuisine. (3)
   When they were little, they did their homework in the kitchen.
10. Le jour quand il est sur les vacances, il finira son projet. (3)
    The day he is on vacation, he will finish his project.
11. Combien des amis vas-tu parler à? (2)
    How many friends are you going to speak to?
12. Il s'est brossé ses dents trois temps aujourd'hui. (2)
    He brushed his teeth three times today.
13. Sur samedi nous irons à la plage s'il sera beau. (2/3)
    On Saturday we will go to the beach if it is nice.

GENDER PRACTICE

Based on the patterns you reviewed in the "Nouns" chapter, identify the following nouns as masculine (M) or feminine (F). The words in bold don't follow any recognizable pattern, and yet they are very common. You should try to memorize the gender, especially for those ending in -e that are not feminine. All other words of the exercise fall into the regular categories listed in the chapter.

1. **anniversaire** ______
2. **argent** ______
3. assistance ______
4. bateau ______
5. beauté ______
6. bidet ______
7. bourbier ______
8. carnage ______
9. **cause** ______
10. **centre** ______
11. chauffage ______
12. chauvinisme ______
13. **chose** ______
14. cocktail ______
15. construction ______
16. **couple** ______
17. **culture** ______
18. département ______
19. **dépense** ______
20. diversité ______
21. drapeau ______
22. **église** ______
23. energie ______
24. engagement ______
25. **état** ______
26. évasion ______
27. exception ______
28. gastronomie ______
29. **genre** ______
30. héritage ______
31. **machine** ______
32. **manière** ______
33. miracle ______
34. **modèle** ______
35. **monde** ______
36. **mot** ______
37. naissance ______
38. nature ______
39. nouveauté ______
40. **objet** ______
41. obstacle ______
42. panier ______
43. patience ______
44. pâtisserie ______
45. **planète** ______
46. pommier ______
47. Porsche ______
48. **pouvoir** ______
49. printemps ______
50. proposition ______
51. **régime** ______
52. **rencontre** ______
53. renseignement ______
54. **Rhône** (French river) ______
55. **semaine** ______
56. société ______
57. **sujet** ______
58. tatouage ______
59. **témoignage** ______
60. tennis ______
61. **terre** ______
62. **théâtre** ______
63. **village** ______

CONSTRUCTION GAME

*This exercise spans the whole book and is intended as a review. A page number in the answer key will send you back to the relevant chapter if you need more detailed explanations. Use the provided elements to build a correct sentence. You may have to add a preposition (*à, de, pour, etc.*), an article, or a subject pronoun, but don't move the elements around, as they are already in order. Don't forget to conjugate the verbs and make the necessary agreements.*

1. quand / il / être / petit / il / aller / grand-mère / tout / dimanche

   ____

2. enfants / devoir / écouter / parents

   ____

3. elle / demander / renseignements / agent de police

   ____

4. elle / dire / étudiants / bien étudier / leçon

   ____

5. hier / ils / se parler

   ____

6. profs / préférer / étudiants / avoir / bon / notes

   ____

7. elle / regarder / enfants / jouer

   ____

8. je / penser / tu / avoir raison

   ____

9. tu / ne pas aimer / se promener / dimanche

   ____

10. nous / chercher / bon / solution

    ____

11. si / pleuvoir / herbe / être / plus / vert

    ____

ANSWER KEY

Pronunciation (page 16)

1. Ils ont commencé.
2. Des glaçons.
3. Nous remplaçons la vitre.
4. Je l'ai aperçu.
5. Elle aime la glace.
6. Avançons lentement.
7. Ça m'intéresse.
8. Ils prononçaient mal.
9. Ils s'est fiancé l'an dernier.

Spelling (pages 26–27)

1. Le chien a marché à côté de son maitre jusqu'à la porte, puis il a pris la fuite.
2. Il a réussi à faire des économies et il a enfin acheté une nouvelle machine à café.
3. Pierre a dix ans aujourd'hui. Sa mère a préparé un bon gâteau.
4. À dix ans, un petit garçon commence à être un petit homme.
5. Quand elle a voyagé à Paris, elle a visité tous les monuments et elle a parlé à beaucoup de gens.
6. À quelle heure a-t-il commencé à travailler?

B

1. sûr
2. salé
3. à
4. marché
5. dès
6. sur

C

1. Qu'est-ce qu'elle veut?
2. Qui a dit ça?
3. L'homme a prononcé le oui qu'on attendait.
4. Mon amie s'appelle Emma.
5. Tu as vu cet arbre? C'est un centenaire.
6. Cet enfant n'est pas sage.

7. Jusqu'où est-ce que tu iras?
8. Qu'est-ce qui t'est arrivé? Tu es pâle.
9. J'ai autant d'amis qu'eux.
10. Est-ce qu'ils se sont amusés?
11. Tu l'as lue?
12. Il l'a mis là.

Capitalization (page 31)

1. Nous sommes le 31 octobre.
2. Leur fille a double nationalité: elle est canadienne et brésilienne. Elle parle français, anglais et portugais.
3. Les Français sont catholiques.
4. Sa maison se trouve 22 place du Tertre.
5. Si vous allez en Suisse, vous verrez le mont Blanc et le lac Léman.
6. Les Suisses sont très gentils. Ils parlent français aussi.
7. Quand vous y serez, essayez de parler français et achetez du chocolat suisse.

Nouns (page 54)

1. une femme
2. une Française
3. une skieuse
4. une épicière
5. une sportive
6. X
7. une réceptionniste
8. une Canadienne
9. une hypocrite
10. une jument
11. une chanteuse
12. une femme ingénieur

B

1. des bancs
2. des animaux
3. des jeux
4. des oiseaux
5. des yeux
6. des choux-fleurs
7. des métaux
8. des bijoux
9. mesdames
10. des travaux
11. des prix
12. des chaises-longues

Descriptive Adjectives (pages 69–70)

A
1. bel
2. canadienne
3. nouvel
4. beaux
5. vieilles
6. nouvelle
7. vieil
8. jolie

B
1. américaine
2. inoffensive
3. heureuse
4. agaçante
5. blanche
6. bonne
7. jeune
8. farceuse
9. belle
10. brune

C
1. beaux
2. gros
3. principaux
4. affreux
5. royaux
6. finals

D
1. un nouvel appartement
2. un bel arbre
3. des livres anciens
4. une petite fille
5. une vieille maison
6. un mauvais livre
7. une très bonne tarte
8. une grosse voiture
9. une femme laide
10. un bref entretien

Determiners (pages 88–89)

A
1. un verre / une bouteille / un litre de vin
2. une bouteille / un verre de lait
3. une tranche de jambon
4. un morceau de fromage
5. un kilo / une livre de tomates
6. un pot de confiture

B
1. d'
2. de l'
3. des, de
4. le
5. une, un
6. de l'
7. le
8. X
9. le, la
10. du, le
11. de la, du

C
1. ses
2. son
3. nos
4. vos
5. mes
6. notre
7. leur
8. son

D
1. Cet
2. ces
3. cette
4. Ces
5. Cette
6. Cet
7. ce
8. Ces
9. Cette

E
1. Ils ont beaucoup d'enfants.
2. Il voudrait visiter d'autres pays.
3. Cet enfant a peur des autres enfants de sa classe.
4. As-tu besoin de lunettes pour lire?
5. Mon chat n'a pas de puces!
6. Bébé a de petits pieds.
7. Nous mangerons du poulet avec des petits pois ce soir.
8. Est-ce que tu te souviens des bêtises que nous faisions à 10 ans?
9. Cet homme est coupable de crimes horribles.
10. La plupart des gens aiment le chocolat.
11. Les chats ne sont pas des animaux bruyants.
12. Elle se mêle toujours des affaires des autres.

Numbers (page 106)

A
1. cent-un
2. soixante-et-onze
3. quatre-vingts
4. mille
5. cinq cents
6. cent quatre-vingt-cinq
7. quatre-vingt-un

B
1. vingt-et-une filles
2. trois millions de dollars
3. zéro euros
4. un demi kilo
5. le trois décembre quatre-vingt-neuf
6. minuit et quart OR zéro heure quinze
7. Jacques 1er
8. le neuvième

Subjects, Objects, and Their Pronouns (pages 133–136)

A
1. Ils la veulent.
2. Nous n'allons pas la vendre.
3. Elle l'a achetée.
4. Ils vont le voir.
5. Ils les aiment.
6. Allez-vous le faire?
7. L'entendez-vous?
8. Etienne l'a invitée.
9. Bois-le!
10. Fais-les!
11. Il les a écrites.

B
1. Nous n'avons pas pu lui parler.
2. Tu leur as écrit.
3. Il va lui donner des roses.
4. Le prof lui a donné un livre.
5. Prête-lui ton livre!
6. Leur parles-tu souvent?

C
1. Oui, j'y suis déjà allé. / Non, je n'y suis jamais allé.
2. J'en ai. / Je n'en ai pas.
3. Je voudrais en avoir. / Je ne voudrais pas en avoir.
4. Ils n'en mangent pas.
5. Je les ai vus récemment. / Je ne les ai pas vus récemment.
6. J'en fais souvent. / Je n'en fais pas souvent.
7. Je l'ai visitée. / Je ne l'ai pas visitée.
8. J'aime en parler. / Je n'aime pas en parler.
9. J'y pense souvent. / Je n'y pense pas souvent.
10. Je vais l'apprendre. / Je ne vais pas l'apprendre.
11. J'en ai peur. / Je n'en ai pas peur.
12. Je leur téléphone souvent. / Je ne leur téléphone pas souvent.
13. Je pense souvent à eux. / Je ne pense pas souvent à eux.

D
1. Oui, il nous y a invités. / Non, il ne nous y a pas invités.
2. Je vais leur en apporter. / Je ne vais pas leur en apporter.
3. Je les y ai achetés. / Je ne les y ai pas achetés.
4. Je veux vous en parler. / Je ne veux pas vous en parler.
5. Je leur en ai donné pour Halloween. / Je ne leur en ai pas donné pour Halloween.
6. Je peux t'en prêter un peu. / Je ne peux pas t'en prêter un peu.
7. Il lui en a offert beaucoup. / Il ne lui en a pas offert beaucoup.

E
1. qui
2. dont
3. dont
4. lequel
5. dont
6. que
7. qui
8. où
9. que
10. qui

Types of Verbs (page 149)

A
1. The children are making fun of you.
2. Let's have lunch together on Saturday.
3. What are you listening to?
4. You brush your teeth three times a day.
5. He did not remember my birthday.
6. Look at yourself!
7. Last night, we talked to each other on the phone for two hours.

B
1. Ils s'aiment.
2. Ils ne se parlent plus.
3. Nous nous rendons visite souvent.
4. Ils se sont aidés.
5. Ils se sont rencontrés au parc.
6. Est-ce que tu t'es lavé les mains, Janine? / Janine, t'es-tu lavé les mains?
7. Elle s'est levée à huit heures.

The Infinitive (page 157)

A
1. Il commence à pleuvoir.
2. Es-tu content de partir en vacances?
3. Elle voudrait aller faire des courses.
4. Il peut partir maintenant.
5. Elle vient de partir.
6. Ils apprennent à danser le tango.
7. Je préfère partir tôt.

The Conjugated Form (page 165)

A
1. past conditional, compound tense
2. present, simple tense
3. future, simple tense; present, simple tense
4. present, simple tense
5. conditional, simple tense; past, simple tense
6. past conditional, compound tense; pluperfect, compound tense

The Present Tense (page 173)

A
1. Nous mangeons une pomme.
2. Ils habitent dans cette maison depuis dix ans.
3. Le dimanche et le jeudi, nous allons au gymnase.
4. Mon chat est très affectueux ces jours-ci.
5. Il pleut.
6. La neige est blanche.
7. Nous travaillons ici depuis 1989.

1. commençons
2. t'amuses
3. ouvrent
4. déçoit
5. partons
6. attend
7. logeons
8. se sent
9. dormez
10. me lève
11. réfléchissent
12. appelle
13. espère

The *passé composé* (pages 184–185)

1. Ils sont venus de Lyon.
2. Elles ne sont pas allées en Europe.
3. Avez-vous pris le bus?
4. Tu n'as rien entendu?
5. —As-tu fait la vaisselle? —Oui, je l'ai faite.
6. Vous êtes allés au cinéma, ou vous êtes restés chez vous?
7. Cette fillette n'est jamais tombée.
8. Ils n'ont pas aimé les bonbons.
9. Nous n'avons regardé personne.

B

1. Ils se sont aimés.
2. Ils se sont téléphoné.
3. Vous ne vous êtes pas réconciliés.
4. Elles se sont lavé les mains.
5. Nous nous sommes ennuyés.
6. Ils se sont écrit.
7. Ils se sont retrouvés au café.
8. Ils se sont levés.
9. Elle s'est brossé les dents.

The *imparfait* (page 191)

1. écrivait
2. habitions
3. faisaient
4. prenaient
5. commençaient
6. jouiez
7. étais
8. voyait
9. voyageais, allais
10. étudiiez
11. venaient
12. avions

B

1. Est-ce que tu aidais toujours ta mère quand tu avais douze ans?
2. Quand il était petit, il voulait être pompier.
3. Que faisais-tu le dimanche quand tu étais au lycée?
4. L'année dernière, je me levais à 6 heures du matin tous les jours.
5. Nous étudiions quand tu as appelé.
6. Tous les matins elle buvait une tasse de café.

The *passé composé* versus the *imparfait* (pages 197–199)

1. a décidé
2. faisait
3. ont pris
4. sont partis
5. était
6. ont décidé
7. étaient
8. a commencé
9. ont couru
10. sont entrés
11. faisait
12. n'étaient plus
13. ont attendu
14. ont mis
15. pleuvait
16. brillait

B

1. Quand je suis parti(e) ce matin, il pleuvait.
2. Quand j'avais dix ans, je faisais du vélo tous les jours. Un jour j'ai cassé mon vélo.
3. Hier, je suis sorti(e). Quand je suis rentré(e), j'étais fatigué(e).
4. Je faisais mes devoirs quand le professeur est entré dans la classe.
5. Elle a toujours pris le bus pour aller au travail. Pourquoi changer?
6. Les enfants voulaient sortir mais leur mère n'a pas voulu, alors ils sont restés à l'intérieur.
7. Nous nous sommes amusés pendant notre voyage l'hiver dernier.
8. Quand elle a ouvert sa porte, elle avait déjà peur.

C

1. nous sommes mariés, faisait, avait
2. dormait
3. lisais
4. avait, avait, n'a pas voulu, ont regardé
5. suis arrivé, n'ai pas pu

D
1. passé composé
2. can't tell
3. imparfait
4. imparfait
5. (a) passé composé (b) imparfait
6. (a) passé composé (b) imparfait (c) passé composé
7. passé composé
8. passé composé
9. (a) passé composé (b) imparfait

The Pluperfect (page 201)

A
1. n'avait pas fini
2. s'est réveillée, s'était couchée
3. étions partis
4. sommes arrivés, avait déjà commencé
5. avais compris, n'avait rien compris

The Future (page 207)

A
1. ferons
2. viendra
3. descendrez
4. enverrons
5. étudieront
6. aura
7. verras
8. saurez
9. irez

B
1. Quand je serai grand/grande, je serai steward / hôtesse de l'air.
2. Si le vol est annulé, je rentrerai à la maison.
3. Si vous regardez dehors, vous pourrez voir les arbres.
4. Dès que j'arriverai à Paris, je téléphonerai à mes parents.

The Future Perfect (page 210)

A
1. aura fini
2. seras rentré
3. partirai
4. sortirez
5. allons partir
6. es
7. arriverez
8. va avoir

The Present Conditional (pages 216–217)

A
1. Si nous n'étions pas en classe aujourd'hui, nous serions à la maison.
2. Pourriez-vous me dire où sont les toilettes, s'il vous plait.
3. Ils espéraient que le film serait intéressant.
4. J'irais en Europe si j'avais assez d'argent.
5. Ils devraient aller à la bibliothèque plus souvent.
6. Qu'est-ce que tu voudrais / vous voudriez faire ce soir?
7. Je n'ai pas pu comprendre le message. Alors je n'ai pas répondu.
8. Voudrais-tu que je t'aide?
9. Tu pourrais au moins t'excuser!

B
1. feriez
2. pourrions
3. n'y avait pas
4. partiriez
5. téléphonerais
6. irais
7. seriez
8. étudiiez
9. arriverais

The Past Conditional (page 220)

A
1. Qu'est-ce que nous aurions fait sans vous?
2. Si j'avais su ton numéro, je t'aurais téléphoné.
3. Si tu n'étais pas venu m'aider, je n'aurais jamais fini ce travail.
4. Elle aurait rencontré le loup si elle était allée dans la forêt.

B
1. n'aurions pas raté
2. ne serait pas sortie
3. irions
4. partiriez
5. pourraient
6. serait arrivé

The Subjunctive Mood (page 237)

A
1. comprenez / comprendrez / avez compris
2. conjuguerez
3. fasse
4. soit
5. est
6. ayons
7. buvions

B
1. Je suis surpris que tu ailles en Europe l'été prochain.
2. C'est dommage qu'ils partent tôt.
3. Qu'est-ce que vous voulez que nous fassions?
4. Je suis triste de partir demain.
5. Je voudrais que mes enfants soient heureux dans la vie.

6. Il a peur de perdre son chapeau.
7. Elle ne pense pas qu'il dise la vérité.

The Present Subjunctive (page 241)

A
1. aient
2. étudiiez
3. ne puisses pas
4. fassiez
5. sorte
6. promènes
7. revienne
8. alliez
9. buvions
10. dorment
11. boives
12. payions

The Past Subjunctive (page 244)

A
1. ne soient pas venus
2. ait découvert
3. ait raté
4. puissiez
5. aille, ait attrapé

Reported Speech (page 251)

A
1. qu'elle n'avait pas faim
2. de finir sa soupe OR qu'il finisse sa soupe
3. si le train était à l'heure
4. ce qui s'était passé
5. si nous avions compris
6. lui a dit d'aller au lit OR lui a dit qu'il aille au lit
7. ce que je ferais si je voyais un martien
8. si j'allais l'inviter

Questions and Answers (pages 272–274)

A
1. Avec qui est-ce que tu voudrais danser? / Avec qui voudrais-tu danser?
2. Est-ce que tes frères jouent au tennis tous les jours? / Tes frères jouent-ils au tennis tous les jours?
3. Qui est-ce qui court le plus vite? / Qui court le plus vite?
4. Quel est son métier? (*no* est-ce que *form*)
5. De quel instrument est-ce que vous jouez? / De quel instrument jouez-vous?
6. Est-ce que tu vas réussir? / Vas-tu réussir?
7. Est-ce qu'elles se sont amusées? / Se sont-elles amusées?

B
1. Qu'est-ce que Luc écoute? (*no inversion form*)
2. À quoi est-ce que Luc s'intéresse? / À quoi Luc s'intéresse-t-il?
3. Quelle couleur est-ce que tu préfères? / Quelle couleur préfères-tu? OR Quelle est ta couleur préférée?

4. À quelle heure est-ce que Julie arrivera à la maison? / À quelle heure Julie arrivera-t-elle à la maison?
5. Qu'est-ce que les Français aiment? (*no inversion form*)
6. Qui est-ce que Virginie aime? / Qui Virginie aime-t-elle?
7. Comment est-ce que tu te sens aujourd'hui? / Comment te sens-tu aujourd'hui?
8. Avec qui est-ce qu'il a passé les vacances? / Avec qui a-t-il passé les vacances?
9. Comment est-ce qu'elle rentre à la maison? / Comment rentre-t-elle à la maison?
10. Où est-ce qu'ils ont allés? / Où sont-ils allés?
11. Pourquoi est-ce qu'il dit cela? / Pourquoi dit-il cela?

C
1. Quelle
2. Qu'est-ce qu'
3. Quel
4. Quelles
5. Quelle
6. Qu'est-ce que
7. Quels
8. Que
9. Qu'est-ce que

Words (pages 302–303)

A
1. Il a essayé quatre fois.
2. Tous les gens portaient des chapeaux.
3. Est-ce que tu sais parler italien?
4. Je connais ce poème par cœur.
5. Nous sommes allés à Houston en avion.
6. Il doit travailler ce soir.
7. Il fait beau.
8. Est-ce que je t'ai manqué?
9. Je sais qu'ils se sont connus en Suisse.
10. Fait-il trop chaud?
11. Il a vécu au 20ème siècle.
12. J'ai laissé mon livre dans le métro.
13. Elle a manqué/raté son train trois fois cette semaine.

B
1. She is doing the eulogy of her former professor.
2. She washes her face.
3. Go to the bookstore.
4. They met on vacation.
5. I miss you.
6. His/Her article is scheduled to be published next month.
7. Fortunately, they had already left.
8. He is cold.
9. You miss me.

Prepositions (page 318)

A

1. à
2. X
3. chez
4. à
5. X
6. jusqu'à ce que
7. chez
8. au, en
9. d'
10. dans, dans
11. de
12. d'
13. du
14. dans
15. en, en
16. dans
17. X
18. en
19. chez
20. X
21. À
22. à
23. de

Constructions (page 330)

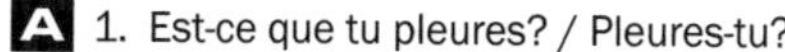

A

1. Est-ce que tu pleures? / Pleures-tu?
2. Est-ce que ce livre est à toi? —Non, il est à Julie. / —Non, c'est le livre de Julie.
3. Ils n'ont pas voulu me dire la vérité. / Ils ne voulaient pas me dire la vérité.
4. Elle veut qu'ils/qu'elles rentrent à la maison.
5. Je me suis blessé en travaillant.
6. Il a des souvenirs d'enfance qu'il ne veut pas partager.
7. Est-ce que c'est quelqu'un que tu connais?
8. Irais-tu? / Est-ce que tu irais?

B

1. ses
2. son
3. notre
4. vos
5. mes
6. notre
7. leur
8. sa
9. son
10. sa

Catch the Blunders 1 (pages 333–335)

A Mardi dernier, Julie est allée chez le dentiste. Elle n'aime pas ce dentiste. Il est brutal et chaque fois qu'elle va chez lui, elle a mal aux dents après. Elle cherche un autre dentiste. Elle espère qu'elle pourra bientôt changer. Pour le moment, elle souffre. Elle sait que des dents qu'on ne soigne pas peuvent devenir un grand problème. Par exemple, l'oncle de Julie a eu beaucoup de problèmes il y a un an. En général, il faut aller chez le dentiste une fois par an. Ce n'est pas agréable, mais c'est nécessaire pour avoir des dents saines.

B Julie est la fille dont Marc a fait la connaissance samedi dernier. Elle est américaine, mais elle vient de Jamaïque. Elle habite à Kingston depuis 6 ans. Son père a acheté une plantation de café dans la montagne il y a 6 ans. Ils ont beaucoup d'argent et elle voyage dans tous les pays du monde. Quand elle est arrivée en France, elle est allée à Paris et elle a acheté un petit appartement qui est agréable. L'immeuble dans lequel est son appartement est vieux mais il est en bon état. Elle a tout le confort dont elle a besoin.

C Marie ne peut pas prendre de douche cette semaine parce qu'elle s'est cassé le bras. Sa mère l'aide et son frère fait les courses pour qu'elle puisse se reposer. Elle aimerait écrire une lettre à son amie Patricia pour lui dire qu'elle ne va pas bien. Les deux jeunes filles ne se sont pas écrit depuis longtemps. Elle se sont parlé le mois dernier mais ce mois-ci, Patricia a dit qu'elle n'avait plus de minute sur son portable et qu'elle ne pouvait pas lui téléphoner. Alors Marie est triste et elle s'ennuie. Elle ne sait pas ce qu'elle pourrait faire pour s'amuser. Elle n'aime pas lire et sa mère ne veut pas qu'elle regarde la télé tout le temps. Elle pense: "Je voudrais que quelqu'un m'aide!"

D Si j'étais un athlète, ma vie serait aussi difficile que gratifiante. Je devrais me lever très tôt tous les matins pour aller m'entrainer. Je déteste me lever tôt. Avant de quitter la maison, je devrais prendre mon petit-déjeuner: il faut qu'un athlète ait des forces. Qu'est-ce qui est bon pour le petit-déjeuner d'un athlète? Je pense que les œufs et les céréales sont bons pour ma santé. Si je gagnais une médaille aux Jeux Olympiques un jour, je pourrais prendre ma retraite et vivre content jusqu'à la fin de ma vie.

E L'été dernier, notre restaurant favori a brulé. On ne sait pas ce qui s'est passé. Tout était calme et tout à coup l'incendie a commencé. Nous avons vu les dégâts à la télé, et nous avons été tristes parce que nous aimions ce restaurant. Quelle horreur! Il y avait toujours beaucoup de gens et l'ambiance était agréable. Un jour un professeur de danse a donné un cours de salsa et nous nous sommes bien amusés. Je voudrais savoir ce que les propriétaires veulent faire maintenant. J'espère qu'ils reconstruiront bientôt.

F Demain dès que j'arriverai au travail, je commencerai à ranger mon bureau. Quand je suis partie hier soir, je n'ai rien rangé parce que je n'ai pas eu le temps. Mon mari m'a téléphoné parce qu'il avait oublié ses clés ce matin. Il m'attendait devant la maison! Alors j'ai dû partir vite pour aller l'aider. Mais je n'aime pas laisser mes affaires en désordre. J'aime que les choses soient bien organisées.

G Je suis en première année à l'université. Je pense que c'est assez difficile mais si je fais des efforts je réussirai. Les autres étudiants dont j'ai fait la connaissance m'ont dit que je ne dois pas m'inquiéter. Ces étudiants ont proposé d'étudier ensemble à la bibliothèque de l'université. Ils sont très gentils, et je suis content de les connaitre. J'ai un joli appartement que je partage avec un autre étudiant. Il est sympa aussi et nous faisons du judo ensemble. Il n'aime pas les études. Il préfère faire du sport tous le temps.

Moi, je veux réussir. Je travaille beaucoup. Le cours qui est difficile pour moi c'est le cours d'italien. Ce cours est le mardi et le jeudi à 8.30 du matin. J'aimerais apprendre l'italien, mais je préfèrerais un cours qui n'est / ne soit pas le matin.

H Samedi dernier nous sommes allés à Dallas en avion pour voir une exposition de peinture. Je n'avais pas été dans un musée depuis deux ans. Il n'y a pas de musée dans la ville dans laquelle nous habitons. Au musée de Dallas il y avait beaucoup de gens et nous avons attendu longtemps avant d'entrer. Dans le musée, il faisait très froid parce que les Américains aiment la climatisation. Nous avons aimé l'exposition, mais quand nous sommes sortis, il faisait très chaud dehors, et à cause de la différence avec la température intérieure, j'ai attrapé un rhume. Quand nous sommes rentrés chez nous, je me suis couchée tout de suite et j'ai dormi dix heures. Quel voyage!

I Ma grand-mère Jeanne était une femme extraordinaire. Elle est née en 1920, à Nice, une ville du sud de la France. Son père était médecin et sa mère s'occupait des pauvres et des sans-abris de la ville. Elle leur donnait à manger quand ils avaient faim, et en hiver quand ils étaient malades, elle avait des médicaments pour eux. Les jours où elle n'avait pas école, Jeanne allait avec sa mère. Quand elle est devenue grande et qu'elle a fini ses études secondaires, elle a décidé d'aller à Paris. Là, elle est allée à l'université parce qu'elle voulait devenir docteur comme son père. Il n'y avait pas beaucoup de femmes à l'université à cette époque. C'était une chose assez extraordinaire quand une femme faisait des études supérieures. Mais aussitôt qu'elle a commencé ses études, la guerre avec l'Allemagne a commencé. Ses parents voulaient qu'elle rentre à Nice parce qu'ils pensaient que Paris serait trop dangereux. Mais elle voulait y rester pour aider les gens qui étaient misérables à cause de la guerre. Comme sa mère elle voulait aider les gens qui souffrent. Elle est devenue infirmière à l'hôpital. C'est là qu'elle a connu mon grand-père. Au début elle n'éprouvait ni amitié, ni affection pour lui, mais petit à petit, elle a commencé à l'aimer... et après la guerre ils se sont mariés. Malheureusement mon grand-père a eu un accident et il est mort assez jeune. Jeanne ne s'est jamais remariée.

Catch the Blunders 2 (page 336–338)

1. Leur fille cadete est parisiene.
   Correction: Leur fille cadette est parisienne.
   See "Forming the Feminine of Adjectives" (pp. 56–59).
2. Elle est très sportife et elle a gagnée beaucoup de trophées intéressantes.
   Correction: Elle est très sportive et elle a gagné beaucoup de trophées intéressants.
   - sportife: *Adjectives ending in* -if *make their feminine with* -ive *(pp. 56–58).*

- gagnée: *There is no past participle agreement with the subject when the auxiliary of the* passé composé *is* avoir *(p. 180).*
- intéressantes: *The noun* trophées *is masculine despite the -e (it is one of the three exceptions along with* lycée *and* musée*), so the adjective must be masculine.*

3. Ils aiment beaucoup de les films français.
   Correction: Ils aiment beaucoup les films français.
   - beaucoup de les: *Even though* beaucoup *is often used to mean "a lot of* **something**,*" when that "something" is not named, you can't use the* de *in French. In this sentence* beaucoup *describes the verb, that is, how much they like French films. It does not express "a lot of films."*
4. Vous préférez du chocolat ou du flan?
   Correction: Vous préférez le chocolat ou le flan?
   Verbs indicating preferences like aimer *and* préférer *are always followed by a definite article (p. 73).*
5. Cet maison a l'air inhabité.
   Correction: Cette maison a l'air inhabitée.
   - Cette: *The form* cet *is found only in front of a masculine noun beginning with a vowel or mute* h. Maison *is feminine. Both the words* cet *and* cette *have the same sound.*
   - inhabitée: *In a sentence with* avoir l'air, *when the subject is a thing as opposed to a person, the adjective must agree with that subject (p. 67).*
6. Paul est un gens qui je vois souvent.
   Correction: Paul est une personne que je vois souvent.
   - un gens: Gens *is always plural and uncountable. The determiner for it can be only* des *or* les *or an expression of quantity such as* beaucoup de. *If a specific number is needed, use the word* personne *instead of* gens *(p. 281).*
   - qui: *This is the relative pronoun subject. In this sentence you need the relative pronoun object. When dealing with relative pronouns, remember that* qui *does not automatically refer to a person (p. 127).*
7. Julie l'a donnée les fleurs.
   Correction: Julie lui a donné des fleurs.
   - l': *The verb* donner *has an indirect construction (pp. 119–120) and the object pronoun is the indirect pronoun* lui, *whether the object of the verb is feminine or masculine. This is a very common mistake due to the fact that* lui *is also the stress pronoun equivalent to* him *(p. 111).*
   - donnée: *The agreement of the past participle does not occur with the indirect object pronoun (p. 177).*
   - les: *There is no reason here to use the definite article* les, *since there is no context. Remember that the "default" article is the indefinite (pp. 78–79).*

8. Si vous auriez beaucoup de l'argent, qu'est-ce que feriez-vous?
   Correction: Si vous aviez beaucoup d'argent, qu'est-ce que vous feriez/que feriez-vous?
   - auriez: *Never put the conditional in a* si *clause (p. 213). Use the* imparfait *instead.*
   - beaucoup de l'argent: Beaucoup *is an expression of quantity and* de l' *is the partitive article. They cannot be combined (p. 85).*
   - qu'est-ce que feriez-vous: *To ask a question, choose either the inversion (*que feriez-vous*) or the formula with* est-ce que, *in which case you cannot use the inversion verb-subject (p. 257). Remember that using the inversion makes a question a little more formal.*
9. Quand ils étaient petit, ils ont fait ses devoirs à la cuisine.
   Correction: Quand ils étaient petits, ils faisaient leurs devoirs à la cuisine.
   - petits: *Adjectives must show the gender (masculine or feminine) and number (singular or plural) of the noun they describe,* ils *here.*
   - ils ont fait: *Usage of* passé composé *versus the* imparfait. *To reflect that an action was habitual, use the* imparfait *(p. 193).*
   - ses: *In French, the possessive adjective must reflect the gender and number of the object that follows, and not just the gender and number of the "owner." This is a very common mistake (pp. 85–86).*
10. Le jour quand il est sur les vacances, il finira son projet.
    Correction: Le jour où il sera en vacances, il finira son projet.
    - où: *This is the relative pronoun that indicates a place and also a time connection.* Quand *is not a relative pronoun (p. 130) so you can't use it here.*
    - il est: *If the main verb (*finira*) is in the future, all the verbs should be in future as well. There are exceptions (p. 207).*
    - sur les vacances: *This is a vocabulary error.*
11. Combien des amis vas-tu parler à?
    Correction: À combien d'amis vas-tu parler?
    - combien des: Combien *is an expression of quantity, and it must be used with* de, *even if the noun that follows is plural.*
    - à: *In a question, the preposition that goes with the verb (*parler à*) must be combined with the question word at the beginning of the sentence (pp. 268–69).*
12. Il s'est brossé ses dents trois temps aujourd'hui.
    Correction: Il s'est brossé les dents trois fois aujourd'hui.
    - ses dents: *When a part of the body is mentioned along with a pronominal verb, it is always used with the definite article instead of a possessive as in English.*
    - temps: *The word "time" in this sense is expressed by* fois *in French (p. 279).*
13. Sur samedi nous irons à la plage s'il sera beau.
    Correction: Samedi nous irons à la plage s'il fait beau.
    - sur: *Never use* sur *before a day of the week. Remember to use* le *if you want to express recurrence (on Mondays—*le lundi*).*

- il sera beau: *A vocabulary issue. To talk about the weather, use* faire *as opposed to* être *(p. 294).*
- sera: *Don't use the future in a* si *clause. In this case, with the future in the main clause, use the present (p. 206).*

Gender Practice (page 339)

1. M
2. M
3. F
4. M
5. F
6. M
7. M
8. M
9. F
10. M
11. M
12. M
13. F
14. M
15. F
16. M
17. F
18. M
19. F
20. F
21. M
22. F
23. F
24. M
25. M
26. F
27. F
28. F
29. M
30. M
31. F
32. F
33. M
34. M
35. M
36. M
37. F
38. F
39. F
40. M
41. M
42. M
43. F
44. F
45. F
46. M
47. F
48. M
49. M
50. F
51. M
52. F
53. M
54. M
55. F
56. F
57. M
58. M
59. M
60. M
61. F
62. M
63. M

Construction Game (page 340)

1. Quand il était petit il allait **chez** sa grand-mère tous **les** dimanches.
   When he was little he went to his grandmother's every Sunday.
   - *The* imparfait *is required to describe a recurrent action in the past (p. 192 on).*
   - *The only way to render "to (or at) his grandmother's" is to use* chez*.*
   - *Don't forget that the adjective* tout *has an irregular plural form: you drop the* -t*.*
2. **Les** enfants doivent écouter **leurs** parents.
   Children must listen to their parents.
   - *In a sequence of verbs, only the first one (*doivent*) is conjugated.*
   - *The verb* écouter *is not followed by a preposition in French.*
   - *All nouns must be preceded by a determiner (p. 71 on).*
3. Elle demande **des** renseignements à **l'**agent de police/à **un** agent de police.
   She asks the policeman for some information.

- Demander *is a transitive verb with two objects: the direct object,* des renseignements, *must come first and then the indirect object,* à un agent de police *(p. 139).*
- *The only preposition that can follow the verb* demander *is* à, *never* pour.
- *All nouns must be preceded by a determiner (p. 71 on).*

4. Elle dit aux étudiants de bien étudier la leçon.
   She tells the students to study the lesson well.
   - *In reported speech (introduced by a verb like* dire*) don't use a subjunctive construction. Instead, use an infinitive construction with* de + *an infinitive:* dire **à** quelqu'un **de** faire quelque chose *(p. 234).*
5. Hier ils se sont parlé.
   Yesterday they spoke to each other.
   - *Pronominal verbs are conjugated with* être *in the* passé composé.
   - *If the verb takes an indirect object in its nonpronominal form (*parler*), don't make the past participle agree with the subject (p. 180).*
6. Les profs préfèrent que **les/leurs** étudiants aient **de** bonnes notes.
   Professors prefer that students make good grades.
   - *Use of the subjunctive (p. 221).*
   - De bonnes notes: *in front of a plural adjective, the indefinite article* des *becomes* de *(p. 80).*
7. Elle regarde **les** enfants jouer.
   She watches the children play.
   - *After a verb of perception (*regarder*), use the infinitive (p. 324).*
   - *Without the translation provided here, the determiner could also be* des *(some) or* ses *(her), since we don't have a context.*
8. Je pense **que** tu as raison.
   I think you're right.
   - Penser *is always followed by* que, *but this is not a subjunctive construction when the sentence is affirmative (p. 227).*
9. Tu n'aimes pas **te** promener **le** dimanche.
   You don't like to take walks on Sundays.
   - *Even when a pronominal verb is in the infinitive, its pronoun still needs to match the subject (p. 141).*
   - *The definite article* le *in front of the name of a day indicates "every."*
10. Nous cherchons **une** bonne solution.
    We are looking for a good solution.
    - *There is no French equivalent to the "-ing" form. Use the present tense if the context is present, the* imparfait *if the context is past.*
    - *The verb* chercher *does not take any preposition in French.*
11. S'il pleut, l'herbe sera plus verte.
    If it rains, the grass will be greener.
    - *This type of* si *clause is not a daydream (also called contrary to fact), so you don't need the conditional (p. 206).*
    - *Don't forget to make the adjective agree with* herbe, *which is feminine.*

INDEX OF FRENCH WORDS AND EXPRESSIONS

SUBJECT INDEX